THE QUALITY TEACHER:
Implementing TOTAL QUALITY MANAGEMENT In The Classroom

by
Margaret A. Byrnes, Ed.S.
Robert A. Cornesky, Sc.D.
and
Lawrence W. Byrnes, Ph.D.

Cornesky & Associates Press

THE QUALITY TEACHER:
Implementing TOTAL QUALITY MANAGEMENT In The Classroom

Margaret A. Byrnes
MLByrnes & Associates

Robert A. Cornesky
Cornesky & Associates

Lawrence W. Byrnes
University of Southern Colorado

1992
Cornesky & Associates Press
PO Box 2139
Bunnell, FL 32110
(904) 437-5401
(904) 439-4317 FAX

CORNESKY & ASSOCIATES, 1992

ISBN 1-881807-01-0

About the authors . . .

Margaret Byrnes is a nationally acclaimed presenter and consultant in understanding the at-risk population and total quality management for classroom teachers. She brings a wealth of experience to these endeavors from the perspective of teacher, school counselor, agency counselor and vocational institute director. She is a trained examiner for the Erie County Excellence Award. Margaret and her husband, Lawrence, live in Pueblo, Colorado. She is a total quality management consultant specializing in K-12 schools. Her address is P.O. Box 11733, Pueblo, Colorado 81001; phone (719) 545-8821.

Robert Cornesky, author of numerous books and articles on Total Quality Management, including *Implementing Total Quality Management in Higher Education*, has over 25 years experience in higher education across the nation. He has served as the Dean of a School of Science, Management & Technologies at a comprehensive state university and as the Dean of a School of Allied Health at a health sciences center. Robert is currently an educational consultant specializing in total quality management. His address is P.O. Box 2139, Bunnell, Florida 32110; phone (904) 437-5401.

Lawrence Byrnes, Director of the Center for Teaching and Learning at the University of Southern Colorado, has many years of educational experience as a public school teacher and administrator of Colleges of Education. He is currently working on an innovative model for training teachers of the 21st century, with school partnerships and a Total Quality Approach. He is co-author of *Implementing Total Quality Management in Higher Education.* His address is Center for Teaching and Learning, University of Southern Colorado, Pueblo, Colorado 81001; phone (719) 549-2681.

TABLE OF CONTENTS

Page

Introduction ... 1

Chapter 1: Approaches and Principles to Total Quality Management (TQM) ... 9

Chapter 2: TQM and Students ... 27

Chapter 3: Leadership ... 39

Chapter 4: Classroom Environment ... 63

Chapter 5: Information and Analysis ... 85

Chapter 6: Strategic Quality Planning ... 103

Chapter 7: Human Resource Utilization ... 117

Chapter 8: Quality Assurance of Products and Services ... 135

Chapter 9: Quality Results ... 163

Chapter 10: Customer Satisfaction ... 173

Chapter 11: Conditions for Implementing Total Quality ... 191

References ... 199

Appendix:

Section I: Total Quality Improvement (TQI) Tools
Affinity Diagram ... 205
Cause and Effect Diagram (Fishbones, Ishikawa Diagram) ... 211
Control Charts ... 215
Flow Charts ... 239
Force Field Analysis ... 247
Histogram ... 251
Nominal Group Process ... 257
Operational Definition ... 267
Pareto Diagram ... 269
Relations Diagram ... 275
Run Chart ... 279
Scatter Diagram ... 285
Scenario Builder ... 287
Systematic Diagram ... 301

Section II: Formula For Determining The Cost of Waste in School Districts ... 303

Section III: Customer-Supplier and Professional Contracts ... 305

Section IV: Quality Index Profile ... 309

Introduction

We recently heard someone comment that "insanity is doing the same thing over and over again in exactly the same manner and expecting the results to be different." In many instances, however, this is precisely what is done while managing the "processes" and "systems" in the classrooms. **Total Quality Management** (TQM), on the other hand, involves procedures where one constantly examines the way things are done and looks for ways to improve the "processes" and "systems" in order to obtain better results. Without alignment with the TQM approach to teaching, true excellence cannot be achieved.

Quality is a way of life. It is a belief system that says one must continue to improve and grow, making every endeavor an adventure. Quality is also a standard of measure. In schools it traditionally means that a few will be singled out for their achievement in the classroom, laboratory, or on the playing field. Rarely do we consider that quality is a measure that can be widely applied. Indeed, current educational systems recognize few students for excellence or for doing quality work, thus eliminating the possibility that approximately 97% of all students will ever be able to achieve this "standard." It is painfully apparent that schools need to adopt a belief system where quality is the standard and that everyone, if given enough time and support, is capable of achieving some measure of excellence.

When one considers this possibility, many of education's sacred cows are thrown into a veritable "tornado". The concept of quality strikes at the heart of standardized tests, grades, ability grouping, gifted programs, honors or remedial classes, and the like, challenging traditional ideas of evaluating students' work. TQM is an approach that provides opportunities for **every** teacher and student to achieve previously unrealized success.

The TQM approach begins with the belief systems of those persons interacting with each other. In this instance, we refer mainly, but not exclusively, to teachers and their students. Therefore, if the teacher believes that the students are incapable, then all lessons, activities, and actions will be geared to proving that belief. If, on the other hand, a teacher approaches each class of students believing that each is endowed with some special gifts, that each has many more capabilities than have yet been discovered, that each can learn far more than previously thought, that each comes with a desire to learn, there will be a different classroom climate and the achievement levels of each student will rise. It follows then, that the teacher with the latter

1

beliefs will come to class with a far different approach, attitude, and higher expectations than the first.

The teacher's belief system is essential to opening the door of quality. We assume that a teacher who believes in quality must clearly understand what it means. This understanding becomes the road map for everything that happens in the classroom. It is not surprising that the **first step** in quality management in the classroom is **establishing a quality statement**, describing exactly what quality means to the class. Once such a statement has been established, it provides the focus of attention for the teacher, students, parents, and administrators. A clearly defined statement about quality/excellence leads to a mission statement that can and should be kept both literally and figuratively at the forefront of the classroom.

Success for All Students

We are not aware of any public schools with missions to "educate some of the students some of the time" or "to provide a quality education for those students who are in the top quarter of their class." All public schools have a mission to "provide an education to all students." What is *really important* is the belief system and focus of those responsible for carrying out the mission of the schools, including school boards, administrators, parents and teachers. Recently we had the privilege of assisting a school district develop some guiding principles for the next five years. When it was suggested that the school adopt an attitude of total success for ALL students and allow that belief to permeate everything that happened within the school, it was considered ridiculous. It was suggested that to do so would reflect poorly on the institution as all failures would be considered institutional failures. Unfortunately in this district as in many others around the country, business will continue as usual with few students receiving a quality education. Some students will go on to college where the cycle will repeat itself; fewer students will receive a quality education.

TQM assumes that everyone is capable of and eager to do quality work. It also assumes that if given the opportunity and an environment free of fear, people will strive to do their best due to a strong desire to take pride in their workmanship. This assumption is the basis for this book: Improving processes and systems by the teacher and student will result in trust; trust will result in an increase in quality; an increase in quality will result in an increase in the pride-of-workmanship; and, as a result, a new classroom culture will be established where **everyone** will expect quality and fun to be the end result. Imagine a school where administrators and teachers believe that *everyone* wants to do a good job. The energy created from such a belief would be contagious. Positive energy helps people reach, stretch, try, and be persistent until success is achieved.

When Basic Needs Aren't Met

We must keep in mind that every human being continuously strives to have five basic needs met. These needs are survival, love (respect), pride (in work and play), freedom (to choose what one does and pursue that which one enjoys), and fun. *Students who are hungry, sick, troubled or depressed cannot function well in the classroom, no matter how good the school* (Carnegie Council on Adolescent Development 1989, p. 32). Evidence of this is clear from the alarming statistics on at-risk students:

> 55.9% of students who use alcohol begin drinking in grades 6-9.

> 29% of students who use drugs begin using them from grades 6-9.

> Between 1980 and 1985 the suicide rate more than doubled for 10-14 year old.

> Since 1960, the suicide rate has almost tripled for those ages 15-19.

> It is estimated that one girl in ten will give birth to a child before she reaches her 18th birthday.

> 2.4 million cases of child abuse were reported in the United States in 1989.

> In New York City, half of all abuse reports are repeat cases of children who have had to be rescued before, only to be returned to an abusive home.

> As many as 7.5 million children—12% of those below the age of 18—suffer from some form of psychological illness.

> 1 of 4 of the nation's youth do not graduate from high school with their classmates.

> In Pennsylvania, during 1986-87, the stated reasons for dropping out of school were: 32.4% disliked school, 24% wanted to work, and 17.5% had academic problems.

> Over 1 million teenage girls became pregnant in 1985 (ages 15-19).

> Approximately 30% of all students are minority. Minority children are more likely to be affected by poverty.

> Children represent 40% of the nation's poor.

> In the United States a student drops out of school every 16 seconds of every school day.

When individual needs are not met within the confines of an institutional structure, they will eventually seek and find a place where their needs can be met. Students who are not honor students, gifted athletes, or who do not fully subscribe to the culture of the school, who are kept out of the "club" that is school will find other organizations to which to belong. Involvement in cults and gangs is evidence of this. Students out of the mainstream of school learn early that they will be treated differently by teachers, administrators, and fellow students. There is evidence that isolation and separation begins in Kindergarten and by the end of the third grade is often well determined. Most frequently this is done using two criteria: basic skill level and behavior. A student who is already feeling left behind will dramatically begin altering behavior by the fourth grade. This behavior is likely to continue throughout his/her school career. Thus, many discipline problems are born out of frustration, embarrassment, and shame. Unless the child receives some form of intervention the cycle of acting-out and failure will continue. Ultimately these are the majority of school drop-outs.

Cost of Waste

TQM addresses the high cost of waste, *e.g.* not doing the job right the first time. Nationally this cost is extremely high, and one wonders whether or not the various school systems of the United States can afford to continue doing "business as usual." For example:

> Each year's class of dropouts will, over their lifetime, cost the nation about $260 billion in lost earnings and foregone taxes.

> In a lifetime, a male high school dropout will earn $260,000 less than a high school graduate and contribute $78,000 less in taxes.

> In 1987, the United States spent more than $19 billion in payments for income maintenance (AFDC), health care, and nutrition to support families begun by teenagers.

> In 1980, alcohol and drug abuse in the U.S. cost more than $136 billion in reduced productivity, treatment, crime, and related costs.

> 85% of all juvenile offenders are illiterate.

> A year of preschool costs an average of $3,000 per child; a year in prison costs $16,500.

> In 1989, 1.8 million teenagers between the ages of 14 — 18 were arrested.
> Nearly 1.5 million teenagers not in school are unemployed. This is nearly twice the overall unemployment rate.
> Dropout rates among migrants are estimated to range between 45% and 90%.
> Approximately 25% of public school students drop out. The rate for some inner city schools reaches 75%.

Local Cost of Waste

The following is an actual example of the potential projected cost of drop-outs to one school district in Pennsylvania for the period of 1990-1994 when 100 students did not return for the 1990-1991 school year.

Loss to the school district in state education funding

Lost state revenue per student = approximately $2,000

Total lost revenue for 1990-91 school year = $200,000

Approximately 6.0 faculty positions lost due to loss of $200,000 in state funding.

Drop in enrollment over 4 year period (Assume an equal number of students fail to return for each of next three school years) = 400 fewer students than 1989-1990.

Lost state revenue for 1991-92 school year = $400,000 (200 students)

Lost state revenue for 1992-93 school year = $600,000 (300 students)

Lost state revenue for 1993-94 school year = $800,000 (400 students)

$800,000 equals a loss of 24 faculty positions over a 4 year period.

Over 4 years, therefore, the conservative estimate of the total lost of revenue to this Pennsylvania school district is **$2,000,000!**

Cost to taxpayers in lost federal, state and local taxes
  Assume a high school graduate would earn approximately
$10,000/yr.
  Approximate loss of local, state and federal revenue (taxes)
$975 each

                    Year 1: $975 x 100 = $ 97,500
                    Year 2: $975 x 200 = $195,000
                    Year 3: $975 x 300 = $292,500
                    Year 4: $975 x 400 = $390,000
Total lost tax revenue by the end of 1994 = $975,000

Cost to taxpayers in public assistance programs:
Assuming half of the students who drop out are single parents
with one child, and receive general assistance (a program for
single persons or non-custodial parents) funds, the following is
the approximate cost to taxpayers in welfare benefits (including
food stamps, Aid for Families with Dependent Children
[AFDC], and General Assistance [GA] programs).

For the purposes of this example, we assume half of 100 (50)
non-returning students take advantage of some public assistance
program.

Year: 1990-91
25 AFDC $316 x 12 months x 25 households = $94,800
25 Food Stamps $193 x 12 months x 25 households = $57,900
25 GA $153 x 3 months x 25 individuals = $ 11,475
25 Food Stamps $105 x 12 months x 25 individuals $ 31,500
Total benefits paid in 1990-91 = $195,675

Assuming there are no changes in numbers of households
receiving public assistance and there are no changes in the
numbers of individuals served, the total conservative estimated
cost for cash assistance and food stamps over the four year
period is **$782,700!**

This does not include:
    WIC (Women, Infants and Children) payments
    Medical Assistance
    Legal Assistance
    Cost of Judicial System
        court costs
        jail (currently $20,000 per inmate per year)
        restitution
        victim expenses

JTPA (Job Training Partnership Acts) programs
Adult Basic Education and GED (high school equivalency)
instruction (currently approximately $1500/person)

**The estimated grand total for not properly
educating students over four years is $4,282,700!**
In order to estimate the cost of waste in your school district
the reader is referred to the Appendix for a worksheet.

The aforementioned figures represent only a small
portion of the loss to the community and the district specifically.
One also has to consider the cost of medical assistance, justice
system, prison, adult literacy and basic education programs,
WIC (Women, Infants, and Children), and JTPA (Job Training
Partnership Act) programs. It is staggering to realize the real
cost of waste in education. We hope this exercise has allowed
the reader to understand that the problem of not doing the job
right the first time affects each of us. Resolution will come only
when teachers, administrators, parents, and the community at-
large begin working collaboratively to alter the way schools do
business. The time for finger pointing and blaming others is
long over. Now is the time to take action!

Why Total Quality Management?
One of the reasons that the TQM approach works is because it
encourages teamwork and collaboration. What is classroom
TQM? **It is a procedure wherein everyone in the class
knows the objectives of the class and adopts a quality
philosophy to continuously improve the work done to
meet the objectives.** The general principles and tools of
TQM encourage everyone in the classroom to identify inadequate
processes and systems and recommend improvements. This
occurs when teachers effectively cultivate the arts of active
listening, analyzing, and implementing. **TQM is not a rigid
set of rules and regulations but processes and
procedures for improving performance.**
This text will clarify TQM processes and procedures and
demonstrate how they can be used in the classroom. It is an
introductory guide to teachers interested in implementing TQM
in their classroom. In Chapter One, we summarize briefly the
TQM approaches of two quality experts, namely Dr. W.
Edwards Deming and Dr. Philip Crosby. Chapter Two shows
how TQM works with students, especially the "at-risk"

population. Chapters Three-10 examine a specific point of the Quality Index Assessment and discusses specific ways to integrate each within the classroom. (Most of the indices are modifications of the Malcolm Baldrige Criteria.) Each chapter ends with the Quality Index Assessment criteria for that point. In Chapter Eleven, we suggest the conditions that are necessary for successfully implementing TQM in the classroom. Finally, the Appendix contains the Total Quality Improvement tools, examples of Customer-Supplier contracts, and a personal Quality Index Profile demonstrating how individual teachers would rate on the overall assessment.

Chapter One: Approaches and Principles to Total Quality Management

Everyone doing his best is not the answer. It is first necessary that people know what to do. Drastic changes are required. The first step in transformation is to learn how to change.

W. Edwards Deming
Out of the Crisis

Approaches to Total Quality Management

This section will introduce the principles of total quality management (TQM) by briefly (1) reviewing the ideas of TQM leaders, and (2) discussing how their ideas apply to the classroom.

The Deming Approach

Few doubt the genius of Dr. W. Edwards Deming. His focus on constant improvement and quality has transformed Japanese industry. Deming has outlined his philosophy by listing 14 points for managing quality and productivity. These points were designed primarily for the manufacturing sector, but apply to the service sector as well (Deming 1986).

Deming was born in Sioux City, Iowa, but he is best known in Japan where, after World War II, his advice was heeded and, as a result, helped their industries rebuild their nation.

Deming is the father of Total Quality Management. He stresses statistical process control (SPC) and a 14-point process for managers to improve quality and productivity. At the same time his approach is humanistic and treats people as intelligent human beings who want to do a good job. Deming has great disdain for managers who allege that workers are responsible for problems of poor quality. Applying this to the classroom, Deming would dislike teachers (managers) who blame the students (workers) for not doing a quality job.

The following are Deming's 14 points:

1. *Create constancy of purpose for improvement of product and service, with the aim of becoming competitive and staying in business, and to provide jobs.*

2. *Adopt the new philosophy. We are in a new economic age. Western management must awaken to the challenge, learn their responsibilities, and take on leadership for change.*

3. *Cease dependence on inspection to achieve quality. Eliminate the need for inspection on a mass basis by building quality into the product in the first place.*

4. *End the practice of awarding business on the basis of price tag alone. Move toward a single supplier for any one item on the basis of a long-term relationship of loyalty and trust. Minimize total cost by working with a single supplier.*

5. *Improve constantly and forever every process for planning, production, and service, to improve quality and productivity, and thus constantly decrease costs.*

6. *Institute training on the job.*

7. *Adopt and institute leadership. The aim of supervision should be to help people and machines and gadgets do a better job. Supervision of management is in need overhaul, as well as supervision of production workers.*

8. *Drive out fear, so that everyone can work effectively for the company.*

9. *Break down barriers between departments. People in research, design, sales, and production must work as a team to foresee problems of production and those that may be encountered with the product or service.*

10. *Eliminate slogans, exhortations, and targets for the work force that ask for zero defects or new levels of productivity. Such exhortations only create adversarial relationships, since the bulk of the causes of low quality and productivity belong to the system and thus lie beyond the power of the work force.*

11. *a. Eliminate work standards (quotas) on the factory floor. Substitute leadership.*
    b. Eliminate management by objectives. Eliminate management by numbers, and numerical goals. Substitute leadership.

12. *a. Remove barriers that rob the hourly worker of his right to pride of workmanship. The responsibility of supervisors must be changed from sheer numbers to quality.*

b. Remove barriers that rob people in management and engineering of their right to pride of workmanship. This means, inter alia, abolishment of the annual or merit rating and of management by objective.

13. *Institute a vigorous program of education and self-improvement.*

14. *Put everybody in the company to work to accomplish the transformation. The transformation is everybody's job.* (Deming 1982, p. 23)

What follows is a brief look at Deming's points and how they might be applied to the classroom.

Point 1: Create a Constancy of Purpose

Many classes in our schools have ill-defined and confusing objectives. We recommend highly that both teacher and student become jointly involved in producing an action plan which concentrates on focused objectives that are responsive to both present and projected societal trends and needs. Such an action plan should represent the best stretch goals (albeit realistic ones) for the classroom, the school, and its budget. Regardless of the objectives, innovative teaching and learning strategies within the context of a total quality improvement (TQI) strategy should be carried out by teachers well educated in TQM principles.

Point 2: Adopt the New Philosophy

Once goals and objectives of the class are established, it is important that the teacher *and* the students accept them. This will only happen when the teacher seriously adopts a plan based upon quality and trust.

Point 3: Cease Dependence on Inspection

Quality must be built into the processes of the classroom in order for each student to achieve his/her maximum potential. Inspections that are done at the "end of the line" are too late. For example, at the end of the year, when students are considered for promotion to the next grade is too late. Whatever chance there was to improve the student's skill levels has been lost. By using the TQI approach in the classroom, teachers, students and parents working together can identify problem areas, thereby enhancing the opportunity to make necessary changes so all students can achieve quality work. Inspection is only helpful if it provides one with information leading to continuous improvement. Build quality into the classroom from the very first day, thus decreasing the need for inspection.

Point 4: End the Practice of Awarding Business on the Basis of Price Tag Alone

This is probably the most difficult of all Deming's points to relate directly to the classroom, as each teacher's suppliers are parents, previous teachers and those that supply curriculum materials. Since it is impossible to accept only certain students coming from certain teacher's classes, this point can only be applied to curriculum materials suppliers. This is usually a school district decision, with recommendations coming from a committee of teachers. Quality teachers will volunteer (for membership on such committees) as they will want a voice in the selection process for curriculum materials. The seriousness of these decisions cannot be overstated. The cost of textbook selection does not stop when the books are delivered, but continues as long as that book is used in the classrooms. Textbooks must contain information and be written in a manner that will be most helpful to students in their quest for quality work. Therefore, one must give careful consideration to factors other than cost when making any selections. Textbook and other curriculum materials companies that are sensitive to the needs of schools (teachers and students) are not necessarily those that simply *sell books and materials*.

A textbook selection process that promotes the use of critical thinking skills and depends less on factual content may provide the best dollar value even if it carries a higher price tag.

Point 5: Improve Constantly and Forever

Educators know that the basis for learning is constant improvement. Since it is impossible to achieve "mastery" in every facet of life, one must strive always to improve. This is as true for teachers as it is for students. Quality classrooms exemplify this point. Everyone (teachers and students) are constantly seeking ways to improve the systems within the classroom that will allow for greater achievement levels while enhancing the fun of learning. When learning is fun, everyone will want to contribute to the continuous improvement process.

Point 6: Institute Training on the Job

Quality will not happen unless everyone is provided with adequate training. This happens when teachers systematically provide students with information about TQM and TQI. Since this approach is unique and without precedence in the K-12 sector, everyone will have to be educated about the system and ways to implement it. This training will be crucial to the total effectiveness of any attempt to implement TQM. Without adequate training, those involved will not be able to fully implement the TQI process.

Point 7: Adopt and Institute Leadership

The aim of TQM and TQI is to allow students to achieve their maximum potential. By adopting a different style of leadership within the classroom, teachers can empower students to become responsible for their own learning and for the success of their fellow students. This can only happen in an environment created by the "leader" teacher totally committed to the notion that all students can and want to learn. From here, each teacher will be totally committed to empowering each student through a variety of leadership roles to become responsible for improving his/her own learning and for the success of the class.

Point 8: Drive Out Fear

Fear must be removed from the work setting so that all students can work constructively. When students feel that they are trusted, they will take more pride in their work and quality will increase. As quality increases, the classroom becomes a fun learning place, rather than one of drudgery. A fun learning place develops and promotes a continuous cycle of collegiality between students and teacher.

Using the traditional A-F grading system instills, rather than drives fear out of the classroom. Additionally, it increases barriers between students, and between students and their teacher. This archaic system fosters embarrassment and shame for many students, thus disenfranchising them from the class and school.

Point 9: Break Down Barriers Between Departments

Traditionally in education, teachers have viewed their classroom as their private domain. In many districts there is little communication between teachers. Deming believes that we must break down these barriers, and begin working together to identify problems and implement changes in the processes that will lead to quality improvement. Without such communication, education will continue to be fragmented and quality will continue to be a problem.

Point 10: Eliminate Slogans

Slogans and exhortations are ineffective in improving quality. Many classrooms are littered with posters and banners urging students to improve their performance, or to "reach for the stars," but none of these are effective in demonstrating to students how they can improve. In other words, they are meaningless unless the teacher shows students how they can achieve such lofty goals.

Point 11: Eliminate Quotas and Numerical Goals: Substitute Leadership

Deming believes that having quotas and numerical goals impedes quality more than any other single working condition. Grades based solely on a paper and pencil tests tends to discourage students from taking an active interest in their own learning, and often encourages them to do the very minimum. It also promotes isolationism since competition increases. Imposed quotas (grading on the curve) and numerical work standards (performance on nationally standardized exams) do as much as anything else to discourage collegiality between the students and teachers.

Point 12: Remove Barriers that Rob Employees of their Right To Pride Of Workmanship

Trust is vital to the TQM classroom. Without trust and other empowerment techniques such as teaming and problem solving, students will lack encouragement to achieve quality work. Only classrooms that operate with a clearly defined mission statement, allowing students to set stretch goals with meaningful assignments will produce active, enthusiastic life-long learners. Every effort must be made to eliminate busy work, traditional grading scales, and boredom from the classroom. These elements foster minimal interest in learning and achievement. Pride in workmanship comes from working to resolve real problems, often within a team setting.

Point 13: Institute a Vigorous Program of Education and Self-Improvement

In Deming's plan it is imperative for teachers to actively engage in a program of education and self-improvement. This presupposes that a professional development plan would be well thought out, with each step leading to greater self-awareness, as well as improvement in teaching techniques and strategies. The Quality teacher will be cognizant of the need for personal growth as well as professional growth, and will therefore, vigorously pursue a continuous self-improvement plan.

Point 14:   Involve Everyone in the Transformation to Quality

Deming's last point encourages universal involvement in the transformation to quality. Often, student contributions to resolve classroom problems are not sought, or, if offered, are ignored. The control issue is a big one for many teachers and as a result, they proceed to give orders (becoming boss-managers) rather than openly seeking and accepting student input. They must keep in mind that *the brain comes free with the student's body.*

In summary, the Deming philosophy reduces variability in the work processes and establishes a management style that is supportive of ongoing improvement. It should be noted that Deming believes that the **main reason for working is to have fun**. To have a truly fun learning environment, however, quality must be part of the classroom culture because one cannot have pride in workmanship without quality, and without pride, fun is not obtainable.

Deming believes that quality is never a problem, but a solution to a problem. He and Juran (1988) support the concept that the organized human activity of work takes place within a system where at least 85 percent of the systems are controlled by management (teachers) and 15 percent or less is under the direct control of the worker (student). Since students work in the system, the main job of the teachers is to work on and to improve the systems. This is done with the help of the students, however, so a higher level of quality can be achieved. Deming believes a quality manager is one with the ability to respond to the problems of systems and the problems of people simultaneously.

The Crosby Approach

The Crosby (1984) philosophy seems to appeal more to the human resource type of manager. Crosby enforces the belief that quality is a universal goal and that management must provide the leadership to ensure that an enterprise **never** compromises quality.

Crosby defines quality as conformance to requirements. He believes that **the system of quality is prevention;** that appraisal is done now, on-the-spot, not later. He encourages a performance standard of zero defects and says that the measurement of quality is the price of non-conformance—doing something over rather than doing it right the first time. He believes that **managers should be facilitators** and should be considered as such by the employees, rather than as punishment sent from God.

Like Deming, Philip B. Crosby (1984, p. 99) has fourteen steps for quality improvement:

1.   *Management commitment*
2.   *Quality improvement team*
3.   *Measurement*
4.   *Cost of quality*
5.   *Quality awareness*
6.   *Corrective action*
7.   *Zero Defects planning*
8.   *Employee education*
9.   *Zero Defects Day*
10.   *Goal setting*
11.   *Error-cause removal*
12.   *Recognition*
13.   *Quality councils*
14.   *Do it over again*

We would like to examine briefly Crosby's points and consider how they might be applied to the classroom. In place of "management" or "managers" we will be inserting "teacher" as s/he is the "manager" of the classroom.

Point 1:   Management Commitment

Before lasting change towards quality can be realized, the teacher must be trained in quality processes and systems, and it must be clear that s/he is going to support the commitment towards quality.

Point 2:   Quality Improvement Team

In order to involve the entire class in adopting the new quality philosophy a team should be formed consisting of individuals representing all factions of the student body. As problems are identified, additional teams are established to work on an action plan for resolution. The training and education processes require a minimum of 30 classroom hours and probably 60-90 hours of reading.

Point 3: Measurement

Baseline data should be gathered in order to evaluate the improvement process. Both the students and the teacher will become frustrated when such data are not available; consequently they won't know how they are doing.

If the teacher and the students are uncertain as to how they are progressing towards announced quality goals, they will become frustrated and will operate under their own rules.

Point 4: The Cost of Quality

The teacher should conduct special training for all students in record keeping so they can establish a procedure for the evaluation system. We recommend that the evaluation procedure be consistent throughout the TQI process.

Point 5: Quality awareness

Quality must become part of the class culture. Students, parents and administrators should understand that the teacher is committed to quality, hence *quality is the policy.* The students must also be educated about the cost of not doing a task correctly the first time.

Point 6: Corrective action

The main purpose of corrective action is to identify problems and then to take the actions necessary to eliminate the root cause. This should be a cooperative group project. Corrective action is **not** having a student redoing their own work or, in case of group projects, redoing someone else's mistakes. Rather, it focuses on utilizing data to eliminate system and process mistakes. Corrective action procedures should be based on data and can only be effective if the system under investigation is statistically represented.

Corrective action steps require student empowerment to bring to the teacher's attention things that are not only done incorrectly but also things that could be done better and more efficiently within a non-punitive/no blame atmosphere. Corrective action requires teamwork between teachers and students and between groups of students.

Point 7:   Zero Defects Planning

According to Crosby, corporations often "plan" mistakes by setting their allowances for defects in advance. He believes that it is imperative to plan not to allow *any* defects. It is easy to recognize this when the product is a manufactured item, but far more difficult when considering the education of children. Planning comes from identifying problems and implementing a

TQI process to eliminate them. Everyone benefits from zero defects planning since it presupposes that no one will leave the classroom with less than "mastery."

Point 8: Employee education
After the teacher is educated about Total Quality Improvement (TQI) and Total Quality Management (TQM), students must be trained in the philosophy and procedures of these approaches. This may take several hours, or the equivalent of several class periods. The depth of TQM and TQI training must take into account the ages of the students. Naturally, training must be developmentally appropriate. Another alternative is to begin classes several weeks earlier and train the entire student body. The best approach to training students is to have an entire course on Continuous Improvement.

Point 9: Zero Defects Day
Crosby believes that a celebration is important when the group is trained and ready to launch its' zero defects day. In the classroom this might mean a special celebration when the students are educated in TQI and make a commitment to a major curricular assignment. The celebration recognizes the success of everyone, and therefore the success of the group and the importance of each individual's contributions to the group are highly valued.

Point 10: Goal Setting
Goal setting is crucial to the success of every student and every teacher. They provide a road map to achievement. By making goal setting a regular, integral part of the school day, each individual will have a clear focus that will direct all behavior towards quality.

Point 11: Error-cause Removal
When errors are recognized, it is important to institute a program to eliminate them quickly. The TQI process becomes an integral part of Crosby's plan as the root causes of problems are identified, and action is taken to remove them so they are not repeated. One can easily see the wisdom of this for educators, as they assist students in realizing where process mistakes are made and provide corrective action. The problem-solving approach to teaching and discipline is a key element in TQM and TQI.

Point 12: Recognition
Crosby believes in providing recognition for achievement. He recognizes that team efforts are more important than

individual efforts. Teaming is one of the cornerstones of the TQM movement as it empowers the workers to resolve problems and work for the success of the organization.

Point 13: Quality councils

Crosby (1984) states that... *[t]he idea of quality councils is to bring the quality professionals together and let them learn from each other* (p. 119). This is an excellent way to keep the organization focused on "quality" issues and to prevent slippage to the traditional manner of operation. Whereas Deming encourages total involvement of the customer and the supplier, Crosby's point on instituting "quality councils" necessarily ensures the constant and persistent reminders necessary to keep everyone in the classroom focused in the same direction.

The Imai Approach

Though we will not discuss in detail the Imai approach (it is incorporated into both the Deming and Crosby philosophies), we do want to provide a short overview. Imai (1986) supports a continuous improvement process encouraging people to focus on the processes and systems in which they work rather than on the results. He believes that continual improvement in the processes and systems will create a better product or service. This has become known as the "P" or process approach (also known as the Kaizen approach), rather than the "R" or results approach.

In the "R" approach, management examines the anticipated result(s), usually predetermined by Management by Objectives, then rates the individual(s) performance. Performance is influenced by reward and punishment, that is, by use of the "carrot and stick." In the "P" approach, management supports the individuals and the teams in their efforts to improve the processes and systems leading up to the end result.

The continuous improvement approach has a long-term, undramatic effect on a process or system. Change is gradual and consistent. The approach involves everyone, and the resulting group effort focuses on processes and systems rather than on one person's performance evaluation. The approach requires little monetary investment, but a great deal of effort on the part of management to maintain the group process. The Kaizen approach is people oriented.

The typical approach to classroom problems (K-12) is totally different from the "P" approach. Most teachers seek a quick, dramatic fix to their problems and "problem" students. The traditional approach (if they are not learning, fail them; if they are not behaving, suspend them) used by many teachers utilizes a short-term, but dramatic approach that often results in abrupt and volatile changes.

Principles of Total Quality Management

In the previous section, we identified the TQM and TQI models of Deming and Crosby. Although different in some respects, they have common elements. The purpose of this section is to examine the common elements of these quality experts and suggest how they may be applied to the classroom.

The seven common elements that bind the foundations of total quality management (TQM) and total quality improvement (TQI) by Deming and Crosby are:

1. Processes and Systems
2. Teaming
3. Customers and Suppliers
4. Quality by Fact, Process, and Perception
5. Management by Fact
6. Complexity
7. Variation

Let us examine each of these common elements.

Processes and Systems

All of the combined tasks or steps necessary to accomplish a given result are defined as a process. Even though Imai can be considered the champion in using the **process** ("P") approach over the more commonly used **result** ("R") approach, the other leaders in quality also stress improving the processes and systems in which employees work in order to increase constantly the quality of goods and services. Deming and Crosby stress that since management controls at least 85 percent of the processes and systems in which the employees work, most poor quality is the direct result of poor management.

Every work activity is a part of a process and system. It follows that classroom learning can improve only if the processes and systems in which the students learn improve. If teachers improve the processes and systems, they will receive better quality results and also higher levels of productivity.

A "system" as used in this text means an arrangement of persons, places, things, and/or circumstances that makes, facilitates, or permits things to happen. Here are a few examples of classroom systems: organization of the classroom, teaching methods, materials, grading procedures, discipline procedures, and assignments. The very nature of a system will determine what will happen and how it will happen.

   Most teachers inherit students trained by previous teachers in methods and procedures not directed towards the TQM philosophy. They face the challenge of maintaining the strengths and eliminating the weaknesses of systems established by their predecessors. Most likely they have entered situations where anticipated results yield predictable attitudes and behaviors. This cycle of predictability is not only difficult to alter, but it also inhibits change towards quality. This is illustrated in Figure 1.

Figure 2.1:   Process inhibiting change to quality.

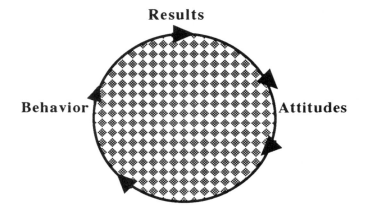

   If we assume that the teacher controls 85-90 percent of the classroom processes and systems, each teacher can influence students to seriously commit to quality. Students will most likely work hard if convinced that quality will be the result (Glasser 1990, p. 433). We agree with Dr. Glasser's comment *. . . quality is contagious* (p. 435). If the teacher directs all of his/her energies toward improving the processes and systems for quality results along with student reception of the service, we are confident that quality results will lead to an improved attitude, modified behavior, and eventually to a classroom culture directed toward achieving quality. An example of this process is displayed in Figure 2.

Figure 2.2:   Process and results of introducing change to quality.

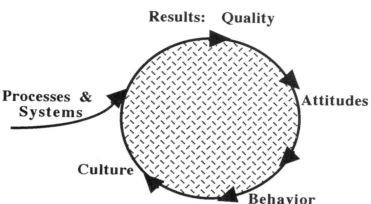

Teaming

Teams and teamwork are extremely important in producing a quality service or product. Although hierarchy is needed within all organizations in order to avoid chaos, most classroom learning can be accomplished across, not within, organizational boundaries.

The informal power structure and the resulting culture in classrooms do not readily permit collegiality in a management system based upon hierarchy; however, properly done teaming (cooperative learning), is invariably found in classrooms producing quality work.

In their recent books Waterman (1990) and Levering (1988) stress the importance of teamwork in effecting change and in keeping morale high in American businesses. The same is probably true for the classroom.

Waterman (1990), in his book *Adhocracy: The Power to Change*, refers to means for motivating active involvement in embracing and effecting change. He suggests that people under the proper leadership will participate in meaningful activities with the intention of changing their organization from one of non-quality to one of high quality. We believe that this can also be applied to the classroom setting as well.

Customers and Suppliers

Generally, the concept of customers within educational institutions differs from the private sector's because in education "repeat customers" are usually undesirable. It can be argued, however, that if parents, alumni and current students are well satisfied with their school experience, they will recommend the institution to others, such as Realtors who often direct families towards available housing in the better quality school districts. Likewise, colleges and universities who are well satisfied with the high school graduates may admit additional graduates from that school. Thus, students, alumni, and employers do share some of the characteristics of traditional customers.

A further parallel to the customer concept lies in the relationships among various teachers within a building or district. For example, parents, alumni and current students who are well satisfied with their quality experience with a given teacher will recommend the teacher to others. Virtually every teacher/student interaction within a classroom is a customer/supplier interaction. The customer/supplier philosophy can be applied by concentrating on each classroom as a user of processes and systems to supply service to students, parents, and society.

The customer/supplier relationship is very important for effective teamwork. Teachers must develop an understanding and appreciation of the concept in order to promote trust, pride, and quality. Central to applying the concept of quality in the classroom itself is the acceptance of the student in the customer/supplier relationship!

Likewise of prime importance is the removal of the top-down (boss-manager) model of management from the classroom. Instead, leadership training for all teachers and students should be undertaken so that everyone can reach her/his maximum performance. In fact, the decentralization necessary to stimulate effectively a customer/supplier attitude requires a participative atmosphere. Empowerment of all teachers and students is necessary for this atmosphere to exist within institutions. With empowerment comes trust; with trust comes pride-in-workmanship; and with pride-in-workmanship comes teamwork for total quality improvement. Manz and Sims (1989) have published an excellent reference for developing self-leadership skills.

Quality by Fact, Process, and Perception

Each of the quality leaders examines quality from at least three different perspectives. They examine it by fact: that is, does the product or service meet the specified requirements? They examine the quality of the process: that is, does the process and/or system produce the product or service as intended? And finally, they examine quality by perception: that is, are the customer's expectations met?

It is conceivable that a course can have quality by fact and of process, yet the perception of the customers, either the students or the parents for example, may be one in which quality is not evident. In this case, total quality has not been achieved. This is usually but **not always** the result of poor past performance.

Management by Fact

All leaders in the study of quality emphasize the need for complete and comprehensive data prior to making major decisions.

One simple rule must apply in determining the mission of the course or even in setting out to improve a simple process: Research data should be complete, accurate and made freely available to everyone. Information serves no purpose unless made available to those directly involved in the workplace. The free availability of information serves at least two purposes. First, when people know the facts, they can offer essential advice. Second, they can call attention to a serious flaw in a developing plan, avoiding additional problems.

Whenever possible, decisions should be based on data rather than hunches. Data and facts have a tendency to uncover the root of the problem rather than the symptoms; thus, permanent solutions can be offered rather than quick fixes.

Complexity

All of the quality leaders realize the complexity of most processes and systems which produce a product or service.

Within a classroom setting, complexity can be defined as extra steps added to a process to deal with errors in the preceding educational experience of students, or steps added to recover from errors occurring in the present classroom experience.

Variation

Every process involving humans and/or machines displays variation. In education, for example, we see wide variation/diversity in incoming students as well as in the teaching/learning process and in the quality of the graduates. Excessive variation, however, causes the processes and systems to be erratic and unpredictable. Mediocrity and generally poor quality result.

Since every process shows variation, no two products — components, services, reports, teaching effectiveness, or graduates—will ever be identical. The goal, therefore, is to increase the uniformity of the process. Universal involvement in studying processes and identification of potential sources of variation can accomplish this.

Once a system is under control, one can determine common and special cause variations by the use of simple statistics. Common cause variation is the inherent variation of a system resulting from many small sources of variation. Special cause variation is a large, sporadic variation unusual to the system under study. For example, the first snowfall of the year is likely to heighten young student's excitability and distract them from their work. At the high school level, championship games often produce a similar effect. These would both be considered special cause variations. An example of a common cause variation is boredom.

Chapter 2: TQM and Students

*People can't have pride in a company that
treats anyone harshly.*

Philip Crosby
The Eternally Successful Organization

At least twelve of the first eighteen years of any American's life are traditionally spent in some type of formal educational setting. Other formal educational settings are provided for three and four year old children. The learning curve during this time period is greater than at any other time in our lives because one's greatest opportunities for learning arise out of mistakes. Yet interestingly, perception of mistakes are at the core of so many educational problems. The reflections of those around us are crucial to the development of self-esteem. Therefore, as educators we must recognize the important part mistakes play and how these lessons can assist students to grow, blossom and reach their full potential. Viewing children's mistakes as windows of opportunity (for continuous improvement) rather than as disasters of misjudgment or inability will help all children become willing to continue taking the necessary risks to become self-confident, responsible citizens.

Unfortunately, as individuals age many believe that they must be perfect. Usually perfectionism is instilled very early in one's life and is founded on the fear that imperfections mean one is unlovable, unacceptable, and therefore inherently flawed. These lessons learned from parents and others, often drive children to continuously and forever strive to please parents and significant others. In far too many cases, particularly when coming from dysfunctional homes, children have had their fears realized through emotional if not physical abandonment of the parent(s). It is easy to understand why children with these experiences become individuals frightened to make mistakes, eventually deciding not to risk anything for fear they won't be successful. Others may have been severely punished, ridiculed or shamed when they made mistakes as very young children.

Sometimes adults (teachers included) become frustrated and angry with children and teens who make mistakes, believing that they should "know better" and resorting to inappropriate coping skills of their own, occasionally becoming brutal in their verbal or physical attacks on children. Often teachers will use red checks, sad faces, and other symbols indicating mistakes. The at-risk child often sees this as further testimony to inherent flaws. The shame-based child will feel embarrassed, guilty, and shamed when teachers approach mistakes this way. Frequently these feelings will trigger an angry outrage from the child, frightening teachers and other students.

When mistakes involve disruptive or destructive behavior, teachers and administrators, out of their own sense of anger and frustration, may resort to coercion or punitive methods. Too frequently these methods involve shaming the child, resulting in deeply felt rage and a sense of worthlessness. Many eventually turn to drugs and alcohol or other addictions when they believe that they cannot do "anything" right. This allows them to float through life, masking the pain of imperfection, rejection and a sense of abandonment. We are not suggesting these behaviors go unrecognized, but rather that better ways exist to resolve student behaviors than coercion and punishment. Of course, when "acting-out" behavior involves safety issues, the problem must be dealt with immediately in order to protect everyone in the classroom. Our concern is the ".way" such behaviors are addressed.

Perfectionism is a "killer" disease since it immediately sets one on a course of failure. Children quickly realize their inability to be perfect in every aspect of life. The contradiction between what one believes others expect and what one can deliver often fragments the child, frequently leaving him/her unable or unwilling to risk any attempt. This unwillingness to risk paralyzes the child from attempting assignments perceived as difficult. Even if an assignment is very similar to one just finished and failed, the child will resist trying again if the teacher uses traditional coercive or shaming tactics. Often this results in a child withdrawing and simply giving up, believing s/he is truly "no good," and hopeless. As the young child receives more and more punishment, "put downs," and negative messages, s/he will experience periods of depression and a sense of worthlessness. In these cases the "system" let him/her down. **In any successful system there is a place for trial and error. It is this that spawns continuous improvement projects.** *In school, students work in a system while the teacher works on the system.*

The approach of adults to any child's mistakes sets the tone for life-long self-esteem issues. Children who are risk takers have probably been accepted and loved in spite of their mistakes. Persons with poor self-esteem are those who are repeatedly put down, punished, or ridiculed because of their mistakes, appearance, heritage, or socio-economic level. These people seldom rise above a situation, because they remember futile past attempts. We must all accept the responsibility for abolishing our biases towards people due to heritage, appearance or economics and refuse to allow ourselves or others to ridicule them. Likewise, we must recognize that children (especially at-risk children) *lack the coping skills to rectify their mistakes.* Consequently teachers and administrators have an obligation to students to educate them in developing new coping skills to ensure the continuation of growth. Trial and error within a non judgmental, supportive atmosphere allows students the opportunity to practice problem solving without the risk of isolation from their peers and teachers.

Students at risk constitute the soft underbelly of our nation. They make up 'the third world' in education. They are alienated from the mainstream of school life. They are disconnected from their fellow students and from the education offered in traditional schools, in traditional ways. (AASA Critical Issues Report, 1989, p. 15) Therefore, it is essential for all educators to reassess approaches that are used when working with these children, recognizing that no human is perfect and that mistakes are opportunities for growth.

The Total Quality Management (TQM) approach encourages every teacher and student to embark on a path of continuous improvement. By accepting students "where they are," we assist them in identifying areas of their personal and academic life that can benefit from the continuous improvement process. Within a framework of an open, friendly atmosphere with no shaming or blaming, students can learn ways to resolve their own problems. The key element in the TQM model is individual problem solving techniques that will prove invaluable over their lifetime. Children who learn these techniques in the early elementary grades will be happier, more eager to learn and less likely to engage in anti-social activities in or out of school. It is **the** way to prevent problems!

Teachers should consider taking a holistic/wellness approach to educating children. Truly well people are physically, mentally and morally fit. They look at the systems within which children live and focus on prevention rather than band-aiding problems. Prevention demands careful scrutiny of symptoms to discover root causes and root effects of any problem; treating the symptoms will never result in wellness. Educators must begin focusing on examining the symptoms of children's problems so everyone (including each child) can identify the real ones. Once the problems are uncovered, a plan must work to resolve the problem so it doesn't recur. This is never the result of a punitive, coercive approach.

One might question how one individual can solve the problems of dysfunctional homes, poverty, etc. It is true, that educators cannot solve problems of dysfunctional homes. Still we suggest that every educator begin to think differently about the cause and effect of the problem(s). They can educate students to resolve their own problems at school, and thereby have successful educational experiences. Schools have a captive audience since students are obligated by law to attend. True gains in self-esteem only follow positive internal feelings. Exhortations and self-esteem units will not achieve the desired results unless one fully empowers each child to believe they have inherent worth. Then, every adult and child within the school will have to treat each other with respect. In his book, *The Eternally Successful Organization,* Crosby (1988, p. 90) states *[p]eople will just not give their all to an organization that won't give them proper consideration.*

Learning new coping skills and problem solving is critical for any positive behavior change. Unfortunately, our jails and drug and alcohol treatment centers are filled with people who have never learned to solve their own problems. Many grew up in homes where perfectionism was expected; consequently, they could never meet the expectations of home, school, or community. This inability to learn positive coping skills led to their disenfranchisement from society. At-risk children are products of homes such as these. Is it any wonder they have difficulty in school? Imagine a world where the educational system focuses on assisting all children to learn to cope, manage stress, and resolve problems. These learned skills will not come without a formal process for educating each child. This is the key to prevention of additional problems and it allows each child to embark on a personal continuous improvement program in other areas of his/her life. TQM allows this to happen naturally within the classroom setting.

A major study done by the Institute for the Study of At-Risk Students at the University of Maine, (Davis and McCaul, 1990, p. 38) reported the following:

FORCES/FACTORS THAT PLACE STUDENTS AT-RISK

Society	School	Student
Poverty	Inappropriate Curriculum	Low Self-Esteem
Minority Racial/ Group Identity	Ineffective Teacher-Student Interactions	Low Aspirations
Non-English or Limited English Background	Insufficient Support Services (e.g. Counseling, Remedial)	Lack of Interest or Motivation Chemical Abuse
Family/Home Homeless Latchkey Child	Unrealistic/Inappropriate Standards	Dangerous Sexual Practices
Child Abuse/Neglect Single Parent Family Dysfunctional Family Educational Level of Parents	Repeated Failure (cycle) School Climate Not Conducive to Positive Development Lack of Sensitivity to Diversity	Lack of Self Discipline Cognitive Deficits
		Emotional & Behavioral Deficits
		Learning Deficits
		Sensory Deficits
		Medical/Physical Deficits
		Different Value System (Incompatibility)
		Excessive Work

Upon closer examination of their findings, one can clearly see how inadequate systems and processes within the school and classroom have contributed significantly to the problems of at-risk students. Indeed, many if not most, of the student risk factors are either a direct result of, or at least subject to a major effect of the inadequacies of the school factors. Success for everyone is precisely why adopting a TQM/TQI approach is crucial.

Unfortunately, few schools in this country are dedicated and committed to the total success of every student. Those that are enjoy an atmosphere of excitement about learning and have students with high achievement levels. Many of these schools have been recognized by the United States Department of Education as *Blue Ribbon Schools*. A list of the winners can be obtained by contacting your state department of education.

The sad fact is, many schools are based on *fear*. This phenomenon is not unique to public schools, but exists in many private and parochial ones as well. We believe this is largely due to the improper training of teachers and administrators. One of the first things a prospective teacher learns from a college or university education program is "one must gain control of the class right away." While this book does not discuss the control issue in detail, we believe it is germane to the TQM style of classroom management.

In the past, when a student did not conform to the rules of the school s/he was suspended and eventually dropped out. Younger students endured countless humiliating and punitive acts carried out by teachers and administrators. While this may have resulted in short term compliance, there is no evidence that this approach elicited enthusiasm about learning.

Throughout the years, behavior modification programs were popular, with teachers using many different kinds of reinforcers. In the 1970's, Lee and Marlene Cantor developed Assertive Discipline (1976). Many school districts adopted this as their district disciplinary policy. Both of these disciplinary systems were predicated on the teacher being the "authority" figure, while demanding student compliance. Each of these systems works periodically for some students but neither allows the child to learn how to resolve his/her own problems. It is top-down management at its worst. Neither has proven effective over the long haul in terms of engaging students in their own education, and helping them become life long learners.

The belief that one can control another's behavior is at best sheer folly. Imagine the husbands and wives who have spent lifetimes trying to alter their spouse's behavior. It doesn't work for adults, and it doesn't work for children either. Sometimes adults can be fooled into thinking they can control a child, largely because of their intimidating size. Children may comply, but they will neither respect the adult nor cooperate willingly.

The control issue for schools is much more complex than first glance would suggest. For example, many teachers attempt to "control" students because their administrators expect them to "keep the students quiet," since many believe that a quiet classroom is an indication that a great deal of studying and learning is taking place. Of course, old ideas and sacred cows are difficult to change.

It is our belief that humans flourish best in environments where they have the freedom to grow, make mistakes and continue to take risks within a nurturing environment. We also believe that all humans have a strong desire to know the parameters under which they are expected to operate. It is the idea that: If you tell me the rules of the game, I can play. However, if you never tell me the rules then I'll never be able to play it right because I'll never know what is expected of me. Therefore, there is no doubt about the need to provide a safe environment for all children at school where everyone clearly knows and understands the rules and the consequences of violating the rules.

Motivation from outside sources will not alter our educational system to reach the America 2000 goals (discussed in Chapter 6), nor will it allow us to graduate citizens prepared to meet future challenges of the 21st century. Coercion and punishment are old, tired methods that simply have not resulted in inspiring students to become enthusiastic, life-long learners. Power struggles have circumvented the work of education and resulted in students willfully choosing not to learn and worse, becoming a disruptive force within the classroom.

The TQM approach to managing the classroom allows children to become members of a team in establishing classroom rules and consequences, under the guidance of the "super-leader" teacher who recognizes the value of empowering all students and teaching them problem solving as a way of achieving success in school and in life. We believe this approach works best with all students, especially those at-risk.

Outcomes-based (or competency-based) education is a natural tool of TQM. It empowers all students to become successful by eliminating the traditional A-F grading system. Outcomes-based education recognizes the ability of all students to learn and succeed within their own time-frame. It acknowledges that some students will grasp some concepts quicker than others, allows students to become responsible for their own learning, and encourages students to help each other to succeed.

We believe firmly in this approach to learning. In school districts where it is currently used, achievement levels are very high. Johnson City School District, in Johnson City, New York, pioneered the outcomes based model. Teachers, administrators, students and parents work together to assist each child become successful. Teacher's expectations are high, and 80% is considered mastery. Outcomes are clear and all assignments are geared towards meeting the goals and objectives of each class.

There is no mystery learning in this model. Students not achieving mastery within the time allotted for any unit are not punished, failed or otherwise made to feel bad. They continue working with the class, using activity periods and after school tutoring sessions to work on correctives necessary to achieve mastery in any previous unit. Self-esteem and achievement levels are very high, while drop-outs and disciplinary problems are few in Johnson City.

On the contrary, children who have received a number of failure messages by the end of the third grade exhibit more behavior problems than others who experience academic success. They strive to gain attention and acceptance and when they cannot accomplish that by doing well in school, they will find another way, often disrupting class and sometimes threatening or physically hurting themselves or others. Often these students' rage frightens teachers and other students.

Teachers know that some students crave attention almost all of the time. Since this is a basic biological need, it is easy to understand why the at-risk student often is the one who seems to demand most of one's attention and energy. These children are least likely to have their acceptance (respect and love) needs filled at home. Unfortunately, students who cannot get the acceptance they need and crave through regular channels will find other, less desirable ways to receive it. Recognition is vital to everyone and simply saying teachers won't tolerate acting-out behavior denies the role this need plays in life. Since all children want/need acceptance (love and respect), educators must find ways to educate them in acceptable means to attain that end. As mentioned previously, these children lack the coping skills necessary to know how to gain love and respect within what most would consider "normal" bounds. We suggest that adopting a coercive, top-down management style that focuses on controlling all student behavior denies the need humans have for respect and love.

Using the TQM model allows teachers to establish trusting relationships with all students. Indeed, teachers who show *respect for all students* will have more success than teachers who either rely on coercion for some, or selectively respect others. This strikes at the very heart of the human need for power. Teachers attempting to take away a student's right to have power and control over their own behavior will find themselves caught in a power struggle where neither the teacher nor the student will emerge as a winner. Once such a power struggle begins, the student and teacher will be locked into it, and very little or no learning will take place. The student will be so focused on the power struggle that s/he will keep it in the forefront of all encounters with that teacher. The more coercive tactics used by the teacher, the more the student will resist. Even if the teacher wins a particular battle, the war will continue because the student will become angry, defensive, and will continue to fight. If the student does not directly carry-on the battle everyday with the teacher, he will continue to do so by ridiculing and criticizing the teacher, the class and school. This negativity will spawn seeds of more discontent throughout the class. Teachers who recognize their contribution to these power struggles are taking a giant step toward altering their own behavior, which will result in student empowerment.

Over the years we have heard many teachers say, "but I have to treat some of these students that way because that is all they know and can relate to." Usually the teacher is referring to a rationalization for ridiculing or otherwise verbally, mentally, or physically abusing a student. This argument is very weak. Since all teachers and all students are human beings first, we are reminded of the basic human needs of: survival, love, power, freedom, and fun. Sometimes as adults, we forget that children also have these needs. Unmet needs are the struggle of life. Because many children lack necessary love and nurturing in their home situations, they constantly strive to find it. If they cannot find it at school, they will strike back to the best of their ability to "protect" themselves, much like an adult would (only within their limited coping abilities). One must recognize that because one was mistreated in a given environment, it does not give one a license to mistreat another. Put-down messages in any form are abusive. These messages can be changed to lift-up messages, making the student feel better about him/herself and allowing each to alter attitudes about teachers, school and school work. Implementing the principles of TQM permits the teacher to provide a framework within which all students can become empowered.

Student empowerment is the key to successful classrooms. This should not be confused with lack of discipline. On the contrary, students who are fully empowered will not act-out. In fact, one will discover that empowered students will seek to cooperate and will be able to maintain a better focus. And, when acting-out behavior does occur, the students will have learned problem solving skills and will be able to resolve them. In actuality, TQM is a freeing experience for both teachers and students.

For at-risk students empowerment may well be the most important thing that can happen to them at school. We say this because people who are made aware of their personal power, and who have the skills to maintain that power will have high self-esteem and know they can overcome even the highest odds. These youngsters need to learn goal setting and problem solving to become successful adults. Using the TQM model allows everyone to participate in governance and goal setting within the classroom. This experience enables students to learn to get along with others through teaming activities. When everyone in the classroom is perceived as an important contributing member, everyone benefits as self-esteem soars.

We cannot stress enough the importance of eliminating biases about all the students in a class and a school. This is one of the basic beliefs about TQM and without it, TQM will not be successful. One can show their respect for all students (without accepting the acting-out behavior) by teaching them different coping and problem solving skills. Remember, we are suggesting respect for each individual as a human being, not necessarily accepting their behaviors. In fact, being a good role model is very important (see Chapter 3). It is urgent, however, that teachers around the country begin looking at this issue differently. As one continues reading about TQM, we believe that each will see how this management style works to empower them to become super-leader teachers and empower students to become active problem solvers eager to engage in quality work. Unless we find a way to internally motivate all students to want to do quality work at school, we will always have a rather large segment of the student body left outside the arena of success.

The amount of support, appreciation, and help you are getting is all you can get, given the current strategies you are using (McKay et. al, 1989, p. 75), should be one's focal point as they embark on the TQM journey. This epitomizes Deming's and Crosby's belief that management is responsible for at least 85% of all problems and therefore, empowering teams of people to assist in problem identification and action plans to alter the current strategies (be they teaching or otherwise) is the only way to establish long-term positive results. *Students can and will alter the way they behave and the quality of the work they achieve only if current strategies are changed.* Some students will require additional education and support as they embark on the continuous improvement trail; these students come to school with disadvantages requiring great patience, persistence and support from the teacher and each classmate. Positive changes can and are occurring in many schools and classrooms throughout the nation. By examining one's own fears in implementing TQM in the classroom, one can recognize the fears of the at-risk student. Putting aside one's fears for the purpose of establishing a classroom where each individual is empowered and can take pride in their work is the first step. One can do it and the rewards will be far greater than one ever imagined!

This book is intended to follow two threads. One, implements a Total Quality Management approach within the classroom by empowering students to engage in continuous improvement practices for the betterment of the class. The second engages each student in a continuous improvement process of his/her own. This involves a recognition of the importance of learning from one's mistakes, feeling confident to make and reach stretch goals, and taking pride in one's work through achieving quality work. Throughout there are references to both classroom practices and individual practices. We believe each of these two threads are important in weaving the cloth of a successful TQM classroom.

Chapter Three: Leadership

Nothing great was ever achieved without enthusiasm. And true enthusiasm comes from giving ourselves to a purpose.

Ralph Waldo Emerson
Circles

We suggest that the reader take the time to briefly answer the following questions prior to reading this chapter and answering the questions on the checksheet at the end.

1.0   Leadership

This category consists of six subcategories which examines your commitment to leading the students in achieving quality work.

1.1   Describe what quality means to you. If you have a formal statement, please include.

1.2   How has the quality policy and/or mission statement been deployed among the students.

1.3   Describe your leadership, personal involvement, and visibility in communicating the quality program to your colleagues, parents, the community, administration, and other groups.

1.4   Describe your preferred teaching styles.

1.5   Describe the nature of any on-going education/training you have had to keep up with the latest trends in your content area.

1.6   How do you define quality in your own work, and explain the ways you exemplify that to your colleagues.

Leadership is probably the most important ingredient in establishing quality in any organization, including the classroom. Leadership takes center stage in all of the quality philosophies. For example, the importance of leadership is targeted in Deming's seventh and eleventh points:

> 7.   *Adopt and institute* **leadership.** *The aim of supervision should be to help people and machines and gadgets do a better job. Supervision of management is in need overhaul, as well as supervision of production workers.*

> 11.a. *Eliminate work standards (quotas) on the factory floor. Substitute* **leadership.**
> b.   *Eliminate management by objectives. Eliminate management by numbers, and numerical goals. Substitute* **leadership.**

If we take the liberty of substituting words that might be applicable to the classroom, Deming's seventh point might read: Adopt and institute **leadership.** The aim of **teachers** should be to help students do a better job. Supervision of **teachers and students** needs to be overhauled. His eleventh point might read: Eliminate the traditional, standardized grading system from the classroom. Substitute leadership making sure that what the students learn, they learn well. Eliminate management by objectives and numbers. Substitute **leadership.**

The quality teacher becomes a leader rather than a manager. It's true that a good manager deals with complexity, but a leader deals with innovation and change (Kotter 1990). Quality teachers, in their role as leaders, must have the ability to empower students to bring about change in the traditional classroom. The importance of leaders having the ability to empower others has been recognized by Bennis (1990); Tichy and Devanna (1986); Manz and Sims (1990); Glasser (1990); and Gardner (1990).

The Quality Teacher as Super-Leader

One of W. Edwards Deming's key observations pertains to the systems within which people operate. According to Deming, 85% of the systems in which people work are controlled by managers, while only 15% are controlled by the workers. Since management controls the systems, 85% of the problems within any organization are the result of poor management. This statement speaks loudly to school districts, and only recently have many begun looking seriously at management as a meaningful place to begin restructuring schools. Here, we will focus on the classroom (rather than on the school as a whole) considering teachers as (leaders) managers, and students as workers. Still, the importance of educating and getting the support of principal, superintendent, and the members of the school board cannot be overly emphasized. But we will not address this issue at this time.

The concept of teacher as management is unique because they've been viewed historically as workers with the administration designated as management. This follows closely the definition of teacher, which is a person who teaches or instructs. Random House College Dictionary (1984) defines *teach* as: to impart knowledge or skill. These suggest that teaching is a one-directional endeavor, from the teacher to the student; this supports the notion of the teacher being the worker within the classroom. This one-directional model clearly no longer fits society's needs as John Goodlad, Al Shanker, Terrell Bell and others would testify.

Using the **Quality Teacher** philosophy expands one's view of the teacher's role. Teaching for critical thinking, for example, cannot be accomplished in a one-directional style; there must be on-going dialogue, questioning, researching, evaluating, etc. Critical thinking skills demand that the teacher become a "leader," guiding the student through a process which ultimately ends with empowerment and expanded knowledge for the student.

As super-leaders, quality teachers will have to assume different roles in the twenty-first century. A major goal of super-leader teachers will be not only to have all students achieving at the 85% level or higher, but also to have students always searching for ways to improve their world, their beliefs, and their society. Students who have been taught in this manner will survive and thrive in our complex, ever-changing technological society. The students will not be frightened by change because they will have been taught to accept change as a way of life.

School boards, communities and administrators must be educated in **TQM**. There must be recognition that the role of teachers is vastly different now. They must accept, and indeed encourage, teachers to become super-leaders. Super-leader teachers believe in the worth of **all students** and encourage each student to stretch their intellectual limits to achieve superior knowledge and problem-solving capabilities. Such a teacher reaches not only the academically gifted student, but also those students who may need additional time to learn a fact or concept. This teacher establishes a classroom climate conducive to universal success.

To establish a new climate within the school and the classroom, teachers must alter the way they think of themselves and their roles to include the super-leader concept. The teacher who assumes a leadership role will instill in all students a sense of inquisitiveness and desire for learning. This requires knowledge about the characteristics of super-leaders (also called Quality Teachers). It requires teachers to take a very different role within the classroom, one that will require more preparation, more flexibility and more questioning from the students. Teachers who are super-leaders will expect excellence of themselves as well as of their students.

As super-leaders, teachers will be comfortable empowering students to gain maximal learning. Central to Quality Teaching is the role of modeling. Modeling involves attention, retention, behavior reproduction and motivation; the teacher must be a role model for student's learning. By being a model of self-discipline, yet having relaxed confidence, maintaining a keen interest in learning, questioning, and respecting others and their opinions, the teacher will provide some benchmark information for students. Teachers who are able to encourage students to behave in a like manner and empower them to become increasingly more responsible for their own behavior and learning, will see students stretching their abilities and interests. One must always encourage students and provide opportunities for them to become self-leaders as appropriate to the time and setting. Motivation through encouragement and the provision of interesting educational lessons will allow students to accept the teacher as sincere while allowing them to stretch and grow continuously. Success in using this model requires that the teacher be comfortable with questioning and critical thinking.

While moving in the direction of super-leadership one must be aware of the difficulty people have with change. (We are continuously reminded about this as it relates to each of us, and the reader may find a mirror of his/her own behavior.) **The TQM model is predicated on continuous improvement, aka: change.** Continuous improvement indicates areas in the systems or processes which, if approached differently could result in better performance, product, etc. Implicit in this is a teacher willing to allow students and others to examine the current systems and processes within the classroom noting those that are flawed. It also requires the Super-Leader teacher be a role model for non-defensiveness and acceptance that no one is perfect. At the same time, the TQM approach frees teachers who can feel the fear of the process and move through it, since identifying the problem areas within the classroom gives the entire class the opportunity to become a team for problem resolu-

tion. It thus becomes everyone's problem and everyone assumes a role in resolving it; no longer is it just the teacher's
problem. None of this comes, however, without the **total
quality** (TQ) teacher taking time to educate the students.

A problem may arise if the teacher expects too much from
students without prior preparation/training in TQM principles
and without being given enough time and opportunity to
practice. One might even have the tendency to revert to top-
down management techniques because students will be
constantly testing. One should expect students to "check it out,"
to see if one really means what one is saying. They will, in fact,
test one repeatedly, until they believe we are serious about
empowering them to become more responsible for their own
learning. Once students recognize our sincerity and commitment
to this style, their confidence in themselves and us will soar. As
with the students, each teacher will find the need to continuously
reinforce the *will* to maintain the role of super-leader. This type
of dramatic change will require self-dedication to continuous
education in TQM principles and practices and the willingness to
share this knowledge with the students. Dare to be different.
Avoid letting minor set-backs cause you to lose focus on
changing the classroom management style.

The new primary functions of quality teachers will be that of
coach and cheerleader. In the coaching role one will guide and
reinforce learned processes such as goal setting, self-evaluation,
self-reinforcement, self-motivation and critical thinking skills.
The coach teaches fundamental information and skills upon
which the student can learn ever-increasingly complex concepts.
Part of this will involve assuming responsibility for teaching
adequately the principles and statistical tools of TQM to all
students so they may become empowered to begin the work of
continuous improvement.

The cheerleader provides the encouragement and rewards for
the continuous improvement journey towards quality work on
which each student will embark. In both roles as coach and
cheerleader one will encourage team play and interaction with
other students. Students helping other students grow and succeed are an important component of any successful classroom.
Students engage in teaming activities and are encouraged to
work collaboratively, solving problems of increasing difficulty.
This emulates the best principles and traditions of our
democracy, focusing on justice, fair play, honesty, cooperation
and equality. Using the classroom as a microcosm of society,
students develop the ability to work in teams for the benefit of
the organization. They also attend to issues such as respect for
others realizing that the success of the class depends on the

success of each individual. For all students to have pride in their work, accept themselves as important members of the workplace (classroom) and participate fully in their own governance, they will need a strong *TQ* teacher with a clear vision and complete understanding of TQM.

The *TQ* teacher asks the students to evaluate their own work for quality, recognizing they can learn how to produce high-quality work. Also, within the classroom, students assume a primary role in evaluating each other's work, through working together to resolve difficult problems and collaborating on research projects. All students are trained in evaluative techniques as well as identification of quality work. The students realize the responsibility for critiquing other's work is to approach it in ways that allow each individual maximum opportunity for academic growth. Indeed, in classrooms across the nation where this is currently happening, even students with minimal skills demonstrate improved self-esteem as each becomes a "helper" to fellow students. A wonderful by-product is that these students regain a "real" place within the classroom and, as their self-esteem grows, their rate of academic achievement increases dramatically. Again, the *TQ teacher* recognizes the importance of educating students in helpful ways to critique others' work without negative messages, but with a systematic method for stretching the skills of each other. In essence, each becomes teacher for the other, by discussing points where improvements could be made. This doesn't happen without careful attention on the part of the teacher; however, the dividends are enormous.

Groups of students may evaluate the group's work and/or individuals may evaluate each other's work. While the teacher is instrumental in the growth process and provides support for the process only completed assignments undergo a final evaluation by the student and teacher. Grades take on less importance as mastery learning and quality work are valued outcomes. Students who have not achieved mastery are given additional time to complete assignments. By the time students have implemented self-evaluative techniques and spent time assessing the evaluations by fellow students, most will have completed a high quality piece of work, one in which they can take great pride.

The classroom becomes a beehive of activity with the teacher as the facilitator, providing the necessary tools for students to accomplish their work, establishing some class goals (resulting from input from the students), providing meaningful assignments, and taking the role of cheerleader and coach.

Students will see their work as important and relevant to their place in society.

Remember, according to Deming, 85% of all problems within any organization are the fault of dysfunctional systems. Since management (teacher) controls the systems, change occurs when the systems are altered. Therefore, results can be positive or negative, depending on the changes made in systems and processes. *It is especially important for all teachers to be aware that the only way to alter results is by making changes in systems and processes.*

In classrooms, the systems are those things that determine the climate (or "feel") of the room. Included are such things as: the organization of lessons, teaching style, organization of materials and teaching stations, assignments, evaluation methods, discipline techniques, and arrangement of furniture. These elements control the dynamics of the classroom over which the teacher has direct control. This implies that these are also the only things the teacher can change. Changes in any of the above systems will result in changes in student attitude, behavior and eventually the quality of their work. Some specific ideas follow.

In a second grade classroom one notices the students are very noisy with little concentration following afternoon recess. The teacher is aware of the problem, but never of the root cause(s). A good place for the teacher to begin is to keep track of what the students are doing for the first five minutes after afternoon recess. One can make a small chart with such things as: talking, getting out of seat, and touching. In this instance and in the TQM model, talking among students is allowed and encouraged; however, our example implies students are not focusing their attention on the assignment, but on socializing or arguing about recess activities. For one week, the teacher can simply jot a hash mark after each one of those incidents s/he witnesses in the first five minutes after recess. At the end of the week, the results are recorded into a graph so s/he has a clear visual image of the variances from desired behavior. For example:

Frequency Table: <u>Students not concentrating after p.m. recess</u>

Behavior	Mon	Tues	Wed	Thur	Fri	Total
Talking	IIIII IIIII III	IIIII IIIII III	IIIII IIIII	IIIII II	IIIII IIIII	54
Out of Seat	IIIII III	IIIII I	IIIII II	IIIII	IIIII I	32
Touching	IIIII IIIII	IIIII IIIII	IIIII IIII	IIIII III	IIIII IIIII	46

The above data are shown in graphic form below.

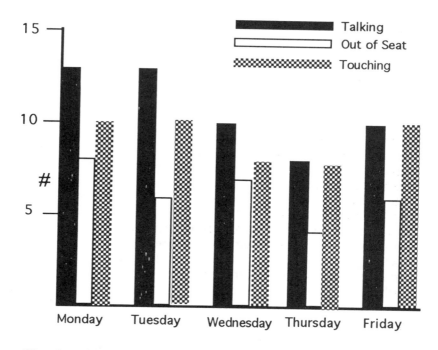

Clearly, this is an area on which to focus a continuous improvement project. By following the steps outlined in subsequent chapters one will be able to involve students in resolving the problem by empowering them to recognize the problem, and then solicit suggestions for resolving it.

One may discover that the students may agree to have the teacher lead them in a relaxation exercise for the first five minutes after recess, or read aloud to them, or have them focus on posture and breathing. Any one of these will give them the opportunity to calm down to begin restoring concentration and focus on learning. *An important point is that the teacher has discussed the problem with the students and after all suggestions for improvement have been heard, the group selects the preferred method of altering the system.* It is vital that all students have been heard and the entire group (teacher and students) has agreed on some resolution. Students must take ownership of the problem and preferred way to resolve it. Once implementation of the suggested solution begins, the teacher will make note of the date(s) and continue to chart the children's behavior. After several weeks of this the teacher analyzes the results while being sure to include students' perceptions of its success. This is the only way to be certain what effect the change has made on behavior. This information is charted (using the tools in the Appendix) and posted in the classroom so everyone can see the improvement. The group may decide that immediately after recess students need time to resolve playground issues and the next five minutes might be utilized best with the peace table example in Chapter 4, **Classroom Environment**.

In another example, let's assume the reader is a seventh grade science teacher. The students are inattentive and many are disruptive. The process you may want to pursue to gather cause and effect data will differ due to the age of your students. One method that might work is using a climate survey to determine students' perceptions of the problems within the classroom. As described in Chapter 6, **Information and Analysis** you may then utilize the Nominal Group Process. Gaining the expertise of the students will be your biggest ally in alleviating any problems encountered within the classroom. In this instance, the students may determine that they are not engaged actively enough in their own learning to maintain interest and concentration. Or, the students may tell you that the assignments don't seem to have any meaningful connection to the "real" world (a key issue that all educators need to address). This may result in altering the assignment, one's teaching style, increasing the numbers of cooperative learning assignments, or perhaps even altering placement of the furniture within the classroom to accommodate these new assignments.

In each of the above examples, data collection was the first step in determining the exact problem within the classroom. This was followed by a team approach to resolving it, with the teacher acting in a leadership role to assist and empower students to take responsibility for continuous improvement. This approach also precludes, however, that teachers assume responsibility for their part in any problems and are willing to work together with students to improve the overall classroom atmosphere.

The *TQ* teacher engages students fully in discussions about the nature of the work they will be expected to do within the quality classroom, and about drawing connections to the real world. Taking time to do this dramatically increases the efficiency of the classroom thus increasing the time spent on instruction while decreasing time spent on discipline and other non-essential activities.

Joel Barker, a noted futurist, discusses this point as well. He claims educators have an obligation to tell students what quality work is, and what they will be expected to know at the end of the unit/semester/year. (Mastery learning not mystery learning.) If we don't spend ample time explaining to students the WHY of education, then we cannot expect them to become actively involved or particularly interested, especially if there is not a clearly defined connection between the subject matter and what is happening in their lives. This reiterates Deming's second point: adopt a new quality philosophy.

Adopt the new philosophy.
The gurus of the quality movement all agree that workers are willing and capable of doing good work, provided they are given the proper education, tools, and time to do it. Many teachers have implied that the biggest problem in our educational system today is that students don't want to learn, are not motivated, have no zeal for learning, and simply will not do the work. Therefore, many teachers have chosen to lower standards to accommodate what they perceive as a general lethargy on the part of the students. Along with this comes the notion that parents are responsible for ensuring that students do their homework, and if it isn't done, somehow the parents are to blame. Blaming students and parents for the current crisis in education has not improved the system nor the results. We must understand that reasons for the problem are complex involving home, society, and school. Blaming parents will not resolve the problem, and in fact may exacerbate them.

Adopting the new philosophy requires major attitudinal changes on the part of all educators, as well as those responsible for making decisions about funding for schools. If one takes seriously the notion that everyone desires to do his/her best, then we simply have to look at our own philosophy and how it drives what is done within the classroom.   Deming, for example, believes that an essential key in effective management is to alter one's thinking about the workers. In schools, this means that we must begin thinking differently about ourselves (as teachers) and also about the students as workers. In order to accomplish one's mission, it is necessary to employ an atmosphere of SUCCESS in each classroom. Commit yourself to maintaining a success orientation. *All students should be included in the new success philosophy.*   Therefore, when one begins the class each fall, one should recognize that each student has gross untapped potential for success and everyone in the classroom will be responsible for working towards personal success as well as the success of the group.

It is necessary but not sufficient, however, to explain to students how they will be evaluated and why we think they should study something. One must also take whatever time and resources are necessary to provide the tools for them to do the job (including examples of quality work), and arrange lessons that will meet the objectives while accommodating a wide-variety of learning styles. The *TQ* teacher has high expectations of students and is dedicated to assisting all students achieve them. These teachers are ready to use any method necessary, and will continue to try new methods until every student has been reached. As the Carnegie Report, *Turning Points* (1989, p. 40) declared, *[s]chools must encourage students who fall short of success to try again and again, and schools must try again and again, using every means available to see that all students succeed.*

The quality teacher shows or models the job so students who perform the job can see exactly what is expected. **Examples of quality work are provided so students can clearly understand specifically what is required.** Expectations are clearly spelled out for all students, and each understands his/her role. Teams of students can work together identifying problems and accomplishing more than the individuals alone, while producing a superior product in which all can take pride. Cooperative learning activities with meaningful assignments exemplify this. Heterogeneous grouping provides each student with a critical and meaningful job and will help all students grow. If the assignments are well thought out, preferably cross-curricular in nature, and have clear and understandable relevance, students will work hard to "produce" a product in which everyone can take great pride.

For activities which involve mastering basic facts, students can work in pairs or small groups to achieve the same end. Learning needn't be drudgery. In fact, we ought to re-arrange our thinking on the whole idea of work. When work is viewed as drudgery there can be little pride in accomplishment, nor can there be much energy to stretch one's limits. A true quality teacher finds ways to approach subject matter with a sense of humor, challenge and creativity. Even mastering basic facts lend themselves to activities that can and should be fun for all. In fact, in the TQM classroom, learning is not only challenging, it is also fun. As such, both students and teacher enjoy being there, working towards a common purpose. There are few discipline problems in classrooms where everyone is having fun! We agree with Deming that the purpose of work should be to have fun. Imagine the peak energy level if this were true in every classroom in every school around the nation; it would assure the achievement of the America 2000 goals.

Throughout the process the *TQ* teacher is a facilitator, providing students with the best tools and a noncoercive and non adversarial atmosphere in which to do the job. There is no penalty for making or correcting mistakes. In fact, mistakes are seen as a natural path to growth—an opportunity to gain greater insight as they spawn continuous improvement projects. The classroom atmosphere is one of genuine friendliness, cooperation, and eagerness to assist others reach maximum potential. There is an excitement generated by the teacher which permeates the class. This excitement is fanned and grows when the teacher encourages questioning and critical thinking. There is no fear in the classroom as the super-leader teacher encourages each student to stretch the limits of their current thinking. Answers are reached together, with the teacher actively engaging in the process.

This brings to mind the true story of a secondary teacher (Mr. B.) who was passing through a colleague's (Mrs. S.) classroom on the way to the school resource room. Mrs. S.'s social studies class was discussing the current political upheaval in the communist countries and how it relates to world economics. Mr. B. (though an uninvited guest) couldn't resist getting involved in the discussion and gave his personal opinion of the subject. One of Mrs. S's students suggested to Mr. B. that if he had knowledge of their studies about the topic he might not take that point of view. Mr. B. became incensed that the student would say this to him. His blood pressure rose while he went to the student's face and began screaming while poking him with his finger. Mr. B. was verbally abusing the student for what he perceived was "disrespect" of a teacher. It all happened so quickly, Mrs. S. seemed stunned at first, then quickly stepped in and quietly suggested to Mr. B. that he leave. Of course, Mr. B. was too angry to interpret her remarks as helpful, and a way for him to remove himself from an embarrassing no-win situation. He did leave the room and went immediately to the principal's office.

Once there, Mr. B. informed the principal that Mrs. S. was teaching her students to be disrespectful of adults and insisted she be appropriately admonished. Since Mr. B. was the president of the local teacher's union and the sponsor of the Student Council, he maintained a powerful position within the school. The next day, with the principal's permission, Mr. B. sat down with the Student Council and insisted they draft a *Respect Oath* which all students would be required to sign. The essence of this oath was that students would be submissive to whatever the teachers' said, and, at the discretion of the teacher, any infraction could be cause for in-school suspension or even out-of-school suspension. A short time later, all students were gathered in the auditorium for a forty-five minute reading of the Respect Oath and lecture on why this was important. Students were required to sign the oath and return it to their homeroom teacher who kept it on file.

Can you imagine what message this incident sent to all the students? Can you imagine the message this incident sent to the student who received Mr. B.'s wrath? Or the other students in Mrs. S.'s class that morning?

This is a prime example of the misuse of power and control. In this instance, Mr. B. was merely using Mrs. S.'s classroom as a shortcut to the resource room. (There were alternate routes he could have taken where he would have not disrupted anyone.) As he passed through the classroom, he chose (again uninvited) to give his opinion of the class discussion. While each of these two points might be considered impolite, Mr. B. had done nothing really wrong. He was culpable, however, when he chose to take offense at the student's comments; which according to Mrs. S. were neither inflammatory nor disrespectful, but simply pointed out that if Mr. B. were acquainted with the facts as they knew them it may have altered his opinion.

We hope the reader can recognize that this entire situation would never have happened if Mr. B. were not defensive at the student's remarks. At this point, Mr. B. became engaged in a power struggle with the student. Mr. B. was fearful that the other students would perceive him as "dumb" based on the students remarks. In what probably started as an effort for him to "save face" unfortunately resulted in inappropriate coping skills. He reacted with anger and became verbally abusive to the student. Getting angry with students inevitably means the teacher will lose. Not only will the teacher lose respect in the eyes of the students, but it encourages students to retort with their own limited coping skills. This is clearly an example of why some teachers have so much difficulty with students. In this instance, the student was not considered "at-risk;" however, if he had been, we feel certain the inflammatory response of Mr. B. would have ignited a flurry of inappropriate retorts from the student. None of us can gain respect by demand.

TQ teachers respect themselves and feel secure about their roles as educators. They work diligently on eliminating biases and demonstrating respect for all students. TQ teachers also recognize the importance of free-flowing dialogue between teacher and student and encourage students to stretch the limits of their current knowledge. Conversely, TQ teachers recognize that there are many ways of looking at problems and maintain an openness with students that suggests they are willing to listen and learn as well. Actions speak much louder than words, and teachers implementing the TQM model are very cognizant of their modeling role.

Using the TQM model, there is no such thing as homogeneous grouping. There is neither a "remedial" nor a "gifted" program. All students are encouraged to participate in the most rigorous endeavors possible. Enrichment materials become integrated as daily activities for all students. The emphasis remains, however, on learning styles and providing the tools necessary to do the job. All students are expected to assist their classmates in achieving the goals of the class, and therefore will work eagerly in partners or small groups to assist their classmates. The *TQ* teacher capitalizes on the human spirit desire to help others by encouraging collaboration among students.

Students are perceived by their teachers and fellow students as wanting to do a good job, wanting to learn, and being willing to assist others. All students are educated in a problem-solving model that encourages independent decision making and responsibility for the consequences of one's actions. This process is carried out in developmentally appropriate ways in each classroom beginning in kindergarten and continuing throughout high school. William Glasser's Control Theory (1990) is an example of such a system that has been proven in a variety of school districts around the country, including Fox Chapel High School in Fox Chapel, PA, and the Johnson City School District in Johnson City, NY. Another example of an effective system for independent problem solving comes from Mrs. Denise Chronicle a third grade teacher in Linden, MI. (See Chapter 4 for more details.)

In the TQM classroom, rules are decided upon by a consensus of the teacher and students at the beginning of each school year. They are few, concise, and easy to understand. *The rule(s) is based upon the principle of respect for self and others.* The purpose of any rules are to provide easily understandable parameters within which the students know they can operate. The consequences of breaking the classroom rules are also reached by consensus after complete discussion (and ownership of consequences) with the entire class in the beginning of the year and periodically as needed. All consequences are related to resolving the problem and are never punitive but rather educational and instrumental in helping each child reach his/her potential. Traditional, punitive, and coercive attempts at discipline do not achieve the object of each individual resolving his/her own problems, and are therefore not considered by the super-leader teacher. This concept is essential to empowering the students. Empowered students will become more active in the educational process, will not need to gain attention in negative ways, will learn to respect self and others, will learn how to solve their own problems, and will enjoy a major rise in self-esteem. Discipline problems will greatly diminish and may even extinguish themselves.

The Deming Way—Adopt and institute leadership

Establish a constancy of purpose

Define your classroom mission and how all students fit into that mission. Maintain a clear focus on the mission. Be specific. Answer the question: "What do you want your students to accomplish and how?" The mission statement should be easily understood and concise. Write it down, distribute it to all your students and parents, and post it clearly in the classroom. Everyone, including the students must understand the mission so that all can retain the focus of attention and work together to achieve the mission.

Establishing a constancy of purpose requires that you have spoken with your administrators, colleagues, and fully understand the school district's mission. The search for a classroom mission is not to be taken lightly. It is likely to send you on a journey into self-assessment and evaluation of your own principles and notions about the teaching/learning process. It presupposes that you will take time to research the latest ideas of educators both within and outside your area of study and put these together with your own philosophy of education. It is important to take this journey thoughtfully, as it will be the guiding force of your work. Avoid the temptation to rush this process, believing that your mission is "a given." With careful thought and research, you can establish some insights that you otherwise may not have and which will provide clear guidelines and direction for all the activities in which your students will engage.

After careful thought and analysis, write down your classroom mission statement. Be certain you allow time for editing and re-thinking. When you're certain that your statement reflects your mission, edit it until you come up with a succinct statement that can be easily repeated and understood by all. This then becomes your mission statement, and your constancy of purpose. This is the statement you will explain and discuss with your students and the one that you will disseminate to the parents.

The mission statement can be printed in each student's *Continuous Improvement to Quality (CIQ)* book. This will help everyone maintain a clear focus. The *Continuous Improvement to Quality* book also becomes vital for teaching TQM principles, goal setting and the classroom rules. Training students in the

TQM principles and statistical process control is necessary for achieving a truly quality classroom.

Additionally educators must view themselves as Super-Leaders, leading students to accomplish quality work, to want to improve knowledge and to achieve a high level of cooperation. The *TQ* teacher also maintains a leadership role within the school district, assisting colleagues, communicating with internal (other teachers and students) and external customers (post-secondary institutions, parents, community, business and industry) and espousing the virtues of quality leadership throughout the area. The true TQ teacher will actively participate in professional activities, continuously striving to improve in subject matter knowledge as well as current best practices. Colleagues will view this teacher as a helper who communicates trust and pride in their work. The end result will be a greater knowledge base, a sense of community, pride in work, and energy to work toward constant improvement.

Super-Leaders are individuals who themselves feel very empowered and can empower their students. Empowering students means showing respect, and trust that they desire to do good work. It means leading students and allowing them to work together or individually, knowing that if they are given the proper tools to do the job, they will want to do it well. A Super-Leader teacher understands the need of all to have pride in workmanship, and will not deprive the students of the opportunity for it. Simply put, the Super-Leader teacher understands that unempowered students will be less inclined to achieve high personal goals or want to contribute to the goals of the class.

Super-Leader teachers see themselves as guides for students. They not only provide the materials with which to achieve the necessary goal, but also act as resource persons. This presupposes that the teacher has done research into the subject matter, has scoured the library for materials, (if the library is devoid or deficient in needed materials, the teacher has made specific suggestions for improving them) and is available to the students to make suggestions regarding the acquisition of additional information. Super-Leader teachers do not see themselves as "experts" knowing all the answers, but rather as resource persons who know where additional information can be gained, and who have a very solid, basic understanding of the subject matter. The teacher in this instance is eager to provide assistance, eager to learn more, and willing to learn from the students.

Important to this process is providing students with examples of quality work, and providing feedback on how the quality of work can improve. This can be accomplished through editing the writing, asking key questions, allowing the student(s) to go back and re-think their answers, and giving meaningful assignments that stretch students academic abilities while giving them something important to study.

Super-Leader teachers will coordinate assignments with colleagues from one or more additional disciplines. In essence, we are suggesting a learning community within each school. An example of this is provided in Chapter 8. Learning communities allow students to enjoy the expertise of more than one teacher while consolidating many assignments into one. The end result is a much greater depth of knowledge and expertise on the part of each student, which translates into pride in workmanship.

Each TQ teacher also recognizes the need for maintaining a personal continuous improvement approach to life. In other words, establishing a regular pattern of goal setting in their personal and professional lives makes them good role models for all students for being life-long learners. Students will quickly sense the amount of energy and commitment they have towards learning. If they sense a teacher who is lacking in energy they too, will lack a commitment to learning. Therefore, one characteristic of a *TQ* teacher is the constant pursuit of knowledge. Professionally, this means establishing professional development plans, and pursuing them with vigor through conferences, workshops, school visitations, university courses, reading professional journals, etc.

Personally, this means recognizing the importance of achieving balance between professional, personal, and family life. Goal setting and planning are important factors in maintaining a high level of satisfaction in one's personal life as well. One may decide, for example that they don't get enough exercise, or should pursue a hobby. With proper time management and utilizing TQM methods suggested in this book, teachers will find opportunities to become more effective TQ practitioners.

The importance of this is noted when teachers expend most of their energy on attempting to resolve classroom problems by themselves and then experience burn-out resulting from dissatisfaction with results. This happens often if the teacher feels s/he has made significant personal sacrifices to do this. In truth, the problems students and teachers bring to the classroom reflect society in general and as such the opportunities for resolution are greatly enhanced, utilizing a team approach. This is true of all problems within the classroom. Since each individual is endowed with a certain amount of energy, it makes sense to use it in the most efficient ways to achieve maximum gain. Therefore, one can see readily the importance of establishing trusting, collegial relationships with all students so each will be willing to assist in resolving classroom problems. There is no need to feel that as the teacher one has the burden of resolving every problem alone. There is a need, however, for each to become a leader rather than a boss-manager of the students. The students will see this approach as one of strength and it will enhance their respect for the teacher. One will also discover that sincerity enables the students to adopt a very caring attitude and the classroom will take on a highly energized, productive, and familial atmosphere, with everyone dedicated to helping the group advance towards quality.

The activities one pursues in one's personal life are important to enhance energy levels and for stress management. Learning something new through a hobby or class may provide one with another way to excite students about learning. The desire and enthusiasm for knowledge and adventure will be a source of renewal each day, whereas focusing all one's energy on students and one's teaching will eventually wear one out. *All* students (especially the at-risk students) need teachers who respect and care for themselves through maintaining a balance in their lives. The students need good role models who demonstrate this balance. The *TQ* teacher is such a role model.

_____

The following is a checksheet tool to help the reader baseline their **Leadership** skills. There are six subcategories that we consider important. Please refer to the various tables and circle the "points" next to the "criteria" that most nearly describes your present classroom situation.

1.1   Describe what quality means to you. If you have a formal statement, please include.

Points	Criteria
1	No formal statement.
2	Quality work is only mentioned at the beginning of the year, with no formal statement or examples of quality work
3	Formal statement is given to students and shared with parents and administrators.
4	A formal statement is presented to students at the beginning of the year; quality work is displayed for all to use as a model; students know what quality work means to their own success and the success of the class and school.
5	The formal statement relates to WORLD CLASS quality results with the teacher and students committed to continuous improvement in the processes and systems of the classroom and the outcomes.

1.2   How has the quality policy and/or mission been translated to the students?

Points	Criteria
1	Mainly "talk" about quality
2	There is a quality manual on display in the classroom with examples of quality work enclosed
3	Quality manual and/or policy statements about quality are distributed to all the students
4	There is training provided to all students on quality procedures and goals
5	The quality policy is deployed with a clear direction, commitment of the teacher and students and everyone works together to integrate the classroom activities.

1.3   Describe your leadership, personal involvement, and visibility in communicating the quality program to your colleagues, parents, the community, administration, and other groups.

Points	Criteria
1	Traditional management role of directing and controlling.
2	Visible in concern for quality issues within the school.
3	Visible in expressing the quality mission outside the school to parents, school board, industry, city officials, and the state department of education.
4	Active in supporting adhocracy and collaborative learning within the classroom and implements suggestions resulting from student input. Is a supportive leader for ALL students as progress is monitored and constantly seeks ways to improve the learning process.
5	Recognized as a leader outside the school for instituting quality.

1.4   Describe your preferred teaching styles.

Points	Criteria
1	Mostly lecture with some question and answer periods.
2	Use of lecture, demonstration, and question and answer periods.
3	More traditional methods interspersed with group work and research assignments
4	A variety, adapting to learning styles of students and including some collaborative learning
5	Mostly student led, collaborative learning with goal setting a major focus. Mastery learning of basic facts is accomplished in a variety of ways. Students with different learning styles are interspersed to provide all with opportunities to contribute in a variety of ways.

1.5   Describe the nature of any on-going education/training you have had to keep up with the latest trends in your content area.

Points	Criteria
1	Meet the local or state in-service requirements for annual increments each year.
2	Subscribe to at least one professional journal, and attend at least one workshop/conference each year.
3	Maintain communication with local and state curriculum specialists, read and implement the latest information, attend as many conferences as possible with the school year.
4	Make recommendations to the librarian for future purchases, send for information on the latest trends in the content area, encourage specialists to come into the classroom to provide demonstrations and/or offer suggestions for improvements, read journals and newspapers to implement the newest trends and make meaningful assignments in concert with world events.
5	Actively engaged in national, state and local organizations, and maintain a network with other professionals. Maintain an on-going, well-planned continuing education program that is well thought out and revolves around a global perspective.

1.6   How do you define quality in your own work, and explain the ways you exemplify that to your colleagues.

Points	Criteria
1	No thought has been given to quality.
2	Quality is defined by the traditional evaluation by management.
3	Quality is defined by the achievements of the students, and this information is presented in written form to my colleagues.
4	The quality of work is reflected in the student's enthusiasm for learning and achieving quality work. As a super-leader, I am available to assist my colleagues.
5	The quality of work is reflected in the "World Class" quality of students' work and their enthusiasm for helping classmates achieve success. The numbers of students choosing to pursue a career in my content area, or who are enrolling in advanced courses in the content area is also a measure of the quality of my work. Finally, we are all having fun while learning.

Chapter Four: Classroom Environment

*Each of our acts makes a statement
as to our purpose.*

Leo Buscaglia

We suggest that the reader take the time to briefly answer the following questions prior to reading this chapter and answering the questions on the checksheet at the end.

2.0   **Classroom Environment.**
This category examines the overall climate of the classroom and its accessibility to achieving quality for all students.

2.1   Describe the arrangement of furniture and equipment in the classroom.

2.2   Describe the climate of the classroom in terms of respect, care and concern for students.

2.3   How do you present a "Success" climate for students.

2.4   Describe how discipline is maintained in the classroom.

Drive out Fear

Unfortunately many schools operate in an atmosphere of fear. Largely, it is a fear of punishment, ridicule, or failure. Fear may drive the more compliant students to "behave" in ways that are socially acceptable, but does little to motivate them to be excited about school or learning. At-risk students come to school very frightened. Some display "attitudes" of arrogance and defensiveness and exhibit other anti-social behaviors designed to fool the adults, however, these are all examples of their fear.

Other at-risk students appear simply unfazed by the coercive tactics they encounter at school. Some students who possess few basic skills and are subjected to a continuous barrage of failure messages will simply give up. For many students, this happens as early as the third grade. As these students progress, it becomes important to hide the fact that they have few basic skills. Imagine the fear these students must feel when asked to read out loud, or take yet another paper and pencil test. The fear of exposure is often the catalyst that results in acting-out behavior. Students who are afraid of "being found out" will often expend all their energy acting-out knowing that whatever negative attention is spawned, at least their biggest fear will not be realized. Students know that if they create enough disruption they will be sent to the suspension room, or perhaps even better, get suspended from school. Teachers lacking education and knowledge about the at-risk population and about TQM generally react to the symptoms rather than address the underlying causes. Is it any wonder that the academic deficiencies of at-risk youth are not improving?

Traditional coercive tactics simply do not work. While they may be successful in repressing the student's behavior at the moment, they do nothing to allure the child to the wonders of learning, school, or wanting to cooperate. Everything we know about human behavior and motivation denies this is the most effective way to gain cooperation and trust. *Students will work harder in an atmosphere that is free of coercion and intimidation. We must find ways to empower students to stretch the limits of their capabilities rather than merely coercing them into behaving.* We cannot stress enough that removing fear from the classroom is essential for teachers and students alike to enjoy a fun learning environment.

Fear can also emanate from sources besides the teacher. Fear of other students can be very destructive to the child who has been victimized by siblings, parents, baby sitters, or other students.

Provide a continuous supportive environment

The Total Quality (TQ) teacher will establish a success oriented classroom which recognizes that some individuals will require more support than others. TQ teachers will use a variety of means to accomplish this including, but not necessarily limited to: peer tutors, mentoring, and support teams. The TQ teacher will be attuned to the necessity of recognizing each student and being a friendly mentor/advisor.

The continuous supportive environment cannot be achieved by simple lip service. It is not enough to have motivational posters displayed in the classroom. (Deming's point #10 - Eliminate slogans, exhortations, and targets for the work force that ask for zero defects or new levels of productivity.) A supportive environment can only be achieved by the determined effort of the teacher to involve every student in the process. Teachers must "walk their talk" each day, and continuously encourage students. For the at-risk student (who is already hyper-sensitive to any criticism) the teacher must be especially cautious to choose only those words that encourage, rather than those that ridicule.

One must be cautious about using praise in lieu of encouragement. Praise is very difficult for at-risk students to accept, since they firmly believe internally all the "bad" things which parents and significant other adults have said about them. Praising one student in front of others may have a deleterious effect on the other students as well. Teachers can probably relate to this in a parable about merit pay. While one person may feel good about it, others may become angry and resentful, thus damaging the teaming effect sought after in the TQM model. Therefore, we caution teachers about using praise or singling out one student over the others. Instead, we recommend words of encouragement for everyone within a gentle, supportive environment that is based on the firm belief that everyone can learn to achieve quality work.

Teachers that display posters with success slogans yet approach the class with biases will confuse students. It is vitally important to walk the talk each day, all day. The teacher is the central figure in establishing the classroom environment. Students will quickly decipher one's level of commitment to total success for all. Anything less than full commitment will backfire, leaving one frustrated and angry.

In addition, the TQ teacher will establish ways and encourage all students to support each other. A truly supportive environment will emerge as individual students begin to work together and take pride in the accomplishments of their classmates. Once that happens, the climate of the class will be totally different and everyone will recognize the difference in the "feel" of the class. As this occurs, all students will attend eagerly and show great desire in learning.

The Total Quality teacher recognizes that this is an on-going daily process, and one that must be guarded and protected at all times. That is, the teacher must be vigilant in ensuring that all students understand there will be no ridiculing, no put downs, and no criticizing or blaming.

Provide for students to succeed

Mastery learning of basic facts is crucial if we expect students to understand more difficult material in any curriculum. Super-Leaders understand what concepts each student has not grasped, and will provide a means for all students to achieve mastery. This may include peer or adult tutoring, skills games, computer games, and independent study with additional information and guidelines from the teacher. Super-Leaders understand that there are different learning styles, and that to achieve total success, students must be allowed to learn according to their style, not according to the teaching style preferred by the teacher.

Recognition of individual differences is important in providing a success climate. Students will come to class with different background knowledge, and abilities. This does not mean that we should place them in some homogeneous grouping however. (Imagine how it would feel to be in a class with three reading groups: Eagles, Red Birds, and Turkeys. Can you guess which group would represent the low level readers? Imagine how these children would feel. Even though our group name "turkey" is meant to be silly, the low group by any name will be well-known by all children. Everyone, including those in it, will attach a label to students in that group, and most likely it will be something like "dummy.") By utilizing the resources within the classroom, including the other students (who may be the primary resources), it is possible to provide necessary assistance to all students to increase their skill level making homogeneous grouping unnecessary.

W. Edwards Deming based the entire TQM model on the fact that all workers want to do a good job and take pride in their work. We have never met a student who did not want to learn, but we've met many students who say that "school is boring" and that "it has no meaning" to them. Teachers often erroneously translate these comments into meaning that the students are unmotivated and they don't want to learn. If this were true, we would see vast numbers of "blobs" who sit around doing absolutely nothing. Some may say that this is exactly what they see in many students. In fact, there are many students who are underachieving in school yet constantly learn new things from their peers after school jobs. Not all of these individuals become involved in criminal acts. Many get jobs during the school year. Research shows that many students quit school because they feel more pride in what they do while working than at school. For these students, schoolwork simply has little value to them. They see almost no carry-over between what is taught in school, and what is happening in their world

Change takes time, however, and teachers will have to continuously remind themselves of that. Therefore, it may be premature to expect all students to become enthusiastic learners, producing quality work within the first three or four months of adopting this new system. One must be consistent, persistent and totally dedicated to the quality management style. When students realize one is serious, has provided them with examples of quality work, and the necessary tools for them to succeed, they will begin to change. Once students hear about and understand the changes in the TQM approach to teaching, there will be more interest in becoming a part of the class. For secondary teachers this means that one's dedication, persistence and success will mean an increase in enrollment in their classes. Students will begin coming with high expectations and a renewed enthusiasm for learning.

Prior to implementing TQM, however, teachers will have to do some soul searching and recognize their own responsibility for problems arising from poor processes and systems within the classroom. This, then, is the place to start, with careful examination of the processes and systems utilized within the classroom. After that, each teacher must recognize that results will be different only as s/he begins to make necessary changes in these functions so that all students can achieve success. This requires courage and persistence, educating in different ways and much time and energy, but the results will be well worth the effort.

Some things can be modified with little or no effort (although changes should only be made as a part of the overall effort towards quality, utilizing input from students, never piecemeal or in an effort to "band aid" the problems). One of these is the organization of the classroom. The arrangement of furniture, for instance, speaks loudly about what the teacher values, and about teaching style. For example, in the most traditional classroom desks are lined neatly in rows, all equally spaced apart and facing the teacher. One would assume in this arrangement, that the focus is on the teacher and that information is provided in a top-down model. Sometimes, this may be the best arrangement, depending on the nature of the lesson being taught, however, such an arrangement rarely represents a commitment to teamwork and interaction by the students.

Ideally, the furniture can be easily moved around and adjusted according to the planned activities for the day. Tables are more easily suited to group activities than individual desks and offer more flexibility.   In some classrooms, there is precious space between desks and tables. If this is the case, teachers may need to exercise even more creativity to determine an arrangement that will produce the greatest enthusiasm about learning.

Case Study: Secondary Physical Education

One year the high school that one of us (MB) taught in was undergoing renovation and consequently the only regular physical education teaching station available for use was one of the playing fields. This provided the opportunity to examine the "classroom" arrangement and needs for modification of the current system.   There were four full-time physical education teachers, approximately 125 students per period with only a football field, track and swimming pool as regular instructional space. Knowing this was going to be the situation, we sat down and brainstormed possible solutions to our collective problem. Before we could think about solutions though, it was necessary to review the mission statement and our classroom goals. Our mission was: To inspire all students to enjoy and integrate physical activity into their lives to enhance the quality of life and life-long physical fitness. The goals for the girls' physical education program varied according to grade level. The ninth grade goals were: (1) All girls will understand their body and learn specific ways to maximize their physical potential. (2) All girls will enjoy physical activity. Our goals were different for the junior and senior students. (After much debate, we agreed to combine boys and girls classes. Thus we became pioneers in co-ed physical education.) Our goal was: All students will have fun while learning a wide variety of life time recreational activities.

With clarity on our mission and goals, we were able to visualize some ways to alter the curriculum, but the issue of space still confronted us. All along the process, our most time-honored "truths" about teaching physical education were tested. We found ourselves becoming energized thinking about new possibilities, while also sensing the changes would forever alter our classes and our roles as teachers. At times, the process was painful, but because our facilities were dramatically altered, it forced us to continue planning a new strategy. We quickly discovered potential instructional space by thinking differently about our two equipment closets and hallways. We also negotiated to include the cafeteria as part of our instructional space.

Once we were able to view our situation differently, we discovered there were five potential indoor spaces and two outdoor spaces (one that with careful planning could accommodate up to three classes at the same time). We then proceeded to discuss the current curriculum and how it could fit into our newly found space. Obviously, we needed make some adjustments. Instead of complaining, we needed to come up with an action plan for our students. It had to be fair and acceptable to everyone. One of the first things we decided was to combine the boys and girls of the junior and senior classes, and focus the curriculum on life-time recreational activities. We taught bridge in the cafeteria and had students themselves teach classes in the latest teen dance steps. We negotiated and utilized local golf, ski and bowling facilities. The ski facility was happy to assist us with instruction at no additional charge. During the spring and fall we were able to teach tennis, archery, and softball.

Among other things, we taught the tenth graders judo, wrestling, gymnastics (floor exercise only) and modern dance in the large equipment closets. The girls received instruction in self-defense in the cafeteria; at the same time the boys were weight lifting and jogging in the hallways.

Swimming classes for freshman and sophomores became a place where the girls determined what they wanted to do. Advanced swimmers were given the option to become peer tutors for a non-swimmer. Enough girls were eager to do this, so that each non-swimmer had a partner/teacher each class period. Options also included synchronized swimming, diving, endurance, basic life saving techniques, and stroke improvement. Each student wrote and signed a personalized contract. Our role was coach and cheerleader. We also added to the environment by turning only underwater lights on and playing music. The results were amazing. Each non-swimmer was able to swim across the pool by the end of the unit. Some were able to swim the length. All could tread water and float. The other girls all achieved or exceeded their contractual agreements. Everyone had fun. Not one girl refused to get involved, and everyone improved their skills far more than if we had conducted the class in a traditional manner.

We also developed an entirely new curriculum for ninth grade girls called *All About Me* which encompassed diet, nutrition, and a personalized exercise program, along with basic movement classes in dance, gymnastics, and swimming. The first thing we eliminated was grading based on the group. We recognized that individual differences in body size and shape meant that some girls would/could be successful at certain sports and others not. Also, we firmly believed it was unfair to give the naturally gifted athlete a better grade for doing something that came natural to them, while "punishing" others, for their inherent physical deficiencies. Therefore, we discussed this with all the girls and provided them with a new plan. It simply was that each would be graded on her own ability and the level at which she improved. This meant we had to develop data on each girl's current physical condition, provide each with a personal exercise program, and discuss the types of activities they would most likely achieve more success based on body shape. Each girl was then responsible for coming up with stretch goals for every activity. We also encouraged each student to assist others in meeting those goals. In fact, that became one of the most often cited positive comments by students. They enjoyed helping others, and being helped without judgment. We made many changes in our procedures to accommodate the new approach, including altering the environment as much as possible to make it more "user friendly." Often, in secondary physical education classes, a certain number of students are very active, and a certain number are on the fringe, avoiding as much activity as possible. We kept a constant focus on our mission and goals and that helped keep the students focused as well.

For example, one of our "user friendly" approaches for the ninth graders was to bring in local experts to teach proper ways to apply make-up and hair styling. Everyone enjoyed this and it fit nicely into the theme of our curriculum, though one would seldom think of this as something having to do with physical education. In a major sense, we broadened our thinking about what physical education was that year.

At the end of the year the teachers and students evaluated the program. We discovered that fun was had by all and the students learned many skills they could use throughout their lifetime. All learned to share and compromise. In fact, it was so successful that we permanently altered the curriculum.

Case Study: Elementary—3rd grade
Mrs. Chronicle, a third grade teacher at Central Elementary School in Linden, Michigan, empowers students in her class by

allowing special needs students to express their concerns about the amount of work required during the school day. For example, one bright child had experienced problems in the first and second grades because she could not complete her work as quickly as her classmates. She was often distracted by the other children and the noise in the classroom. Her second grade teacher suggested that she was immature and perhaps the problems would resolve themselves if she were retained. By the end of the second grade, the student was far behind her classmates. She had been very out-going and courageous only to become frightened to try because she couldn't work as quickly as the other students. Consequently, each night she had a stack of homework papers. This created problems at home because she believed that she was being punished for not being "good enough" at school. The mother was very conscientious and made every attempt to have her daughter complete her homework, but it was too much. This child began to dislike reading and school in general. She became introverted with her peers, was irritable at home, and resisted trying new things. The child's mother realized something was wrong and suggested she be tested for a learning disability. The testing was completed during the summer and a learning disability was indeed discovered. The child had difficulty decoding words and also suffered from scotopic sensitivity. The mother, second grade teacher and the principal met and decided not to retain her in second grade. This was done over the objections of the teacher. The principal recommended the student be placed in Mrs. Chronicle's class because of her previous success with learning disabled children.

Mrs. Chronicle empowers her students in several ways. First, she announces to the class that if anyone is unable to complete any assignments within the allotted time, they can put it into their unfinished work file, take it home and bring it in by 9:30 the following morning and it won't be considered late. Mrs. Chronicle gives no other homework.

Jenny later spoke to Mrs. Chronicle about the frustration she was experiencing because she couldn't write the spelling words five times each in the allotted time. Mrs. Chronicle, in an effort to alleviate her concerns, suggested Jenny write them three times each. Jenny, feeling a sense of empowerment said she felt she could write each word four times. Mrs. Chronicle left the final decision to Jenny who agreed to write each word four times. Since that day, the child has been able to stay on task, feel successful, and keep her promise. Any work she has taken home always comes back complete and correct the next day.

Mrs. Chronicle is astute to the children's learning styles and makes many accommodations. For example, children like Jenny who are auditory learners are provided audio tapes and head phones for test taking. After only ten weeks of school, the student asked the teacher if she could take a test without using the head phones. Her confidence has been restored: she received all A's and B's on her report card. Mrs. Chronicle's expectations have not been compromised and Jenny is having fun and is enjoying school.

Mrs. Chronicle has developed a class pledge that she asks the students to recite at the beginning of each day. It exemplifies her commitment to the notion that all students can learn as well as the things she values as it gives the students a focus.

Room #10   CLASS PLEDGE

> Today I will do my best, to be the best.
> I will listen.
> I will follow directions.
> I will be honest.
> I will respect others.
> I will care for all property.
> I can learn! I will learn!

She has 27 students in her classroom: four are special needs students, and one is emotionally impaired with an Attention Deficit Disorder. She considers about 40% of her students are at-risk. She has no aides, and the only additional services some of the children receive are Chapter I, Reading and Math. Consequently, several students (including Jenny) receive private tutoring for two hours a week. The tutor comes to the school at a time mutually agreed upon by the teacher, tutor and child. The child (in this case, Jenny), teacher, and tutor negotiated the least disruptive time for the student to be out of the classroom. Jenny agreed to give up part of her morning recess in order to minimize the amount of class time she would miss. Jenny knows that it is her responsibility to make up all of the class assignments. She is happy because she is successful. The teacher is satisfied because this child is not acting out in the classroom and is able to stay on task. The parents are satisfied because of the successful negotiations that have led to a happy, successful child. This did not happen though without the teacher recognizing that she needed to be flexible in order for the student to achieve success. The relationship between the parents and Mrs. Chronicle are, as you may have guessed excellent. With each day, this student feels better about herself and is able to take more risks knowing that if she stumbles, there will be no punishment, but a great deal of support and problem solving.

Case Study: Secondary Economics Class

Mrs. Candace Allen, a high school social studies teacher at Centennial High School in Pueblo, Colorado, has been recognized by her peers and by the state of Colorado for her excellence in teaching. One of the classes that she teaches is AP (Advanced Placement) Economics. She has no restrictions on who can enroll in the class, but requires each student to sign a contract stating they agree to do all assignments (including any summer assignments) and to work with a **study buddy.**

Mrs. Allen uses a variety of teaching methods designed to stretch each student's intellectual capability. She thoroughly understands what she hopes to accomplish from each assignment and consequently allows the students freedom to question the way each assignment is to be done. Therefore, any students believing they cannot display their best work within the parameters of the assignment are given the opportunity to discuss it with the teacher. During these negotiations, Mrs. Allen explains fully and thoroughly the purpose of the assignment, and its importance to the learning outcomes of the class (Deming's first point: Create constancy of purpose). Students are then encouraged to discuss their concerns about the assignment. Discussions are free and noncoercive, with both student and teacher fully respecting each other's opinions. **Students who can come up with other methods for achieving the same goals as the stated assignment are encouraged to complete it their way.   Expectations are neither lowered nor raised, although this teacher maintains very high expectations of herself and the students.** Students feel comfortable discussing these issues with the teacher, knowing she will neither be threatened, nor threaten. Mrs. Allen is very focused on her mission. She carefully thinks about the goals each assignment will achieve. There are no "busy work" assignments. Each and every assignment has been thoroughly prepared and analyzed as to the prospective benefit the students will gain from its completion.

The **study buddy** idea came about several years ago when Mrs. Allen recognized the importance of students working together to increase knowledge and achievement. Each fall, students are given the opportunity to provide input into how the study buddies will be assigned. There is spirited discussion surrounding this, since some students don't initially recognize the importance of the selection process and prefer to choose their friends. Sometimes selecting a friend is the way it is accomplished, but not always. Since each student in the class has signed a contract stating they agree to spend a great deal of time studying with the "study buddy," it soon becomes important to each of them. A decision is reached by consensus which is not made lightly. Discussion each fall may take portions of each class period for several days. The students in her classes work very hard, achieve a very high level of knowledge and are fully prepared to pursue advanced work in other classes because of the critical thinking and study skills they've learned from Mrs. Allen.

Discipline

Some teachers might be concerned about empowering students believing that giving students too much power may result in classroom anarchy. After all, many teacher preparation programs urge prospective teachers to **get control of the class on the first day** to minimize discipline problems. Many teachers misunderstand the control issue. In our opinion, this fear represents one of the major stumbling blocks to implementing TQM in the classroom.

Historically, discipline problems were harshly dealt with and in many instances corporal punishment was the desired mode. If a student persisted in being a problem to teachers, he or she was eventually urged to drop out of school, which seemed to work fairly well for everyone. The drop-out could find work in a factory environment and the teacher had less hassle. Now, however, things are dramatically different. We know that coercive tactics and corporal punishment never did work.

Discipline is a complex issue. It focuses on the mission of the classroom as well as on the empowerment of students. If the mission of the classroom is *to have all students become problem solvers and become life long learners*, then attention will have to be paid to the control issue. Students who are successful problem solvers control themselves first and foremost. Students who become life long learners know that learning is fun and self-discipline is necessary to achieve it. Jails, juvenile detention centers, and chemical dependency recovery centers are all filled with individuals who do not know how to solve their own problems. Maintaining a clear focus on the classroom mission, therefore, is vital to the success of each student and to the reduction of disciplinary problems.

Mrs. Chronicle empowers students by having them participate in classroom governance and problem resolution. Each fall Mrs. Chronicle places her third graders into small groups, mixing them for abilities and personalities. She draws the connection for students that, as working adults, they will have to work in groups and learn to get along together. She then provides instruction in problem solving, using a worksheet that students use throughout the year whenever problems arise between students. Mrs. Chronicle is careful to allow students ample time to discuss and ask questions. After the problem solving training, each group must select a messenger, a timer and a recorder. These are leadership positions within the group. Groups sit together all year and make their own decisions about how often these positions are rotated. She encourages students to help each other. Cheating is never a problem in Mrs. Chronicle's class. All children learn they have special ways to help their peers and no one is singled out or ridiculed. (Students not selected for a group leadership role are given other leadership opportunities.)

When problems do occur, Mrs. Chronicle listens to the students and reminds them of the problem solving model and the importance of negotiating with each other. She never intervenes in student problems, rather empowers students to resolve their own. As problems occur on the playground, all parties involved are referred to the problem solving worksheet and given time to work for problem resolution. Mrs. Chronicle says she has never had a situation where the students could not resolve their own problems, and in the process, there are few if any discipline problems within her classroom. She rarely has to involve parents in any discipline problems arising in the classroom, even though she has fully mainstreamed emotionally impaired students within her class. Below is the worksheet used by Mrs. Chronicle.

Problem Solving Worksheet
YOU CAN THINK FOR YOURSELF

Description of your problem.
1. What happened?_____
_____
_____

2. How did I feel?_____
_____
_____

3. What did I do?_____
_____
_____

Brainstorming.
1. What can I do differently?_____
_____
_____
_____
_____

Solution.
1. What am I going to do the next time?_____
_____
_____
_____
_____

_____   _____
Student Signature   Date

_____   _____
Parent Signature   Date

Please return signed to me tomorrow. Thank you.

Dr. William Glasser, in his book *The Quality School,* states it clearly: *In school, the adversarial teacher-student relationship that is destructive to quality starts quickly. As early as first grade, any child who does not do as the teacher says is almost always boss-managed, and the coercion starts. ...and their [the children's] formal education becomes secondary to a never-ending power struggle in which all involved are losers* (1990, pp. 28-29).

The Glasser model of teaching students how to resolve their own problems is excellent. It is working in schools around the country including Fox Chapel High School, near Pittsburgh, Pennsylvania and the Johnson City Public Schools, Johnson City, New York. Each of these schools has successfully adapted Glasser's model. They have dramatically lowered disruption in the classroom and have empowered students to resolve their own problems.

Other problem solving models (including Mrs. Chronicle's) may work equally well. One has to believe that all students, even those in Kindergarten possess the capability and desire to be free. Freedom is a key element in any successful school. However, we must be certain not to interpret freedom as anarchy. On the contrary, true freedom for students can be described by using these examples of school rules:

"Anything I do that will hurt myself or anyone else is forbidden."

"I will respect myself and others."

Within the realm of each of these rules is an underlying assumption that students and teachers alike know and understand their true meaning. Adopting either of these rules will not work unless ample time is provided for the class to discuss perceptions and meanings of them, both written and implied. Without taking the time to discuss thoroughly and listen to the students, neither the teacher nor the students will be happy with the outcome. Children need guidance and the teacher must be a role model for self-control and must allow discussion without coercion.

Case Study: Secondary Metal Shop Class

Mr. ABC is angry. An administrative decision was made to alter his teaching assignment after he successfully taught for many years at another school. He did not want the re-assignment, but felt he had to take it.

Mr. ABC is a perfectionist. He is not comfortable teaching older students, and is impatient with those that are not serious about their work. Mr. ABC has tried to get his students interested in their work, but nothing has worked. He is trying his best, but the students are not responding.

Most of the students in Mr. ABC's classes are doing poorly in their academic subjects and many of them are failing. Most are disenfranchised from the mainstream of students and teachers and all but a few students in his classes are at-risk.

Mr. ABC begins each class with all students standing around a shop table while he gives them instructions for the day. He expects all the students to remain quiet during this time. On observation, however, we noted that he allowed various groups of students to talk while he was talking. This went on for approximately three minutes, during which time Mr. ABC neither said anything nor indicated he was upset. One student (with whom Mr. ABC had difficulty) picked up a hammer that was laying on the table and began tapping it lightly on the table. Immediately, Mr. ABC began screaming at the student, and sent him to the principal's office.

Another shop rule is that every student must wear safety goggles at all times. The students are instructed to wear the goggles when they first enter the shop, yet as Mr. ABC was speaking, only five students were wearing the goggles. Even Mr. ABC did not have the goggles on. Others never put them on during class. When Mr. ABC noticed two students not wearing goggles, he went to them, and with his face very close to theirs, began screaming at them. These young men started screaming back at him. Mr. ABC sent them to the principal's office, where they got a three day in-school suspension just like the first young man.

After class, Mr. ABC told us that he is fearful of an accident and feels he must maintain safety first in the shop. He referred to his students as bums and hoodlums and said they shouldn't even be in school. We agreed that safety must be the first consideration, however, we believe Mr. ABC creates many of his own problems.

Mr. ABC made several mistakes. First, he had rules for the class, but didn't adhere to them himself. Second, he left the hammer on the table, thus tempting students to pick it up. Third, he was inconsistent in his decisions with regards to his rules. Fourth, Mr. ABC's reaction under stress was to scream at the students and "to get in their faces." Fifth, he had strong biases about his students and didn't respect them, making it impossible for the students to respect him. Sixth, Mr. ABC sent each of the offending students to the principal's office where they got a three day in-school suspension, making it even more difficult for them to achieve success in any of their academic classes. When this happens, the other teachers become angry and frustrated because the students are not in class: the students get farther behind in their work; and everyone loses. Clearly, Mr. ABC's discipline policy didn't work.

If Mr. ABC applied the TQM approach to teaching, he would assess those processes and systems within his shop that were hampering quality. By following the techniques in Chapter 5, Mr. ABC could effect positive changes in his classroom environment, and focus on his mission.

Within each classroom one may end up feeling frustrated because the "students don't get it," or that they are incapable of knowing how to discipline themselves. One may feel, as many teachers have expressed, that they have to repeat themselves over and over again. To this, we respond, "right!!" One will have to take every opportunity to reinforce the classroom rule, and when one stops the activity, it is important to let every student know why. For instance, when one sees or hear students verbally abusing others by calling them names, saying disparaging things about their heritage, etc., it will prove worthy of one's time to call a halt to any curricular activity and discuss what is happening. It is fairly simple to relate most anything that happens within any classroom to one or both of these classroom rules:

"Anything I do that will hurt myself or anyone else is forbidden."

"I will respect myself and others."

Failure to do so implies consent and approval. The students will be very aware of the conditions under which one chooses to interrupt classroom activity. The rewards for persistence in adhering to such rules is a classroom that functions as a team, working for a common good, where all feel worthwhile and each shares a spirit of willingness to help the other.

Implementing the wonderful, inexpensive idea of a "peace table" in the classroom will also prove beneficial to all. This suggestion from Dolores J. Kirk from Peace Links in Missouri is one that allows even very young children to participate in problem solving by providing a process within which it can happen. Even if the school does not have a time-out room, or lacks the resources for one, one can arrange a "peace table" (any designated spot) within their classroom. The peace table allows each individual to be heard without fear of retribution. The rule is that any individual wishing to talk must touch the table. This includes teachers, and allows a systematic process for being heard. It is very empowering to all participants. For details see: *Discover the World: Empowering Children to Value Themselves, Others and the Earth,* edited by Susan Hopkins and Jeffry Winters (1990).

Whether one's individual style precludes their use of the Glasser model of Control Theory, the Kirk model of the Peace Table, Mrs. Chronicle's model for problem solving, or some other form of problem solving model, each will work to empower the students, allowing each to develop and grow into responsible citizens, eager to learn. Gone will be the student who works out of fear of punishment. Gone will be the student who cannot seem to control his behavior, or who simply acts as if he doesn't care. Instead, one will see each child gain in self-esteem and confidence as each problem is resolved. An exciting benefit is that the teacher will be relieved of believing that *s/he must control the students*. In truth, we all know that we cannot control another's behavior.

The following is a checksheet tool to help the reader baseline their **Classroom   Environment** skills. There are four subcategories that we have considered important. Please refer to the various tables and circle the "points" next to the "criteria" that most nearly describes your present classroom situation.

2.1   Describe the arrangement of furniture and equipment in the classroom.

Points	Criteria
1	Furniture is arranged in rows. Equipment and supplies are locked in cabinets not accessible to students.
2	Furniture is clustered in small groups. Equipment is not readily available to students.
3	Furniture is periodically rearranged to compliment lessons and student activities. Some equipment is available to students most of the time.
4	Classroom furniture becomes a workstation for student groups and they arrange it as needed.
5	Equipment and furniture are extensions of the work taking place within the classroom. Students may move the furniture to suit their needs. Equipment is kept out and ready for students use. Everyone understands the need to respect others and property is properly handled and cared for.

2.2   Describe the climate of the classroom in terms of respect, care and concern for students.

Points	Criteria
1	Interaction between teacher and students and between students is infrequent.
2	All students are greeted in a friendly manner each day.
3	The teacher takes care to let students know he/she is available to "talk" outside of the classroom.
4	The teacher presents him/herself as a role model for caring and respects all students. There are no visible biases for students or groups of students.
5	The teacher maintains a supportive, caring role when students are ill or troubled and makes time for them.

2.3   How do you present a "Success" climate for students?

Points	Criteria
1	There are some success posters in the room.
2	The teacher posts examples of student work, and provides some individual rewards for "excellence".
3	The teacher is the cheerleader for the group. Students have no fear in the classroom. Students' self-esteem is affirmed even when mistakes are made. Mistakes are accepted as necessary risks towards growth. There is no blaming.
4	The teacher openly displays an unconditional belief in the ability of ALL students to perform quality work and maintains high expectations of self and the students. To this end, the teacher constantly and patiently strives to assist all students to achieve quality work.
5	Students engage in meaningful activities, which allow them to want to achieve quality work. They are encouraged to work collaboratively and help others achieve success. The group goal is to have every student achieve success and in the process gain pride of workmanship and have fun.

2.4   Describe how discipline is developed and maintained in the classroom.

Points	Criteria
1	Traditional punitive methods are developed and implemented by the teacher.
2	Students understand the classroom rules and those who choose to break them are reprimanded.
3	Students assist in establishing classroom rules and the consequences of breaking them.
4	Students are held responsible for their own behavior and disruption may involve "time-out" and includes a contractual arrangement with the teacher to resume regular classroom activities.
5	Discipline problems are few since all students are empowered and accepted equally. Students have no fear in coming to the classroom. All students learn ways to communicate through speaking and in writing that allows them to resolve problems without major disruption to the class. Students are expected to resolve problems with others involved, rather than having teachers or administration solve the problem.

Chapter Five: Information and Analysis

Quality comes not from inspection but from improvement of the production process.

W. Edwards Deming
Out of the Crisis

We suggest that the reader take the time to briefly answer the following question prior to reading this chapter and answering the questions on the checksheet at the end.

3.0   Information and Analysis

This category examines the scope, validity, use, and management of data and information that underlie the total quality system in the classroom. Adequacy of data and information is examined to support a prevention-based quality approach using "management by fact."

3.1   In what areas (materials, student satisfaction, student involvement, parent satisfaction, students entering postsecondary institutions, students adequately prepared for the next level of instruction in any given curricular area, number and type of discipline problems, student retention, time for achieving mastery in any curricular area, etc.) do you have data to illustrate quality trends by function, and/or process in your classroom? Please list. If you have any, please enclose examples of quality trends.

TQM and TQI can never be achieved without collecting data as systems management is based upon fact not intuition. The idea of collecting factual data should not be frightening. Many who work in "people related" careers are resistant to the notion that statistics can drive the system better than some "softer" approach such as human relations. The use of statistical methods helps uncover clues as to on how the class is performing. One may be frightened by data collection and statistical methods because of the belief that "data" will be used against them, and although we cannot guarantee that it will not happen, we encourage teachers to recognize these fears and move forward in spite of them. What will really be important is the quality generated because baseline data was collected and results compared over a period of time.

Teachers may want to think about their classroom as having certain processes and systems that need attention. Things may be happening for which one is unable to assign causes. For instance, a certain group of students may be acting out, or may seem unable to stay on task for very long, or may have seemingly low reading levels or may not be able to spell or write very well. No matter what is tried, nothing dramatic changes. This would be enough to frustrate anyone.

Try looking at the situation from a different point of view— one that implies that the systems and processes within the classroom can be improved to increase the students performance. One then becomes a detective, attempting to determine which systems and processes are weak and need improving. This is just one area where factual, statistical data becomes very important. There are many kinds of data that can be collected and used for baseline information. The statistical data selected for analysis will in part be determined by the grade level being taught. Critical to data selection will be an analysis of the **customers**.

Before collecting any data, teachers will need to do several things:

1. *Establish a small group of individuals* who are directly involved in the situation to assist in the data collection to determine root causes of the problem and to create an action plan.
2. *Decide which problem(s) needs to be addressed.*
3. *State the problem clearly and succinctly.* Be certain to include when, where, and the extent of the problem.
4. *Establish a chart which diagrams the exact breakdown points* leading to the problem.
5. *Agree on the causes* of the problem.

6. *Develop an action plan* designed to resolve the problem.
7. *Implement the action plan and monitor the results.*

Case Study: Ninth Grade English Class

Mr. Waldon had been teaching high school English for over twenty-three years. He was experiencing difficulty in getting his ninth grade students to become actively involved in his English classes. Well over half the students had earned less than 50% of all possible points during the first semester. While Mr. Waldon had never taught ninth graders before, he prided himself on having very high expectations for all his students. He expressed some concern that the students were not doing very well and believed they simply didn't want to learn. In the past, Mr. Waldon had always taught eleventh and twelfth grade college bound classes. His goal was to have all his students increase their vocabulary and knowledge about English literature.

Every Monday Mr. Waldon wrote on the board twenty-five vocabulary words that were selected from a compiled list of words on the SAT. During class, each student was required to look up the definitions of each word. On Tuesday, Mr. Waldon gave a reading assignment from the literature book. Again, students worked independently, doing silent sustained reading for the entire period. Wednesday, the students took a quiz on the word definitions and began reading aloud from the literature book. Thursday, the students were asked to discuss the reading. Mr. Waldon asked key questions and students were guided through an analysis of the reading. Friday all students were given a spelling test on the vocabulary words. At the end of each literature unit, the students were given a major (machine scored) test.

Mr. Waldon was frustrated that very few students received passing grades on the vocabulary or unit tests. He felt they were simply lazy and if they would just study, they could vastly improve their grades. He was unable to understand why the students chose not to participate more fully in the class.

After taking a workshop on applying TQM and TQI into the classroom, the following is an example of a few things that Mr. Waldon did to improve his classroom situation and increase achievement. He first performed a Climate Survey in order to get feedback from his customers—his students, peers, administration, and parents. Although lacking in many respects, including not being statistically valid, the survey instrument demonstrated that the students perceived him to be hierarchic, unfriendly, and boss-like.

CLIMATE SURVEY
(Adapted from Pueblo Colorado School District #60)

I am a:

	Student
_____	Student
_____	Teacher
_____	Parent
_____	Administrator
_____	Community representative

You are asked to respond to each question twice. Mark (√) 1 if you agree or (√) 2 if you disagree.

QUESTION	How Things Are Now		How Things Should Be	
	1	2	1	2
1. This teacher treats students with respect.				
2. Parents are welcome in this class.				
3. This teacher respects those from other subject areas.				
4. Students feel this teacher likes them.				
5. While we don't always agree, we can share our concerns with each other openly.				
6. The teacher is a good spokesman for this class.				
7. This teacher makes students enthusiastic about learning.				
8. The teacher is enthusiastic about learning.				
9. The teacher feels pride in this school and its students.				
10. The teacher develops and maintains a high level of morale.				
11. I feel my ideas are listened to and used in the classroom.				
12. When important decisions are made about changes in this classroom, I have been involved in some of the discussions.				
13. Important decisions are made in this classroom by a team process.				
14. The teacher is seeking new ideas.				
15. There is a "we" spirit in this classroom.				
16. The teacher and students collaborate toward making the classroom run effectively with little teacher–student tension.				
17. Differences between individuals and groups (both teacher and students) are considered to contribute to the richness of the class.				
18. When a problem comes up the class has procedures for working on it.				

19. Problems are seen as normal challenges and not as "rocking the boat."		
20. Students are encouraged to be creative rather than to conform in the classroom.		
21. This teacher really cares about students.		
22. I think my classmates care about me.		
23. The teacher really cares about me.		
24. The teacher tries to deal with conflict constructively not just "keep the lid on."		
25. When there are classroom conflicts the result is constructive and never destructive.		
26. I feel this teacher is friendly and easy to talk to.		
27. The teacher talks with us frankly and openly.		
28. The teacher is available to students who want help.		
29. In this class there is communication between groups.		
30. This teacher knows how to teach as well as what to teach.		
31. Problems in this class are recognized and worked upon openly. They are not allowed to slide.		
32. People in this class solve problems, they don't just talk about them.		
33. In this class students with ideas or values different from the commonly accepted ones get a chance to be heard.		
34. This teacher believes there may be several alternative solutions to most problems.		
35. Students from this class know how to resolve their own problems.		
36. Students from this class take responsibility for their own learning.		
37. This class fosters a sense of teamwork and everyone wants to help others.		
38. Students feel pride in this class.		
39. This teacher shares information and ideas with colleagues.		
40. This teacher displays a sense of teamwork among colleagues, students and parents for purposes of student success.		

Although skeptical at first, Mr. Waldon proceeded to use the following TQI tools to get at the root causes of the problem(s) in the system and to get the students working together as a team to improve their learning: Flow Charting, Nominal Group Process, Cause-and-Effect Diagramming, and Run Charting. The techniques for utilizing these tools are in explained in the Appendix. In this example we will simply show the data, interpretation, and end-results of Mr. Waldon's efforts.

Sometimes it is obvious what the principal problem(s) of a given class is and why it needs to be addressed. In most cases, however, a major "system" that inhibits quality within a unit may not be readily apparent either to the teacher or to most of the students in the entire class. Some say that their classroom or school has so many serious problems that they don't know where to begin. As a result, it is a common mistake among teachers and principals to draw up meaningless long-range plans in an attempt to identify and correct all of the problems within three to five years. The objectives in the plan cannot be met because resources cannot be diverted from the "real" to the "ideal" and everyone who helped design the long-range plan becomes disenchanted as their proposed remedies are not implemented. Morale suffers; and it is business as usual.

In order to concentrate on the major problems within a classroom that detract from that class doing quality work, it may become necessary for the teacher to have each class identify the major problem(s) by one or more of the tools listed in Table 5.1 The actual procedures for using the TQI tools are explained in Appendix.

Using the nominal group process (NGP) and several other tools mentioned below, Mr. Waldon had his classes identify and rank the major problems/processes that were perceived to inhibit learning in his class. The results of the NGP are shown in Table 5.2.

Table 5.1: Several extremely useful total quality improvement tools to identify and rank problem "processes" and/or "systems" in classrooms.

Affinity Diagram
- Used to examine complex and/or hard to understand problems
- Used to build team consensus
- Results can be further analyzed by a **Relations Diagram**

Cause and Effect Diagram (Fishbones)
- Used to identify **root causes** of a problem
- Used to draw out many ideas and/or opinions about the causes

Flow Charts
- Gives a picture of the processes in the system

Force Field Analysis
- Used when changing the system might be difficult and/or complex

Histogram
- A bar graph of data which displays information about the data set and shape
- Can be used to predict the stability in the system

Nominal Group Process
- A structured process to help groups make decisions
- Useful in choosing a problem to work on
- Used to build team consensus
- Used to draw out many ideas and/or opinions about the causes

Pareto Diagram
- Bar chart that ranks data by categories
- Used to show that a few items contribute greatly to over-all problem(s)
- Helps the team identify which processes/systems to direct their efforts

Relations Diagram
- Helps the team to analyze the cause and effect relationships between complex issues
- Directs the team to the **root** causes of a problem

Systematic Diagram
- Used when a broad task or goal becomes the focus of the team's work
- Often used after an **Affinity Diagram** and/or **Relations Diagram**
- Used when the action plan needed to accomplish the goal or the task is complex

Using the NGP approach, Mr. Waldon started by explaining to the class why he was concerned, what the essential problem was, and what he hoped to accomplish by using this technique. This presupposes that Mr. Waldon has respect for the students and was willing to work to establish trust with each student. If only some of the students participate (either the achievers or non-achievers) the results will be invalid. Therefore, it was imperative that Mr. Waldon lay the proper ground work before he began the NGP.

In fact, Mr. Waldon decided that someone other than he should be in charge of facilitating the process. In which case, he chose a middle-of-the-road type student who was fairly well liked by the other students. This helped others feel comfortable about expressing their perceptions.

Mr. Waldon stated his concerns to the class in a non judgmental, factual way. The students were then asked to give their impressions of why student performance was so poor in his class. Mr. Waldon was very careful not to become defensive and to listen nonjudgmentally to all students. By the time all students had finished talking, the facilitator has developed a list of responses shown in Table 5.2.

Table 5.2   The rank and the final values of perceived problems as assigned by the students in Mr. Waldon's classes using the nominal group process.

Rank	Perceived Problem	Final Value
1	The class is repetitious	280
2	The class is boring	230
3	The class is not important	180
4	The class is not challenging	20
5	Others	90
	TOTAL	800

This technique, as well as any of the other TQM techniques will not work unless students feel they are operating within a non-punitive environment. Students who believe in your sincerity to alter the class so they can reach greater levels of achievement will want to assist the teacher in this process. Students who feel threatened, or who feel that there may be some reprisals from the teacher or others will be less apt to be honest, and will not provide you with the required information. It is very important that you take time to explain to the students your intentions, why you decided to do this, and how committed you are in making positive change. Of course, one should already have their mission statement posted and should have spoken to the students about TQM.

Let's follow the problems listed above to demonstrate how various TQI tools were used to solve this "systems" problem.

Using the results from the nominal group process, Mr. Waldon and the students agreed that an action team be established to concentrate on improving the success rate and making the class more fun. After consultation with the students, Mr. Waldon established an action team consisting of seven students, Mr. Waldon, and two parents. The action team was to make specific recommendations to improve the learning system.

The first thing the action team did was to flow chart the system under study. This is shown below.

Flow chart of Mr. Waldon's spelling and vocabulary testing system.

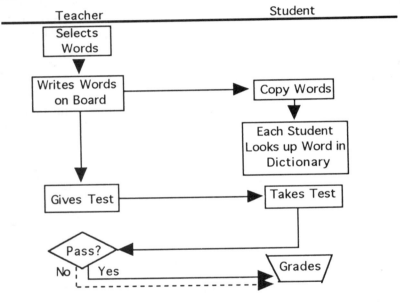

As one can see, there is no feedback loop for those students who do not pass either the vocabulary or spelling test. Therefore, at the end of each week, there are many students who have not learned the words, defeating Mr. Waldon's goal. A major place where the process breaks down is where there is only a one way flow. Students who do not pass, simply fail. There is no opportunity to rectify mistakes. There is no opportunity for these students to become engaged in the process differently. If the flow was different, the action team concluded, the students might be more successful.

On the basis of the results from the Climate Survey and the NGP the action team wanted to get additional information as to the root causes of the unacceptably low student achievement rate. The action team posted a fishbone (cause-and-effect) diagram permitting all students to add their remarks. The completed fishbone diagram is presented below.

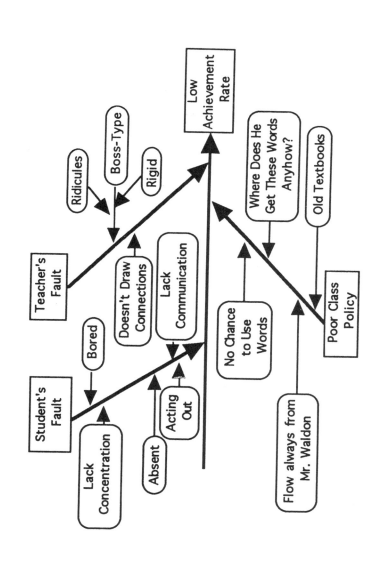

As a result of the data from the above TQI tools, the action team recommended changes in the "system." Mr. Waldon revised the vocabulary and spelling system per recommendation of the action team. The flow chart of the revised system is presented below.

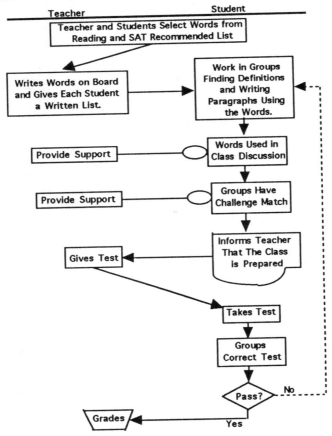

Revised flow chart of Mr. Waldon's spelling and vocabulary testing system.

After the system was modified per the suggestions of the action team, Mr. Waldon did some charting of his own. He compared and posted run charts of the percent of students in his class that received a grade of 90% or better in the vocabulary and spelling quizzes before and after the changes. (Each student was also encouraged to record their personal scores in order for them to determine their best manner for learning.) Mr. Waldon also kept information for each student and found it to be very useful in determining individual learning styles and well as for group improvement.

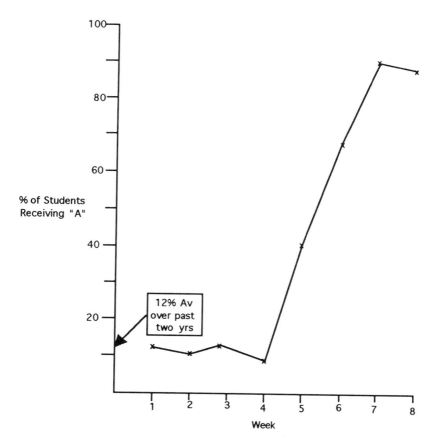

We can't guarantee that everyone using TQM and TQI tools will be as successful as Mr. Waldon, however, two years later an average of 86 percent of his students receive an "A" while 10 percent receive a "B" and less than 1 percent receive a "D" or "F."

Other Considerations

Secondary teachers can also tabulate student's results on such tests as the PSAT, SAT, ACT, and AP tests. Elementary teachers can utilize data obtained from whatever standardized tests are administered within the school. Data accumulated from these tests can be very useful when assessing students' ability to be successful at the next level of education. Although, in these cases, one will be sifting through data from the previous year's students, trends can provide one with excellent clues as to potential problem areas within the class. Actually, analyzing the data and using it to improve the systems and processes within the classroom is the only justification, in our opinion, for giving students standardized tests. For example, students who score poorly in the reading subsection of the SAT might be assisted by teachers of: English, foreign languages, geography, history, science, economics, psychology, etc. Assisting students in interpreting the readings, and implementing other critical thinking skills techniques within the classroom can improve these skills.

Another source of valuable data are attendance records. Graphing or charting absences along with such things as achievement allows clear insight of the resulting effect and may be important to your district. Disruptive student logs allow the teacher to note numbers of disruptions, time of day and how the problem was resolved. These logs can be completed for individuals and/or groups. Time of day is important, as is notation of the teaching methodology at the time the disruption occurred. Analysis of these variables may indicate that children are more apt to be disruptive during a certain time of the day, such as right after lunch. Similar trends may provide valuable information useful for quick resolution of a situation.

Some may notice that certain students act out only during the use of a certain teaching style. This allows the teacher to think differently about the student's behavior. For instance, if a particular student is more disruptive when one is lecturing, but is always attentive when engaged in some tactile learning activity, then one can surmise that the student is probably not an auditory learner. Thus, one can select alternative activities or limit the amount of time the student is exposed to the lecture method.

Other statistical data one may want to gather includes the length of time students take to achieve unit mastery. In outcomes based education models, generally students are allowed to proceed at their own pace until they have achieved mastery (at a level determined by each school district). Some schools have recorded these data and determined the length of time it takes most students to achieve mastery, then used this information as a basis for determining the length of time per unit. It is important, however, to recognize that each of us needs a certain amount of "stress" in our lives. Without it, we would be so bored that we would become more stressed and less able to complete our work. Too, with students, it is a fine balance between pushing too much and not demanding enough.

For those teachers working with graduating seniors it is important to determine the satisfaction levels of both post-secondary institutions and major employers in the area. One way to begin this is to obtain information on which post-secondary institutions have accepted your students. Have any taken the AP test in one's subject area? If so, how many have received a 3, how many a 4, and how many a 5. Do more students take the AP test each year? What does the trend look like? Survey the students after the first year to see how many were successful in your subject matter area. If they were having difficulty, one should seek to discover what could have been done differently that would have helped. For example, perhaps the reading list for the 12th grade English Literature class is not rigorous enough. This information will provide data for re-evaluating the curriculum and selection of materials.

Employers can be surveyed to discover what skills they require for entry-level employment in their workplace. For many clerical positions students need a basic knowledge of certain word processing software. We have found that most larger employers in a given region seem to prefer similar software. Students are at a disadvantage when seeking employment if the school doesn't have such software. Knowing this information provides one with an opportunity to request the school purchase such software. If that isn't feasible, perhaps one could ask local employers using that package to purchase a copy for the school. Other employers have strict rules of grammar in both speaking (answering the telephone) and writing. Students graduating from classes seeking entry-level positions who have poor verbal communication skills, are unable to write a grammatically correct sentence, or spell common words will be unable to maintain such a position.

These are samples of the kinds of data one can begin to obtain and utilize when determining the success of students and the success of teaching techniques. Every piece of data collected should be used to its fullest because: (1) no one wants to provide information if it won't be used, (2) information should be analyzed and represented in ways that can be readily interpreted by all, including students, parents, colleagues, and the school board, (3) the only reason to collect information is to use it to alter the processes and systems within the classroom, (4) all information should be disseminated to students and parents, thus allowing them to become partners in change so that everyone can become a winner, and (5) information becomes a part of the plan-do-check-act (P-D-C-A) cycle which is crucial to the Total Quality Management.

Information becomes a friend. It gives a focus for change. It allows each to plan effectively, then make the necessary changes. Once one has planned, and changed a process or system, the DO part of the cycle kicks in. After additional information is gathered, which is the CHECK stage, one can then ACT (change again if necessary). The cycle continues for the teacher and for the students every day, all year. It is the process by which one seeks constant improvement.

The following is a checksheet tool to help the reader baseline their **Information and Analysis** skills. There is one subcategory. Please refer to the table and circle the "point" next to the "criteria" that most nearly describes your present classroom situation.

3.1   In what areas (materials, student satisfaction, student involvement, parent satisfaction, students entering post-secondary institutions, students adequately prepared for the next level of instruction in any given curricular area, number and type of discipline problems, student retention, time for achieving mastery in any curricular area, etc.) do you have data to illustrate quality trends by function, and/or process in your classroom? Please list. If you have any, please enclose examples of quality trends.

Points	Criteria
1	No data or just the standard evaluation data.
2	Standard retention data, with some information on curricular trends.
3	Use of statistical methods to monitor critical processes and systems.
4	Cost of quality analysis data are collected and available for all (including students) to examine.
5	Within the classroom all processes and systems are analyzed from statistical data and use the Plan-Do-Check-Act (P-D-C-A) cycle to improve the processes and systems.

Chapter Six: Strategic Quality Planning

Your [the] past cannot be changed,
but you can change tomorrow by your
actions   today.

David McNally
Even Eagles Need a Push

We suggest that the reader take the time to briefly answer the following question prior to reading this chapter and answering the questions on the checksheet at the end.

4.0   Strategic Quality Planning

This category examines the teacher's planning process for empowering students to achieve quality work and the short and long-term priorities to achieve or sustain any leadership position.

4.1   Summarize your specific principal quality goals, objectives, and plans for the short-term (3-6 months) and longer term (1-2 years).

Strategic quality planning begins with a firm commitment from the total quality (TQ) teacher who will no longer do "business as usual" in the classroom. This will be an outgrowth of some sense of discontent one is feeling about the operations within the class which probably will include the levels of achievement of **all** students. For years one may have wondered how to engage all the students actively in learning. Like many teachers, one may have tried a variety of techniques. More likely, one noticed that with each change even though more students may get involved, many don't seem to care. Engaging all students in the activities is a key factor in the overall success. This is where the TQM approach works.

One of the first things is to recognize is the need to *include everyone in the transformation.* All students within the classroom will eagerly participate if they are given the opportunity to understand how this approach will help them, and what the changes will mean. An excellent way to accomplish this in the classroom is to provide ample time in the fall for class discussion. Such discussions must be within the context of a trusting, open environment where students feel "safe" in expressing their views (both positive and negative) without fear of reprisal either from the teacher or from fellow students. At first, students will probably be skeptical of this new plan. After all, the very concept of a teacher saying s/he was going to institute an entirely new way to operate the classroom, and that every student would be asked and encouraged to provide input for improving the class is foreign.

This will take time. However, without a proper foundation the students will be confused and unsure of what is expected. This will undoubtedly lead to a lack of enthusiasm that the teacher may view as a lack of motivation or caring. Since the TQM model is dramatically different for the classroom, it will take some time to properly educate the students. It is **essential** that all students receive education about TQM, and in fact, as one goes through the education process with the students their knowledge and commitment to TQM will grow. Without strong leadership and dedication to the TQM model, teachers will be unable to convince students that this is a good way to operate the class. It is crucial, especially in the beginning when students are in the skeptical phase, for the teacher to continue to persist and educate them about TQM. Giving class time to TQM in the fall will pay dramatic, positive dividends by the end of the school year as each student will become involved in the class and will produce higher quality work.

A TQ teacher also informs the administration and parents about the plan in a well constructed written form. It's also important to receive input from the administration and parents. This can be accomplished in a variety of ways, including the use of some statistical tools. One must be certain to lay the groundwork for understanding among these groups prior to seeking input from them. This will be discussed in Chapter 10, **Customer Satisfaction**.

Educating the students, administration, and parents to the TQM model, and how it seeks to empower students to perform higher quality work, will allay many fears, particularly those of the administration and parents. The teacher must take time to ensure all groups that their input is vital to the functioning of the TQM classroom. Let all groups know how they will be informed of the results of this approach, as well as what one will do with the provided input.

Using TQM means that the communication is both vertical and horizontal. Traditional classrooms only utilize the vertical method of communication, essentially excluding students and parents from having any viable say in the operation of the classroom. TQM, however, not only encourages horizontal communication, it is crucial to the success of this model. Teachers, therefore, will need to establish new ways of thinking about horizontal communication and how such communication can be used to ensure continuous improvement.

For example, providing students and their parents with a climate survey several times a year will provide insight as to whether or not some of the changes being made in the classroom are having the desired effect. Results of these surveys should be provided to students and parents as well as the administration. After the data are distributed, part of the continuous improvement process includes meeting with quality councils (groups) and analyzing and discussing the results. The process then reverts to gathering additional information and doing an analysis of the problem areas. This process will include the use of TQI tools such as the "cause-and-effect" (fishbone charts) within the classroom from second grade up. Remember, the basis of TQM is continuous improvement, so *the results of climate surveys and other data must be viewed in a positive way, focusing on the information received and never blaming anyone or any group.* Statistical data simply provides people with ways to identify problems.

It may seem impossible to think about spending classroom time on TQM when one feels pressured about the time constraints of curriculum matters, district policies, state and federal regulations. We have heard many teachers, especially at the lower grade levels complain about not enough time to get through the "academic" curriculum of reading, writing and math let alone having time for art, music, science, social science and physical education. The beauty of the TQM model is that once it is up and running, it takes a tremendous burden off the teacher to be the boss-manager. It effectively eliminates most, if not all serious discipline problems, and engages each child actively in the learning process. This model empowers students to be responsible for and feel good about their work. So, whatever time it takes in the beginning will pay vast dividends in the spring.

Goal Setting

Once the commitment to TQM is made, and the teacher has found a way to include everyone in the transformation, the next step will be to establish **goals for the class.** The goals must be directly related to the mission statement. They will become the map for achieving the mission. In fact, a graphic representation of the mission statement and goals, with some interim short-term goals will be a constant reminder to the teacher, the students, the parents, and the administration as to the focus. The statement and goals should be displayed in a readily observable place in the classroom, so that everyone who enters will clearly understand the direction.

Whether within the classroom or within the school, it is important to establish goals. As alluded to earlier, goal setting provides a map to reach a certain destination. Within the classroom there will be class goals as well as individual goals. The TQ teacher will methodically teach the art of goal setting to all students in the fall, along with the TQM instruction. Students can assist in setting the goals of the group, such as when assignments will be due as well as what the nature of the goals will be (with guidance from the TQ teacher).

Each student will also engage in personal goal setting on a regular basis, and will track his/her progress towards achieving these goals. In the early elementary grades, it may be necessary to have the teacher assist in charting students' progress, but as soon as students are able, each child can and should become responsible for doing their own charting. This will become their record that allows the student instant access to his progress and his educational and emotional/social growth. This feedback is crucial for developing self-discipline as well as maintaining a high level of enthusiasm.

At-risk students are seldom reared in homes where goal setting is practiced, let alone a priority. Yet we know that individuals who don't set regular stretch goals become fragmented and confused, often going through life with little direction. It is especially important, therefore, to recognize the importance of teaching all students how to set goals and how to utilize mapping techniques to enhance the attainment of goals. This will take time, but the rewards will be appreciated by all. Another by-product of utilizing daily goal setting in the classroom is that it provides individuals and groups with the sense of personal accomplishment which enhances self-esteem since it empower students to have some control over their lives.

The following example is from a fifth grade class in which the teacher is alone with 28 students.

Mission Statement: To inspire all students to become responsible citizens, to be responsible, enthusiastic learners achieving their fullest potential, and to accept the challenge of responsibility for the success of everyone within the class.

Long-Range Classroom Goals:
All students will embark on continuous improvement projects aimed at producing quality work.
All students will utilize the problem solving model for resolving personal and classroom problems.
Groups of students will work together to improve their community.
All students will assist each other in achieving higher levels of learning.
All students will respect themselves, each other and the environment.

Short-Term Classroom Goals:
Students will receive training in TQM, including a historical synopsis, the quality principles and theory. *(Begin the first week of school.)*
Students will be taught the TQI tools for Continuous Improvement and track their own Continuous Improvement projects. *(Begin the first week of school and on-going for at least nine weeks.)*
Students will be taught the problem solving model and the use of the peace table. *(Begin during the first week of school.)*

Students will be divided into groups, research a community problem, and plan and carry-out a project designed to effect positive change in the community. *(Begin second nine weeks of school.)*

Everyone will work cooperatively in groups, rotating responsibilities, and coming to agreement on outcomes. *(Begin during the first week of school and make it on-going.)*

Everyone will learn to be peer tutors. *(Established by the end of the first month of school.)*

Everyone will participate in projects to save the environment, and communicating this knowledge to families and others. *(Establish during the first month of school and make it on-going.)*

Homework assignments will be practical, meaningful, and completed in a timely fashion. *(Begin with the first assignment and make it on-going.)*

A volunteer list of parents and others will be established in the classroom to assist students and/or assist groups. *(Have established by the end of the first six weeks of school.)*

Goal setting doesn't end, however, by simply writing them down. Give yourself a specific time frame for achieving each goal. That gives additional energy to the process. Next, map out a strategy for achieving each and every goal. Mapping will allow you and the students to realize the steps that are necessary in achieving each one. The use of systematic diagrams can be very useful as a mapping technique. The reader is referred to the **Control Chart** examples in the appendix to show how careful planning and the use of TQM tools can be used to chart one's improvement.

As you can see from the above list of goals, the TQ teacher will need to provide guidance in the process of establishing goals. Some of the goals relate more to the teacher's responsibility and some more to the students. For instance, a major portion of the short term goal on homework assignments is the teacher's responsibility.

Homework is one area of school that is frustrating for the teachers, parents, and students. Some educators believe that homework is a way to increase self-discipline. That is true, however, the nature and amount of homework assignments must be relevant and something that the student is capable of doing without instruction. It is important that we not simply assign homework for the sake of homework. We have never understood the purpose of giving 25 math problems for homework if the child is going to do 25 problems wrong. Reinforcing the wrong way of doing something simply doesn't make sense. Therefore, doesn't it make more sense to ensure the child thoroughly understands the concept at school, and if you determine that additional practice is necessary to assign perhaps no more than 5 problems? If the children truly understand the concepts, then ask yourself if there is really any reason to assign homework. There is a legitimate case for homework though, and if you thoroughly understand why you are assigning it, then you can also adequately explain it to the children and their parents. It is an issue that needs to be thought about before assignments are given.

Parents of at-risk children often become very resentful of the teacher who assigns homework and then expects the parent to ensure it is done, and done properly. Keep in mind, these parents probably didn't have a good school experience themselves. They may not be able to help their children do the homework because of low basic skills. For many parents, homework may feel like punishment for them. If the child struggles and resists doing the homework, and thus spawns a battle between parent and child, who could blame the parent for being angry with the teacher? At-risk families have so many problems and most are single parents (usually mothers) struggling to survive each day. If you are going to assign homework please consider giving a minimal amount, making certain it is vitally necessary. Then, provide assistance (such as through EXAMPLES) to parents to increase cooperation from the home.

For instance, consider how the homework assignments relate to your classroom goals. Ask yourself, what do I do with the homework when it is returned? Is there any logical sequence to what you are doing? Your students will be more apt to do the homework if you have clearly thought it out, and if you incorporate it somehow into the mission of the class. Otherwise, many students and parents will have a legitimate concern about why you are giving homework. The worst reason for homework is "because the school says we have to." In your own planning and preparing for implementation of TQM and becoming a TQ teacher, you'll want to give serious thought to this one aspect of your class.

Other goals will probably exceed the time frame of one year. For example, you may want to adopt the America 2000 goals as your personal goals. They are:

By the year 2000,

> *All children in America will start school ready to learn.*
> *The high school graduation rate will increase to at least 90 percent.*
> *American students will leave grades four, eight, and twelve having demonstrated competency in challenging subject matter including English, mathematics, science, history, and geography; and every school in America will ensure that all students learn to use their minds well, so they may be prepared for responsible citizenship, further learning, and productive employment in our modern economy.*
> *U.S. students will be first in the world in science and mathematics achievement.*
> *Every adult American will be literate and will possess the knowledge and skills necessary to compete in a global economy and exercise the rights and responsibilities of citizenship.*
> *Every school in America will be free of drugs and violence and will offer a disciplined environment conducive to learning.*

Upon first glance, some of the America 2000 goals may not appear to apply to your subject or grade level. We would challenge you, however, by suggesting that beginning in Kindergarten the outcome of each one of theses goals will be affected by what you do within your classroom. Without some specific strategies for achieving these goals none of them will be reached. Many adults are still eager to point the finger of blame and adopt a doom and gloom attitude, citing a lack of resources, or lack of parental guidance and concern, or lack of leadership, or overwhelming societal problems as reasons for why these goals cannot be met. Some believe it doesn't apply to them or their situation. We urge you to take another, more careful look at each of these goals and see how and what you do or don't do within your classroom will affect the outcome of each of them.

The doom and gloom attitude is not reflective of a nation built on determination and freedom and justice for all. We would probably never have put a man on the moon as soon as we did had not President Kennedy boldly stated that it was a national goal. He then empowered groups of individuals (who were experts in rocket science) to come up with a specific action plan to achieve this goal. Once the plan was in place, the President and Congress made decisions about its' value and provided it with appropriate financing. Few people thought it would be possible to achieve, but by focusing on the goal, and working together, it happened.

There are many readers who will probably take the attitude that the problems faced by schools are overwhelming, and that the government refuses to place enough resources into education to resolve them. While we agree that government funding of education is probably less than it should be for our democracy to survive, we suggest that one way to improve it is by adopting a TQM model NOW. If each K-12 teacher and administrator in this country were to become totally focused on the success of **ALL** students, through empowering students to become better decision makers, and giving them hope for the future, amazing things would happen. Our achievement levels would soar, and money that is currently spent on funding adult basic and literacy programs can be moved to support K-12 schools. If every child in this country had high self-esteem that can come only through empowerment, there would be far fewer drug and alcohol problems, teen pregnancy, juvenile crime, etc. We firmly believe that through a concerted effort, and adoption of TQM in our schools, the America 2000 goals will not only be reached, but surpassed as well.

While we believe these goals are reachable, it cannot happen without proper planning and major alterations in the ways schools are managed and students taught. Focus is of the utmost importance. There are times when it is difficult to maintain that focus when students appear to be out of control, when you lack textbooks, or when you lack parental or administrative support. Therefore, we suggest you begin examining your own commitment to the education of all students, and how the America 2000 goals fit into that commitment. As stated earlier, the time for blame and shame is long over.

Blaming others has not produced any solutions to what is a growing national problem. Let's all agree that each and every individual in the United States has a responsibility for the improvement of the educational system. That is, each parent, administrator, community leader, industry and business leader, politician, government official, teacher and student has a role to play. We must accept responsibility for the problem and then accept responsibility for helping to resolve it. Teachers who adapt the TQM philosophy of **Continuous Improvement** will empower students and parents. Everyone will benefit from increases in student achievement.

It all starts with a commitment and goal setting. You, the teacher, must lead the way, then involve the students and others. Each year reassess your goals, always focusing your sights higher...never lower. When you are beginning to implement the TQM approach, remember that this is an on-going, ever improving process that will continue as long as you are teaching. Do not get discouraged by seeming lack of motivation in the students, but persist on the continuous improvement path, persist in educating students in the principles of Quality, and maintain the focus on the classroom goals. Students, parents, administrators, and your colleagues will be eager to jump on the bandwagon when they see the results. After all, when one reaches goals they feel good and thus become invigorated to aspire to higher goals.

Goal setting is an integral part of the quality movement. Students can work collaboratively with the TQ teacher to establish workable, stretch goals throughout the school year. Goals also provide all students with a view of the future.

Provide hope for the future

Most individuals in the helping professions who are involved with providing programs for at-risk children agree that these children lack hope for the future. By teaching, and utilizing the goal setting approach to learning, **ALL** students learn how effective this method can be for quickly accomplishing a task. In addition, goal setting can then be related to future careers and to life after school. Students should be encouraged (beginning in kindergarten) to think about their future, and imagine what they would like to accomplish. Imagine if yearly or semi-yearly goal setting became a part of each school year, and students not only wrote goals, but learned how to map the steps necessary to accomplish them. In the early years this may consist of things such as: deciding to read 15 minutes each night, or be able to throw and catch a ball, as well as answering the question of "What do I want to do when I am an adult?".

This information can become part of the child's permanent record, and teachers reviewing those records can continue encouraging and building on these goals. Students who show an interest in pursuing a scientific career ought to be continuously encouraged and provided with opportunities to study a variety of scientific opportunities. Likewise, the same would be true for students displaying any interests. Educators who have adapted the philosophy of success for **ALL** students can effectively use this kind of information, and weave it into the child's assignments. It is our duty as educators to assist all students in becoming goal oriented. Without the necessary goals many students will simply flounder, never knowing exactly what they want, nor how to get it.

Teachers will become knowledgeable in mapping, providing instruction and direction to students so they can achieve their goals. Even very young students can become involved in this process, and time should be set aside at the beginning of each semester to allow for training in goal setting and mapping. Students can be encouraged to set stretch goals that will be somewhat difficult for them to achieve. The stretch goals allow students to be individually challenged while recognizing individual differences. Repeating this process at regular intervals helps students learn to make adjustments in their previous goals, but more importantly, the students can see how much they have accomplished and how much closer they are to their goal.

Setting stretch goals puts one on a path to success. It also allows one a process for re-evaluating the direction of one's life. On the map of life, there are many side roads leading to the same destination. These side-roads can offer very different perspectives and are frequently more scenic. Students who learn that it is okay to alter one's path periodically, particularly as one progresses through the life cycle, will ultimately be more comfortable with the necessary changes that are thrust upon each of us.

This is TQM in action.

_____

The following is a check sheet tool to help the reader baseline their **Strategic Quality Planning** skills. There is one subcategory. Please refer to the table and circle the "point" next to the "criteria" that most nearly describes your present classroom situation.

4.1   Summarize your specific principal quality goals, objectives, and plans for the short-term (3-6 months) and longer term (1-2 years).

Points	Criteria
1	Standard goals, based on the district or the state's goals.
2	Numerical objectives related to quality, cost effectiveness, and customer satisfaction.
3	Management by policy deployment where all students have work plan assignments related to the quality goals of the classroom.
4	Quality goals exceed those of the district and/or state, and everyone is committed to achieving those goals.
5	All objectives of the classroom key on achieving "World Class" capabilities in quality related performance which includes process and system orientations.

Chapter Seven: Human Resource Utilization

Everyone might well ask himself every day what he has done this day to advance his learning and skill on this job, and how he has advanced his education for greater satisfaction in life.

W. Edwards Deming
Out of the Crisis

We suggest that the reader take the time to briefly answer the following questions prior to reading this chapter and answering the questions on the checksheet at the end.

5.0   Human Resource Utilization

This category examines the outcomes of your efforts to develop and utilize the full potential of all the students for quality and to maintain an environment conducive to full participation, continuous improvement, and classroom growth.

5.1   What are your key strategies for increasing the effectiveness, productivity, and participation of <u>all</u> students.

5.2   Please describe how you educate students in quality improvement.

5.3   What percentage of current students have ever received education in quality improvement concepts and processes?

5.4   Describe how you positively reinforce students for contributions to quality improvement (e.g. recognition of teams, awards, etc.)

5.5   What have you done to ensure the quality of work life in the classroom, to maintain a supportive education environment and to empower all students to actively participate in the learning process? If you have examples, please include.

Improve Constantly

Continue to improve your classroom techniques until all students have achieved a high degree of success and are doing quality work. This will require continuous updating of teaching techniques, particularly as they relate to differing learning styles. The goal is to maintain a high level of awareness of developments in one's area (or level) as well as how this relates to the student's current and future life. A major thrust will be one's own personal professional development plan which includes training in principles of TQM.

Even the youngest students quickly and accurately assess a teacher's enthusiasm for learning. One cannot expect students to be enthusiastic learners without comparable enthusiasm from teachers and/or parents. Each teacher must become a role model for life-long learning and excellence and then share this excitement and interest with all students. Begin to look at your experiences and consider them as learning opportunities, then be willing to share your philosophy and knowledge with your students.

Continuous improvement in the classroom also requires evaluation of daily happenings. This can be done informally, while observing and interacting with various students or, more formally, by having the students spend several minutes at the end of each class period (or weekly) evaluating accomplishments and requirements that are needed to increase their efficiency and the quality of work. Perhaps this is a matter of altering the flow of activities, or moving the furniture, or providing a few additional minutes to discuss a matter with team members or other classmates. This may involve moving students as well, but never within the context of coercion or punishment. Such feedback provides necessary data to improve methods, materials, organization, and styles of presentation.

Case Study: Elementary Math Class

At Central Elementary School in Linden, Michigan, Mrs. Chronicle prides herself on her ability to analyze each student's **learning style** and use that as a basis for her teaching strategy. The Linden School District recently adopted a new math textbook. It is markedly different from the previous one, requiring a great deal of reading. At least six students in the class are auditory learners while three students are tactile learners, requiring the use of some kind of manipulatives. When these third graders work on math, a host of supportive strategies are integrated. You will recall in Chapter 4, we discussed how Mrs. Chronicle used groups as a basis for her classroom activities. She also arranged to have the students with similar **learning styles** sit in such a way (unbeknownst to them) that she can easily move a chair between them and work directly with several at the same time. Thus, the student groups are clustered so that four students with reading problems sit on toward the inside of each group, making it possible for Mrs. Chronicle to sit in the midst of all of them to help read the math instructions. See example below:

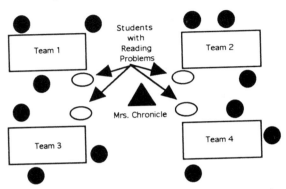

Mrs. Chronicle realizes that the success of each of these students depends on what she and their classmates do. Each group works together at problem resolution, helping each other along the way. Each table is provided with manipulatives so groups can assist those students needing graphic representation of the concepts.

The class will generally end with a lively game involving the math problems for the day. Students are numbered and the teacher asks challenge questions, testing to see if each group and each student has understood how to do the problems. Students see this as "fun," and it provides valuable feed-back to Mrs. Chronicle. If all students haven't understood the concepts, then Mrs. Chronicle begins the cycle of continuous improvement.

Constant improvement also alerts students to the notion that they must become change-oriented individuals. Our technological society no longer permits or tolerates individuals who are resistant to change. That is, those who refuse to retrain as their jobs become obsolete, or who refuse to move as the company relocates, will likely become disenfranchised in the 21st century. In fact, teachers who refuse to change to accommodate students will find themselves isolated, as more educators recognize the need for change. Indeed, changing the system of education means dramatic change for every K-12 teacher. A major part of the educational process must be to role model flexibility, adopting a change-orientation for students, and teaching them ways to follow suit. This entire procedure allows students to become flexible with the learning process, permitting them to recognize many ways to improve along the way.

Institute a vigorous program of education and self-improvement

In order for students to understand and utilize this new way of approaching learning, they will need to be trained in the techniques of Quality. Training can begin in the very earliest grades within a developmentally appropriate context. Begin this training by using the conditions for implementing Total Quality in the Classroom. Give an overview of what TQM means, and describe how it empowers students to achieve higher goals. Answer the question: *"Why are we doing this?"* Mention the leaders of quality and the impact each has had on the world, then focus on those aspects of Deming and Crosby as described in this book. Draw connections between the **Quality** movement and what has happened in the world and how the Japanese have used TQM to help overcome the tremendous economic problems faced at the end of World War II. Talk about the auto industry and what has happened because the Japanese have successfully implemented TQM. Explain how students are "workers" within the classroom and describe your role as the manager. Describe the differences between the new leadership role of TQ teacher rather than the traditional top down "boss" manager. Discuss how each will be involved in working on a continuous improvement plan and give some specific examples of how that will happen.

It is also essential to communicate with parents about one's decision to implement TQM and TQI in classroom, giving an overview of how one intends to pursue it. Include information about the purpose of and necessity for TQM training and its impact on both children and the class as a whole. When classroom goals are established, it is important to have the students (either personally, or a small group) create a "memo" for parents detailing what the class is doing along with the mission and the goals.

Education in the principles of TQM is critical to producing quality work. Each individual in the classroom must be provided with the requisite concepts involved in TQM, including statistical process control (SPC) and Deming's continuous improvement cycle of plan-do-check-act (P-D-C-A). The TQ teacher implementing TQM within the classroom will have to take time to educate all students in these processes. **This requires each teacher understand appropriate TQI procedures for resolving any problems within the classroom.**

For example, at Mt. Edgecumbe High School in Sitka, Alaska, all students are provided ninety minutes per week of quality improvement training and school wide problem solving. This displays the entire school's commitment to quality. Achievement levels have improved dramatically, students have driven out fear, and accepted responsibility for their own learning.

Next one needs to discuss the concept of "customer" with the students. We believe that with careful planning, and age-appropriate language, all students can understand and grasp these concepts. Get students involved immediately in assisting you with both long and short range classroom goals. TQM training cannot be completed in an hour, or a day. One will want to begin training the first day of school, then continue training throughout the school year. Training will become an integral part of the school day, often through practicing and repeating the P-D-C-A cycle.

By the end of the first week the mission statement and long and short range goals will be printed and posted. Once the classroom goals are set, the teacher and students will focus on individual goals.

In fact, we recommend the reader begin to correspond with teachers of similar grade levels and subjects in the schools mentioned here and other outstanding schools around the nation. Reach for your own stretch goals through learning from others. One may think of these individuals as valued guides. In the words of John Noe (1986, p. 116):

> *An expert guide is...[able] to assess the capabilities and limitations of the person being guided. The expert guide also knows how to communicate what must be done to reach the high goal and to spot and correct mistakes before they become critical. He inspires confidence.*

The challenge is twofold when one begins to implement TQM in the classroom. One, there is an on-going need for self-education and (hopefully) a mentor or a colleague in your school who will provide a sounding board. Two, one needs to educate the students and parents many of whom will view you as their mentor in this process, making personal leadership and enthusiasm a key element in achieving success.

Remove barriers that rob people of their right to pride in workmanship

Who can take pride in mediocrity? This may explain why many good teachers leave education. Depression is more likely in schools where expectations for both students and teachers is low. In fact, low expectations for teachers translates into lowered expectations for students. Surely no one is fooled into believing that we need to lower expectations because students aren't doing quality work. When people feel no one cares about their work, pride in workmanship disappears and work becomes drudgery for both students and teachers. No one is happy. No one seems to really care, and nothing of quality happens. On the other hand, the TQ teacher will provide challenges for students that require them to stretch their limits without resorting to shaming tactics.

TQ teachers recognize that everyone wants to do quality work and that it takes some students longer to accomplish it. Quality begins with providing examples of quality work from other previous classes or other students. If no one has done any quality work in your classes (and quality work really is a high level of accomplishment), take time to prepare some examples of your own. This is part of **mastery learning** as opposed to **mystery learning**. It is unfair to expect students to achieve quality work when its not clearly defined.

Students who have never been expected to do quality work will have no idea what it is. Furthermore, they will be unable to do quality work unless the TQ teacher: (1) believes they can do it, (2) is available to coach and assist them, and (3) provides the feedback and the opportunity to improve until quality is achieved.

The concept of quality work is one with which even teachers may be unfamiliar. This should not be too surprising, especially if the school standards are not very high. Sometimes those teachers who set high standards are ridiculed by their colleagues. Unfortunately, the standards in so many schools are so low that students have given up trying. It is a mistake to believe that quality is a known concept to teachers and students any more than is the concept of *normal behavior* to the individual from a dysfunctional home. Therefore, each teacher must seek out examples of truly quality work for their students to model. If no examples exist from your previous class or even within the school, seek out information from schools identified as Blue Ribbon Schools. Such a list is available from the United States Department of Education. A list of schools currently involved in the Total Quality movement was published in the October, 1991 issue of *Quality Progress*.

One should not diminish the work of students who require more time than others. Individual differences make up the wonderful mosaic that is humanity, and we must recognize that the quality of the work is vastly more important that the requisite time any student takes to accomplish it.

Pride in workmanship involves having the proper tools and equipment to do the job which implies that teachers will have to prepare their students to perform the task. However, avoid the temptation to blame lack of resources for lack of student achievement. There are many examples of schools where students lack resources but do outstanding work.

Preparation for work is essential. This again speaks to the mastery learning versus the mystery learning cycles. Students who understand expectations and the outcome are more likely to produce quality work. Preparation also means students focus on the assignment. The groundwork has been laid, as students have been introduced to the topic by the TQ teacher. This does not imply that the teacher will "give the answers" to the class, on the contrary, the introduction encourages students to ask questions; to become interested and captivated by the assignment. The students will want to discover the answer to the assignment, whether it is a cooperative learning activity or an individual problem.

Judy Scaletta, a math teacher at General McLane High School in Edinboro, Pennsylvania, begins her "Trigonometry and Calculus" classes by having students get into groups to solve a puzzling question of higher order mathematics. The group is instructed to become a model detective, looking for clues to solve the puzzle. Each individual is given time to ponder the question first, and jot down his/her thinking. Then, the group discusses it and determines whether or not the group can come up with a consensus. Class discussion is lively as each as each group then proceeds with their logic and conclusions. Mrs. Scaletta uses this as a demonstration for engaging students into the logic of higher mathematics and to point out the possibility for more than one method to determine the answer. Discussions proceed to careers and the uses of mathematics in virtually every endeavor her students wish to pursue. By the end of the period, she has managed to eliminate many of the student's fears about how "difficult" the course will be, and instead the students have expanded their views of mathematics.

Indeed, mathematics education is becoming revolutionized. Many now advocate having all students work in groups on all problems. Imagine presenting a real-life math problem to the students, then asking them to get into groups to discover the answer. Each group keeps notes on the steps followed so when the class comes together to discuss the answer, each group checks their logic for accuracy. Self-discovery often arises as students recognize flaws in their logic. No one is made to feel bad and every member of the class understands the concepts presented by that particular math problem. Groups may use manipulatives or not, depending on the group.

In Mrs. Scaletta's classes, students use computers, calculators, paper, and manipulatives to accommodate their learning style. Groups are often seen using one or more of the above tools. She also has groups of students applying the formulas in construction projects. Such projects provide students with a greater sense of the application of higher order mathematical principles.

This foundation is a tool required to do the job. Additionally, the students will need other tools such as access to books, computers, and other data, not to mention paper, pencils, etc. Many teachers we've known have become very creative in developing or adapting materials to fit the needs of their class when funds have not been available. While we recognize this is a major problem in some schools, we hope it will not be an excuse for "blaming" the educational system for today's problems. Remember, blaming won't resolve the problems, we must become proactive and involved in problem resolution.

Another factor of student pride in workmanship is the need to do meaningful work. Meaningful class assignments can increase greatly student motivation to complete the work and do a quality job. Assignments viewed by students as busy work, boring, or unnecessarily repetitive simply will not be taken seriously. The TQ teacher must spend a good deal of time deliberating on the nature of all assignments. At all grade levels, subjects can be made relevant to happenings within the student's life. If all students can easily understand the connections between what they are asked to do in school, and the "real world," they will be motivated, if not eager to become active participants in school. Unfortunately, teachers have tended to move away from recognizing the importance of this issue on class participation. Meaningful assignments may, and most likely do, include cross-curricular assignments. In elementary schools these are often referred to as "thematic units." Students know that things within the "real" world don't happen in a vacuum, and in English class, to do only things such as grammar, reading and writing without somehow linking them to other curricular areas or life is not going to instill in students the drive to do quality work in English. Seldom have we visited an English class where the teacher relates all of the preceding components to the other classes students are taking. Doesn't it make sense to do more of this? Communication is vital to success and studying English is really a study in communications. We recognize this is much easier to accomplish at the elementary level, however, we suggest that each secondary teacher can also make a concerted effort to point out areas of cross-over.

Teachers would also do well to draw connections between their course work and the real world. This process can begin as early as first grade. Some students are naturally curious and will learn everything the teachers ask of them; however, there are many more curious students who will choose not to work hard and produce quality work unless drawn into the assignment by the teacher. These students often view school as a convenient place to meet friends rather than an intellectually stimulating place where important work happens.

Finding assignments that relate closely to community happenings also make class work meaningful. For instance, relating historical issues with governmental issues of today. Science classes can take the "global perspective" and/or interweave local issues into the subject matter. Throughout the K-12 curriculum there are ways to establish relationships between book learning, critical thinking, and ways to improve one's town, state, region, or country. TQ teachers actively seek to provide these kinds of assignments for their students as part of their continuous improvement plan to achieve success with all students.

Examples of Meaningful Assignments

Elementary School (We thank Tom Parker for helping us with this suggestion.)

Language Arts—Class discussion of hunger and ways the class might help resolve the problem. Following the project completion, all students write a story about their experience.

Social Studies—a study is made of the community hunger problem. Discussion follows around how the food bank operates and how many are served. Map skills are employed to show the area the local food bank serves. The class decides on a community volunteer project to collect canned food to donate to the food bank. Students work in pairs. After the collection campaign, students take a field trip to the Food Bank where they are given a tour and shown how food is distributed to needy families.

Math —Students sort (size and type of food) and count cans. They also weigh the cans and keep track of the totals. Charts are made showing progress towards the goal of 1,000 pieces.

Health/Nutrition—Students discuss the food groups and sort cans accordingly. Students keep track of their food intake for one week. They use charts to determine if they are eating "healthy."

Art —Students draw a picture depicting one aspect of the community service project.

Middle School

In another area of the country around the Great Lakes, the following examples may be appropriate:

Science —Study the ecological system of the Great Lakes. Include information about zebra mussels and the impact they have had on water systems, local economy, and the ecosystem of the lake. Take a field trip to a state park or a fish hatchery. Take a water sample from the lake, examine it under a microscope. Research pollutants in the lake. Where do they come from?

Social Studies —Study the historical significance of the Great Lakes to surrounding states. What was the significance of the War of 1812 to the Great Lakes region? What significance do the Lakes have today on the economy and life of people living on their shores? How is industrial pollution affecting the Great Lakes?

Geology/Earth Science —How were the Great Lakes formed? What are the current weather patterns that affect surrounding land masses?

Reading —Read stories about waterways, boating, fish and water fowl. Research social studies and science projects.

Math — Work on the concept of volume.

Art —Make a paper mache fish or some other marine animal that comprises the ecological system of the Great Lakes.

Writing —Write a story about an important event that happened on the Great Lakes. Write letters to corporations responsible for polluting the waters of the Great Lakes urging them to save our environment. Write letters to the newspaper, government leaders and others urging everyone to save the environment by not polluting the waterways. Write research papers for science and social studies.

Culminating activity—Each group will create a manuscript about the Great Lakes including research papers, drawings, and maps. Groups will share their work with each other. One member from each group will be responsible for leading a discussion on the Great Lakes Ecological System. Parents will be invited to a program about the Great Lakes with recitations and sharing of the art projects

Secondary School

In California the following examples may be appropriate:

Science— What is a Mediterranean fruit fly? Gather some of these fruit flies and examine them under the microscope. How do they differ from ordinary fruit flies? What is their genetic make-up, and why are they difficult to eradicate? What are their natural enemies? Research the problem using sources including data collected from the U.S. Department of Agriculture and any other sources that might be helpful.

Geography—Where do the Mediterranean fruit flies come from, and what pattern of migration did they take to get to the United States? What effect, if any, do weather conditions have on the spread of this fruit fly, and on its eradication? Draw a map showing the origin of the Mediterranean fruit fly, the path of migration and provide an overlay with various weather conditions that have affected this problem.

Economics— What is the importance of the California citrus crop to the food supply of the country? What is the likely economic outcome of a disastrous citrus crop in California? What will the likely by-product of this be for consumers locally? nationally? Research the problem and write an analysis.

Social Studies— What is the historical significance of the citrus crop in the United States, and in California specifically? How has that affected the growth of California? Research the historical roots of the California citrus industry and include information on key individuals or groups that have influenced the growth of this industry. Debate the pros and cons of using pesticides to eradicate the problem and the effect of pesticides on health and world wide food supplies.

English—Research papers on this issue will be presented in the American Psychological Association format. Standard English will be used throughout. Footnotes and the bibliography will be properly documented. The paper will be examined for format, spelling, grammar, punctuation and general readability. The English teacher plays a key role in teaching all students the proper way to footnote and document the bibliography. As students work on drafts of their papers, the English teacher will be assisting them with style and readability as well as grammar, spelling and punctuation.

Keyboarding—All research papers will be completed using a typewriter or computer. The keyboarding teacher will teach students the proper way to set up the page with margins, etc., and will assist them with editing. This teacher will be looking at the final product to determine if the style is correct, the spelling accurate, and whether the approach /format is followed.

Math—Any research papers requiring scientific data can be examined by the math teacher. Statistical data can be presented and students can learn ways to best represent their data. The math teacher will assist students in understanding how statistical data can be used to present information in graphic form.

Culminating Activity—Students will assist in all areas of research, and individual students will each prepare a paper selecting the topic from the research. Groups will work on all research, keeping notes and records of information gathered for members to utilize when writing. Data presented in research papers will come from the group efforts.

Many meaningful assignments can be established well within the confines of the current curriculum. We recommend that one relate as much of the material as possible to the community, state, region, country or world. Certainly, by the time students reach secondary school, assignments should reflect a global perspective. If you approach your subject matter from this perspective, you'll recognize the importance of creativity in assignments and the part assignments play in student's enthusiasm for learning. We're not familiar with any inherently boring course of study.

Students also need to feel that they can make some contributions to the entire class. This involves planning, as well as the actual activity of the classroom. Students are most closely affected by the teacher's actions and, therefore, are in the best position to make some positive contributions to the class. This will require some courage on the part of the teacher, but it will reap great rewards. Students can be polled for their opinions as climate surveys can be regularly taken (at least twice a year as described in Chapter 5) and students can be made to feel that each and everyone of them makes an important contribution to the class as a whole.

Every student is unique and possesses special gifts. The TQ teacher will begin the first day of school, determining what each student has to offer, and will allow each the right to share their gift with the class. Students who feel they are contributing in a variety of ways will be eager to participate and willing to assist other students to achieve quality work.

Institute a vigorous program of self-improvement

TQ teachers will become role models for continuous self-improvement. This will be accomplished by a well thought-out personal development plan involving conference attendance, subscription to a variety of professional magazines, newspapers, and journals, as well as knowledge of the latest trends in one's subject matter. The self-improvement plan will also include data collection from students, parents, teachers and other customers to continuously improve not only the climate of the classroom but also the delivery of lessons, etc. Each TQ teacher will become actively involved in helping all suppliers (such as parents, previous teachers, text book publishers, and curriculum materials specialists) to continuously improve.

Role models of life-long learning show their enthusiasm for learning in their personal lives as well as their professional lives. As such, teachers who view experiences as opportunities for growth will share this enthusiasm with students. If the leadership of any classroom is not committed to continuous personal improvement, no major changes will take place within the classroom. Walking your talk is vital to your success.

The following is a check sheet tool to help the reader baseline their **Human Resource Utilization** skills. There are five subcategories that we consider important. Please refer to the table and circle the "point" next to the "criteria" that most nearly describes your present classroom situation.

5.1   What are your key strategies for increasing the effectiveness, productivity, and participation of <u>all</u> students.

Points	Criteria
1	No formal strategy.
2	Strategy is dependent on the curriculum
3	Formal and flexible strategy which encourages the students to participate in assessing the classroom climate and offer suggestions for improving it. Students are empowered to work for the success of all.
4	The classroom environment is completely without fear, and cooperative learning opportunities are a pivotal part of each day; therefore all students have a part in the success of the group.
5	The teacher assumes the role of TQ Teacher, challenging students to reach untapped potentials. Students evaluate their own work as well as others' for quality, offering suggestions and encouragement.

5.2   Please describe how you educate students in quality improvement.

Points	Criteria
1	Students receive no education in principles of total quality improvement (TQI).
2	Students are educated only on subject matter skills and receive no TQM or TQI training.
3	All students are educated on the principles of TQM and TQI.
4	Students are educated on the principles and processes of quality including SPC and PDCA, and utilize these in their daily work.
5	Learning is based on the continuous improvement of <u>all</u> students as the keystone to the success of all.

5.3   What percentage of current students have ever received education in quality improvement concepts and processes?

Points	Criteria
1	0%
2	Less than 25%
3	25 to 60%
4	61 to 90%
5	91 to 100%

5.4   Describe how you positively reinforce students for contributions to quality improvement (e.g. recognition of teams, awards, etc.)

Points	Criteria
1	Traditional grades are the reward for achievement.
2	Typical performance reviews focusing on individual efforts.
3	Commendations and other rewards are dispensed at the discretion of the teacher.
4	Commendations and other rewards are dispensed at the discretion of both the teacher and students.
5	Team recognition and incentives for efforts are based on the improvement of the processes and systems where the teacher's role is to support and facilitate the efforts of the team. Information about team rewards is sent home. There is a system in place for distributing information to parents, community members, and school colleagues.

5.5   What have you done to ensure the quality of work life in the classroom, to maintain a supportive education environment and to empower all students to actively participate in the learning process? If you have examples, please include.

Points	Criteria
1	The classroom environment reflects an attitude of: be quiet, do your work and don't question or make suggestions.
2	Administration's suggestions are considered and discussed.
3	Only certain selected students' suggestions and ideas are discussed.
4	Participative management approach where all students are encouraged to make suggestions, discuss options and collaborate with others to implement group decisions.
5	Upside down pyramid where the teacher's role is to be a leader and to support quality work and all students are performing that work. Adhocracy at its best.

Chapter Eight: Quality Assurance of Products and Services

Poor quality begets poor quality and lowers productivity all along the line, and some of the faulty product goes out the door, into the hands of the customer.

W. Edwards Deming
Out of the Crisis

We suggest that the reader take the time to briefly answer the following questions prior to reading this chapter and answering the questions on the checksheet at the end.

6.0 Quality Assurance of Products and Services

This category examines the classroom's systematic approach based primarily upon quality improvement processes and systems, including the control of procured curriculum materials, equipment, and services.

6.1   What methods do you use to evaluate student's academic performance?

6.2   How do you define waste in your classroom, and what preventive measures do you take to reduce waste?

6.3   How do you elicit improvements in quality to those supplying goods and services to you, including those students coming to you?

6.4   How do you evaluate and integrate the quality of skills your students use that they've learned from other classes within your school?

How do you define WASTE?

Quality leaders define waste as the cost of non-conformance. For educators, therefore, waste would include drop-outs, individuals retained in a grade, a student who fails to achieve mastery in any subject or class, teen pregnancy, drug and alcohol problems, juvenile crime, truancy, etc. All processes and systems within the classroom that do not function optimally, including poor or inappropriate teaching methods and an inadequate disciplinary system, contribute to waste. Problems with any or all of these will lead to inefficiency and under education for all. The price of non-conformance is ... *all the expenses involved in doing things wrong* (Crosby 1984, p. 85).

The TQM approach pays close attention to the high cost of waste. An example of the high cost of waste is illustrated in the Introduction where the cost of waste to a community in lost state school aid, lost taxes and cost of public assistance monies for each school drop-out was computed. See the Appendix for computing the cost of waste in your school district.

An example of the federal government's lack of faith in the public school system in our country is the thirty percent increase of the U.S. Department of Education's 1992 budget for Adult Basic and Literacy Education programs. This clearly represents the cost of K-12 schools not doing the job right the first time. We recognize the current problem is twofold: (1) we must remediate (re-work) those individuals who the system failed in past years, and (2) we must also take the necessary steps to ensure that the pattern of school drop-outs does not continue. A major goal the U.S. Department of Education might want to set would be: By the year 2000, the budget for Adult Basic and Literacy Education will decrease by fifty percent due to a lack of persons requiring the service. That would free a tremendous amount of money for K-12 programs, which is where it should be.

While we admire greatly the work done by adult educators, it is a vivid example of the high cost of waste in the K-12 system. By focusing on eliminating waste in the K-12 system, we will have saved taxpayers billions of dollars in lost taxes, and greatly decreased money needed for public assistance. Referring back to the Introduction one can see from the statistics listed many examples of waste in education. In fact, take a moment and reflect of the ways in which waste in education has cost our nation. Now answer the question of whether or not we can afford to continue doing business as usual in education.

Even though one's school district may not be inclined to adopt a Total Quality Management approach, it is possible to make major changes within the classroom and subsequently reduce waste. In his book, *Let's Talk About Quality* (1989, p. 72), Crosby   says:

> *All work is a process... Whenever anything*
> *goes wrong in one area, the shock waves are*
> *felt throughout the organization. That is why*
> *it is so important for everyone to be involved*
> *in efforts to do things right.*

Taking the TQM viewpoint allows everyone to identify problems and set upon a course of action for improving the system and, consequently, improving the product. It is better if entire school districts adopt the TQM model, however, each classroom teacher has an obligation to take the lead and improve the processes and systems within his/her classroom and discontinuing improper and ineffective teaching.

As in business, doing things right the first time will keep costs down and increase customer satisfaction. Prevention comes first in identifying waste within the classroom, although identifying waste isn't enough. Once it is identified, one can implement the Plan-Do-Check-Act (P-D-C-A) cycle. Ignoring waste in the classroom is no longer excusable from an economic or service perspective. In fact, school districts around the nation would do well to have each teacher and administrator complete the Quality Index Profile at the end of this Chapter. The process of identification can eliminate some of the waste rather quickly.

Other problems, of course, will take time and will depend on a variety of society's institutions teaming together to eliminate them. One such problem is teen pregnancy. Another is drug and alcohol use. This does not mean, however, that individual teachers cannot make major strides toward eliminating these problems for students in their classes. Empowering students to become responsible problem solvers, and driving fear out of the classroom will make school a **fun** place to be, where all students will feel welcome and will work to achieve their best is one way to help eliminate these problems.

Cease dependence on inspection to achieve quality

Schools have typically handled inspection somewhat differently from industry. In the industrial sector, traditionally only the end product receives inspection from the quality control people. Quality control in most cases has relied on the judgment of the quality control inspectors to check and see if the product has met the company's specifications. In most companies, mistakes or variances are allowed within certain limits. Nonetheless, many companies produce products that are far from acceptable, often discovering this at the end of the line when the quality control inspectors do their work. At this point (end of the line), inspectors will either throw out any pieces of the product that don't meet specifications, or send them back to be re-worked. This is known as non-value added work and is the price of non-conformance. This is the cost of waste. Sometimes, quality control inspectors allow defective products into the marketplace, causing customer dissatisfaction, which over a period of time leads to anger and finally loss of business. Poor quality will always lead to higher costs and eventually the entire business will suffer.

Customer dissatisfaction leads to the need to recall any defective products for replacement or repair. Repair services are one price corporations pay for non-conformance. In fact, many corporations lose millions of dollars per year repairing or replacing defective products, the major flaw of depending on final inspections to determine quality.

Consider the above information as an analogy to our present K-12 school system. As most schools operate, inspection is twofold. The first line of inspection is accomplished by quizzes, unit tests, homework, etc. The second line of inspection is standardized tests or teacher-constructed final exams. A compilation of both of these usually lead to a grade for the class and used as the basis for decisions regarding moving to the next grade level or taking the next course in a sequence at the secondary level. Final inspection also determines whether or not a student graduates.

Consider the folly of what happens in most classrooms and schools. Inspection is done and results are ignored, since there is a need to get through the curriculum. There is no place in most schools for students to focus on the process of learning. Generally the focus is on the final product with no regard for how it is attained. Students who do poorly on quizzes, tests, homework, research papers, etc. are often left behind. They have not mastered the material, but the unit is over and everyone must move on. Even when a majority of students do poorly in a class there is no attempt to consider when or where things went wrong and worse no plan on how to eliminate root causes of the process and system problems. In short, it is deemed the student's problem. Rarely is it considered a problem for the teacher or the school. When inspection is carried out in this fashion it is meaningless. It does nothing to improve the student's learning (product) and therefore is a complete waste of time. Students who do not understand the work usually know they don't understand, but the system breaks down when nothing is done to remedy the situation. It is at this point that students can be very helpful to quality teachers.

In *Let's Talk About Quality* (1989, p.102), Crosby says: *Each and every person in the organization must understand his or her personal role in making quality happen.*

Isn't it foolish to label people as failures when the institution has not given them the proper tools with which to become successful? Can you imagine how that feels? Can you imagine what might happen to you, if over a period of time, you've been "stamped" as a failure or reject? Like most students who have dropped out of the system, you would become filled with shame and probably give up trying, thus becoming a financial burden on society.

This is one example of the price of waste in our educational system. Can we afford to continue? Clearly, every sector of our nation is sending educators a loud message that says, "we won't stand for it anymore." The cost of waste in education is far too high. Business as usual won't work. Band-aiding the problem by infusing additional money into programs that don't work won't resolve the problem. Educators must realize that the current systems and processes by which schools operate do not work. Waste will be reduced if systemic changes are made which empower students to achieve pride in workmanship.

TQM allows teachers and students to focus on the process, rather than the outcome. By discovering flaws in the process, the total quality (TQ) teacher and the students can alter the processes that lead to the breakdown in the system. If both teacher and students are totally focused on the processes and systems within the classroom, and both have agreed on a path for achieving the classroom goals, there will be no need to continually check and inspect whether or not students are working to achieve quality.

Classroom goals should never focus on numbers. For example, 76% of all students will learn to add, subtract, multiple or divide. (If that is one's goal, then which 24% of the student body will be excused from coming to class, already assuming they will not learn?) Numbers excite everyone, particularly when it comes to standardized test reporting. When the media reports these statistics, the focus is always on what percentage of students at any school achieve at or above the national average percentile. The folly of this is in how testing companies report their scores. Statistical representation of test scores will always reveal that 50% of those taking the test will be below the average. How then, can one expect that every student will achieve success if one depends solely on such scores as the standard measure?

Standardized test scores may ignore other, more important measures of student knowledge. Standardized tests will never be the best way to measure student achievement in learning critical thinking skills or problem solving. We should strive for maximum achievement and realize that this potential is higher than previously imagined by most. Dependence on standardized tests limits our thinking about learning and, worse, it is used as a punitive measure for both students, teachers and school systems in general.

Subscribing to the idea of mastery learning and having the students maintain accurate records will eliminate much of the need to inspect students. Remember, this returns to the basic belief (one of the tenets of TQM), that everyone is capable of and wants to do quality work in which they can have pride. Trust is an important factor in this process. As you develop the trust and sense of teamwork within the classroom, you can feel more comfortable with students evaluating each other's work. In Candace Allen's high school economics classes, the students not only critique classmates work, but are also given guidelines for suggesting improvements. This allows students to interact with each other, discuss the strengths and weaknesses of arguments and answers, then provide opportunities for students to work to strengthen the assignment. Using this process also allows each student to evaluate his/her own thinking, enhancing the knowledge base of each. Through such discussions, each student assists the other and the overall achievement rate of the group is raised.

Outcomes based education is one tool for ceasing dependence on inspection. It allows both teachers and students to focus on the process of learning. In Johnson City Schools, the teachers maintain only one grade per unit, which is the unit mastery test grade. Students are not given the test until their teacher is reasonably sure, based on other classroom work and assignments, that there is clear understanding of the desired knowledge. Students who do not achieve mastery are said to need "correctives." They will require additional work to master thoroughly the material. Once they've completed the additional work, they are given a different form of the unit test. Eighty percent is considered mastery in Johnson City Schools. It is the student's responsibility to make-up any correctives. No matter how many times a student takes the test, the only grade they will eventually receive is the grade indicating mastery. Grades are never averaged together.

An example of an instructional process in a TQM classroom is described in the Flow Chart below.

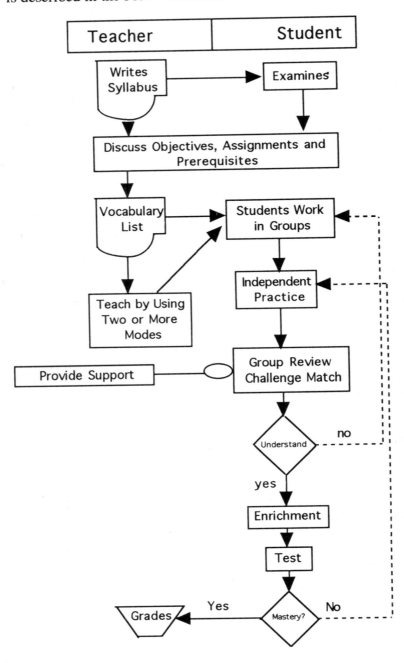

This system recognizes that not everyone can learn at the same pace. However, if one's school has adopted an outcomes based approach, it's important to maintain a clear focus and understanding of one's classroom mission. For instance, schools that use outcomes-based models focus on a belief that all students can achieve success. It is important to be wary of reverting back to "standard classroom procedure" of teacher inspected homework, quizzes, etc. Instead, empower the students to focus on the classroom mission and goals, and make changes in the systems and processes within the classroom so that students learn to do it right the first time.

The outcomes based model is a major step toward fully implementing TQM in the classroom. By its very nature, many discipline problems (simply because one eliminates failure and the need to act out) will be eliminated through its use.

To fully implement TQM, however, requires one go beyond the outcomes based model. Specifically, educators must dramatically alter their thinking and recognize that those directly involved in the activity are most qualified to suggest ways to improve the system This presupposes that one allow students to critique all classroom systems and processes, in a non-coercive, non-judgmental environment. Naturally, student age must be taken into consideration, and teachers of very young children must alter the TQM training appropriately. Nonetheless we believe that all students are capable and will become eager participants helping to resolve classroom problems. When one allows this to happen, **the students** will become involved and take responsibility for their own learning. The outcome from utilizing the TQM approach will be superior to that achieved thus far.

Provide for success

Mastery learning of basic facts is essential for continued mastery of more difficult material in any curriculum. After all, the greatest athletes spend most of their time working on fundamentals. In elementary schools, this is an accepted part of the job; however, many students still arrive at middle and high school with inadequate fundamentals. Isn't it a paradox that excellent teachers rarely teach remedial classes? In many schools, teachers in the remedial classes are new to the school district and/or older teachers being "punished" for some known or unknown previous mistakes. Therefore, when problems of waste arise, we ask the least able teachers to solve them, generally without giving them to tools to do the job. As a result these teachers cannot take pride in their work. They become frustrated and burned out. Imagine the message that is being sent to the students and parents. It is as if we don't care enough about these students to give them our very best effort to bring them up to speed. There is something dramatically wrong with these situations.

Low reading skills are a problem for both teachers and students. Since most of what happens in schools depends on reading ability, doesn't it make more sense to give these students the very best teachers, using the TQM approach to enhance reading skills? The same could be said for math teachers. We will need to dramatically alter our thinking and our priorities if this problem is to be resolved. Teaching fundamentals needn't be drudgery. In fact, working with these students could prove the most rewarding. In order to move all students forward and give them the opportunity to succeed, one cannot overlook this problem. This is one price of nonconformance and we will continue to pay as long as the basic problem is ignored. If the TQM approach were instilled in every classroom in the nation, the problem of "re-doing" past mistakes would disappear.

Judy Scaletta, from Edinboro, Pennsylvania, is teaching ninth grade basic math as well as advanced trigonometry, and calculus. She took this position without realizing the positive benefits that would come from working with students at both ends of the math spectrum. Mrs. Scaletta believes she has learned a great deal about teaching from the basic math classes that she has applied to her advanced classes. She has adapted lessons for all students based on learning styles as well as raising the expectations of her basic classes. She first surveys the students for their biases about math and uses that information to create meaningful assignments. Consequently, students in Mrs. Scaletta's classes enjoy a high rate of success and many go on to enjoy mathematics.

TQ teachers understand what concepts each student has not grasped while providing a means for all students to achieve mastery. This may include, but is not limited to, peer tutoring, skills games, cooperative learning, study groups, and independent study with additional information and guidelines from the teacher. TQ teachers understand that there are different learning styles, and success can only be achieved if students are allowed to learn according to their style, not the style preferred by the teacher.

Recognition of individual differences is also important in providing a success climate. Some students will undoubtedly come to class with different backgrounds, and abilities. This does not mean however, that the answer is to place them in a homogeneous grouping. By utilizing the classroom resources, including the other students (who may be one's primary resources) it is possible to provide necessary assistance to those students to increase their skill level.

This reminds us of the philosophy of W. Edwards Deming, who based the entire TQM model on the fact that all workers want to do a good job and take pride in their work. Indeed, we have never met a student who did not want to learn, but we've met many students who say that "school is boring" and that "it has no meaning" to them.

Teachers often erroneously blame the students by saying they are unmotivated and don't want to learn, when, in fact, it is the student who often doesn't see a need to learn what teachers want them to learn. This is one of the most frustrating things to teachers. Yet, if you really think about it, it clarifies the need for telling students what you want them to learn and WHY. The "why" question is key and the answers given to students must be other than, "Because I said so."

We must make a concerted effort at explaining our purpose in teaching our subject matter. This is true of all subjects at all levels. If students understand and agree with the "why" question, they will rise to your expectations and probably exceed them. An excellent example of this type of teacher is Jaime Escalente, upon whom the movie, *Stand and Deliver* was based. His success hinged on his ability to convince his students that learning calculus was essential to their future happiness and survival, and **the belief that together they could achieve success.** Had he not drawn the connections for his students between the classroom activities and the real world, they would never have reached the heights they did. Research suggests that many students quit school because they feel more pride in what they do while working (even in a fast food restaurant) than at school. It simply has more meaning to them. It behooves each reader to give a great deal of thought to the question, "why do we have to learn this?"

Additionally, teachers must do some soul searching and recognize their responsibility for the problems within the classroom. This is the place to start. Teachers must examine the processes and systems utilized within the classroom, and realize that results will be different only when they begin to make the necessary changes in these functions so that all students can achieve success. As Crosby says, *[a]s long as things can go out without being right, no one will believe you are serious about it* (1988, p.86). This will require courage and persistence, educating in different ways, with much time and energy; but the results will be well worth the effort.

One can assist students by describing and demonstrating how they can implement statistical process control (SPC) and the plan-do-check-act (P-D-C-A) cycle to assess their own work and that of classmates. Each student should have a personal **Continuous Improvement to Quality (CIQ)** book where his/her own records are maintained in some graph form. This is an easy way for all students to see their progress while making use of these procedures as a regular part of classroom evaluative activities. The **CIQ** book has the classroom mission statement and classroom goals printed in the front. Space is provided for students to list their personal goals for achievement in each class or subject. Each student's short-term goals should be updated at least weekly while the long range goals should be adjusted as the students advance to the following unit and/or grade. A graph or some other chart should record the progress daily. Students (grades three and higher) can be responsible for keeping track of their own progress, and can learn to become involved in their own continuous improvement process on the basis of this information. When students take an active role in assessing their own progress they will feel empowered and will want to achieve higher levels. Students who keep journals of their accomplishments will achieve more, especially when they have a written record of their path. Better yet, students who see the data in graph form clearly understand their progress. This scientific approach to learning could be used easily in all curricular areas.

Classroom wellness depends on students understanding how they can continuously improve. If this process begins in the early grades, and students know and understand quality work, they will far exceed expectations. Students must be provided the tools to grow and improve their work continuously from day to day, month to month, and year to year. When problems of poor quality arise, it is the responsibility of the student (with support and guidance from the TQ teacher) to recognize problem areas and ways to improve.

Traditional teachers have taken all this away from students, leaving them outside the system and feeling impotent about their own future. When people (even the youngest) learn ways to resolve their own problems, they feel stronger, have increased self-confidence and become eager to do more. This is what must be taught to all students. Students involved in this process will become responsible for their own learning, thus taking the drudgery out of your work. As you drive fear out of the classroom and begin to empower students, you'll recognize why TQM is a workable approach to successfully educating all children.

The students will each maintain their own records of accomplishment. As stated earlier, such record keeping will be the responsibility of the K-2 teacher, but can be turned over to the students as early as third grade. Some teachers get so mired down in grading papers that they become resentful of the time it takes. By following the suggestions, a TQ teacher is relieved of the burden of continuous inspection. However, it is vitally important for the teacher to know how the students are doing in order to become better coaches for the students. Neither teachers nor students involved in a functioning TQM classroom will be bogged down in inspecting student work. Students will be involved in the continuous improvement process and will become "self-inspectors." Classmates working together in cooperative learning groups will not only evaluate their collective work, but also each other's work, through written and oral evaluations. The focus of any evaluation, however, must always be on continuous improvement, and never be punitive, coercive or shaming! **Dependence on standardized test scores will decline in importance; however, implementing TQM will undoubtedly improve test scores immeasurably.**

Even if one's school district operates on a A-F grading system, there are alternatives available to the TQ teacher. A much more sensible approach to evaluation includes a yearly or semester portfolio of the student's work. Students and the TQ teacher can work together to determine exactly what the portfolio will contain. Parental input should be sought as well, as they are external customers. The teacher will need to guide students and parents through this process, however, since seeking their input to this degree may be considered a radical idea. At first, they may not want to become involved so one must lay the groundwork and educate them about TQM. A portfolio might include an assessment of the student's intellectual curiosity, perhaps based on research s/he did, some special project undertaken, and examples of writing, math, critical thinking, and special learning needs. Portfolios might also include examples of re-working some paper or project, indicating the growth from the first draft to the achievement of quality work. This information, along with the student's charted information can provide valuable information. Each student should be fully cognizant of what is included in the portfolio; indeed, they will have access to it daily and will be placing assignments in it. If operating within a standard, traditional grading system the portfolio will provide more information upon which to determine the final grade

The portfolio shouldn't contain every paper or homework assignment as that places too much attention on inspection.

Instead, in the elementary grades, it will probably include examples of growth in each of the core areas—critical thinking, self-discipline, creativity, cooperative learning, and the CIQ Book. It is important to show growth, so parents, administrators, and others can clearly see the child's progress.

At the junior high or middle school level, portfolios will be kept in each class or within the team, if the school district uses that model. Each portfolio will demonstrate growth in critical thinking, the ability to self-evaluate and correct mistakes, and the results of cooperative assignments, as well as the thought processes that went into the completion of such assignments.

In high school, it is important that cross-curricular assignments are kept in an agreed upon place. These will demonstrate the student's learning within a wide range of curricular activities. Research papers will demonstrate the steps leading to the final product as well as the quality result. Discouraged students, with the help of the TQ teacher, can quickly access their strengths and evidence of their growth. Imagine how empowering this will be for students who begin to feel bogged down, or for those needing an additional boost.

At all levels, the portfolio might also include evidence of goal setting, disciplinary action required within the classroom and the problem-solving the student undertook to ensure problems would not be repeated. Evidence of growth in problem solving will also empower the student. This is just an example of things one might want to include in a student's portfolio. When parents and students become involved in the process, they will undoubtedly add additional items. Remember, nothing about the portfolio is fixed. Be flexible but certainly include any evidence of growth in critical thinking, problem solving, and quality work.

As you gather evidence of quality work, display it for all to see. Students need concrete examples of quality work so they can emulate it. It returns to the idea, that if you show me what you want me to do, I can do it; but if I'm never sure what you want, then how will I ever be able to know if I do it? Be as clear and concise as possible about the definition of quality work. Continue to raise standards with each class. Students will rise to one's expectations if the TQ teacher is committed to quality and fully believes in each student's desire to learn.

At the end of each year, encourage those students or groups of students who have completed the highest quality work to make copies of their excellent examples for following classes. This will be very helpful when one begins the TQM and TQI training each fall. It also increases the possibility that these students will act as mentors for the younger students.

Continuous improvement means, for example, that once a student learns the proper way to write a fully documented research paper, s/he will continue to do it that way for the remainder of his/her formal education. This is the beauty of TQM. The continuous improvement process means that teachers will not have to start at "square one" every time an assignment is given. Much less attention will have to be given to remediation (price of nonconformance) and much more energy and attention can be paid to critical thinking and higher order thinking skills. Students will learn to critique everything they see, hear and read, allowing them to broaden their understanding.

At this point one has exerted a great deal of energy trying to establish a **quality classroom**, and may feel some irritation and frustration with colleagues in the lower grade levels and parents of students with inadequate skills and disruptive behaviors. What can be done to ensure improvement in the quality of those supplying goods (students) and services to the TQ teacher? We know this is a difficult issue as it pertains to work of one's colleagues'. Unfortunately, this is likely to remain an issue if you are the lone TQM teacher in the building. You can ill afford to ignore this problem, however, since as long as students come to your class without minimum competencies, remediation and boredom are likely to become a way of life. It will be a slow process that begins with trust, and continuing with conversations regarding what you notice about the students who coming to you from a colleague's class. Again, one possible problem is that people will get caught up in blaming others. However, that is not going to resolve any problems. Approaching colleagues with problems is best done through a positive, non judgmental approach. Become the corporate rebel!

Curriculum teams across grade levels can be an approach, ensuring minimum competencies for all students prior to the end of each grade level. The competencies must be clearly and objectively spelled out, with agreement on the terminology and a time frame. This will avoid any "fuzziness" that may otherwise occur. Another method is to have staff meetings (across grade levels) in the spring of each year to discuss the deficiencies of a group of students and then to begin working on the P-D-C-A cycle with these individuals. A plan for corrective action should be the key element in each of these meetings. The TQ teacher must help colleagues understand the principles of TQM and continuous improvement and explain the successful educational experiences you have experienced because of it. You will probably win converts to the TQM model through a willingness to share experience, expertise and results.

Parents can and should become your partner in TQM. An important part of this is establishing a trusting relationship. It may take awhile, especially with parents of at-risk children, since many of them are undereducated and had poor educational experiences in school, but the long-term dividends of this will be excellent cooperation and a willingness to assist the children achieve success. There are many ways this can be accomplished, however, the important element is that each teacher begin working towards establishing trust from the first day of school. We have presented two excellent case studies of communication with parents below.

Establish Trust
Case Study: Elementary School— Mr. Tom Parker, Edinboro Elementary School, Edinboro, PA

September, 1991
Dear Parents:

As you all know, your son or daughter is in Mr. Parker's class this year. This note is to introduce me; let you know a few things about your child's schedule and inform everyone about a few rules and policies.

My name is Tom Parker. I am married and the father of two: our young man is a senior in college; and our little girl is five and is in her second year in preschool. I have a B.S. degree in Elementary Education and an M.Ed. in Guidance and Counseling. In addition, I have ten years counseling experience and ten years experience in the world of business. On a more personal level, I have traveled most of North America from the Arctic Circle south and have traveled throughout Europe. I am also an avid outdoor person and love sports, nature, art and music. My wife, kids and I live in McKean, in the middle of her family farm, and are involved in many community activities as well as in our church. If you have any questions, please call or write a note and I'll get back to you as soon as possible.

Some parents have asked about our special classes. We have one special each day. They are:

Monday - Gym (Physical Education)
Tuesday - Library
Wednesday - Music
Thursday - Art
Friday - Health

Starting last year, second grade classrooms are self contained; a change from the past. This means the students are with me for all subjects except the specials, and do not change classes for any other subject. This is especially good because we can coordinate math learning with science material; social studies with reading and spelling, and so on. It also allows for flexible small groups in the classroom and keeps your child from becoming labeled high, average, or low. It also allows the students to learn from and share with each other. This is not to say that there are no problems, but simply to state that the positives far outweigh the negatives, especially for younger students.

I like to have a parent teach or talk to my class at least one time per week. If you are interested and able time wise, please contact me in the very near future. This will allow scheduling to fit your free time. You might talk about your hobby, vocation, special interest, vacation, family, or anything else appropriate to second graders. The kids absolutely love to have parents around—and, in part because of this, the program was very successful last year. I am anxious to get it going this year and hope you will make a contribution.

Some other notes:
1. The second Wednesday of each month is early dismissal.
2. Birthday and holiday treats may be sent to school. Please let me know in advance.
3. If your child is absent, please send an excuse the day they return.
4. Please send a note if your child will ride a different bus or has other transportation home.
5. Please take time to read to or with your kids every weeknight. Check their understanding of the stories.
6. Help them with their spelling words...the list comes home Monday, tests are Friday. Have your child find these words in the newspaper or a magazine. Discuss the words and their meanings.
7. I would like the students to know their addition and subtraction facts up to ten. Try a few simple problems with your child. If there is any hesitation, you might consider making flash cards for practice. Try them Sunday nights...I'll see the difference on Monday.
8. Encourage your kids to tell what they are doing in school. Try this every couple of days.

One final comment. My door is always open and you are welcome anytime. Please visit or observe class in progress and please join your parent-teacher organization.

My goal as a teacher is to inspire these children and to make them life long learners. I am looking forward to meeting each one of you, and to a successful year.

Sincerely,

James T. (Tom) Parker, III

Case Study: Secondary School— Mrs. Judy Scaletta, General McLane High School, Edinboro, PA

Dear Parent:

Your child has enrolled in the Calculus course which I will be teaching during the 1991-1992 school year. The course is designed to develop the analytical skills, problem solving techniques, logical reasoning and effective communications skills needed for future courses in the physical and social sciences, engineering and mathematics.

The scope of this Calculus course is equivalent to approximately one and one-half semesters of college Calculus. The material is challenging but is presented through real-world applications. This curriculum also satisfies the requirements of the Advanced Placement Program administered by the College Board. Students can earn three to four college credits and/or advanced standing by taking the Calculus AB Advanced Placement Examination in May. I will be providing students with detailed information on this. Be sure to review the information with your son or daughter. Please contact me if you have questions regarding this topic.

In order to help your child have a successful experience this school year, I have listed below some of my expectations for students in this class.
*   > Homework will be collected and graded. Homework is an essential part of any math course. It allows the students to internalize the concepts discussed. Please encourage your child to complete daily*

assignments. You will be notified if your child is falling behind in this area.

> Students will be expected to participate in the presentation of problems at the board. The ability to communicate ideas clearly is an essential skill that students must develop.

> Tests and worksheets will be cumulative to stress retention. A semester exam will be given in January and a final exam will be given at the conclusion of the course.

> A day-by-day syllabus of the course, listing topics covered, all assignments and test dates will be provided to each student. Should absence occur, a student can readily make-up the necessary work. Should a pupil miss a test, he or she will take a make-up test upon returning to school.

> A scientific calculator is required.

> A 3-ring binder (not a spiral notebook) will be required. This will facilitate the organization of notes, homework, tests, and handouts. At the conclusion of the course, you child will have compiled a calculus reference manual to take to college.

> Each activity period, I sponsor a calculus study group. This is a very informal gathering during which time students may ask questions on any topic, receive extra help, or investigate problems that have sparked their interest. These sessions are not mandatory, but most students find them very helpful.

To keep you informed of your child's progress, you will receive a Progress Report halfway through each grading period. This is a thorough profile of your child's performance in class which will list individual test scores as well as comments. Space is also provided for your comments. I ask that you sign the form and have your child return it to me.

Working together, we can make the senior year a valuable learning experience. Should you have any questions, please feel free to contact me. I look forward to meeting you at open house on October 9.

Sincerely,
Judy Scaletta

Both of these letters contain valuable information for parents, and each solicits trust (albeit in a different way). The elementary school example is very informal, and Mr. Parker presents himself as a personal, approachable individual. Parents probably experience friendly feelings for him. This is the beginning of trust. Mrs. Scaletta's letter is more formal, however, she sends a strong message of organization, expectations and caring for each of her students. Both are examples of engaging parents as partners in the educational process.

These teachers give specific examples of "why" they organize the class in a certain way. Mr. Parker emphasizes a cross-curricular approach without labeling students. Mrs. Scaletta explains why students are expected to perform certain functions and the relevance of Calculus to her student's future.

Each of these examples also gives parents specific suggestions for assisting their child. This is important and as with everything else in TQM must be done with a clear understanding of the desired outcome. Finally, each teacher invites parents to become part of a team to ensure the student's success.

What follows is an example of an introductory letter to parents about TQM and the impact on their child. In the Appendix you will find an example of a Customer-Supplier Contract.

Dear Parent:

    Welcome to our classroom family. _____ may have told you class is very different this year. We are embarking on a Total Quality, continuous improvement journey. The Total Quality approach is different in that it focuses on satisfying the customer. For our purposes, you are both my supplier—that is, you supply me with your child, and my customer—that is, I return your child to you with different skills and abilities (the "product"). It is upon these skills and abilities that you will be asked to evaluate _____'s classroom experiences this year. It is important that we work closely together as customers and suppliers to achieve the greatest end result.

    In this class, I will ask you to assume some responsibilities as my supplier so that I receive students ready to learn. I will also ask you to evaluate the class for friendliness, efficiency, and rapid response to your concerns. This will happen several times during the year and certainly at the end of the year. Your responses will enable me to embark on continuous improvement projects aimed at eliminating errors forever from this classroom.

All students will work with me to improve our class. This means taking an active role in determining causes and recommending changes that will lead to everyone's success. Your child will participate in this process throughout the year. Ours will be a truly democratic classroom that will seek long-term solutions to classroom problems so they do not recur. Some of these may include: rules, discipline, teaching techniques, assignments, and the arrangement of classroom furniture.

I believe that 85% of all problems within the classroom are management controlled. The students and the quality of their work are affected by each of these. I believe this is the major reason why students don't reach their potential in schools today. In order to identify and resolve problems I will need help from students and parents. I am committed to altering those processes and systems that are the cause of inferior student work and poor attitudes towards learning.

Your child's future depends on our making school a safe, interesting place where s/he can take pride in doing quality work. My classroom will become a place where everyone enjoys:

TRUST (teacher-student/student-student)
QUALITY (excellent work)
PRIDE (resulting from quality work)
FUN (the result of high interest and excitement of
*   learning)*

My mission is to have each child develop a love of learning based on the enthusiasm and pride generated from doing quality work, and to become good citizens through working together to resolve problems. The success of this classroom is based on the successes of the group continuous improvement projects.

This is not "business as usual" and I am eager to gain your input and have you visit our class. Please sign the attached contract and return to me by Friday. Thank you for your cooperation.

On a more global scale, the teacher can and should be working toward collecting data from customers regarding students after they have left the classroom. Tracking students at each level is necessary to implement one's own P-D-C-A cycle. For example, French I students entering French II classes can be tracked for such things as retention, speaking skills, and vocabulary. One might also note the numbers of students who choose not to enroll in French II, and the reasons they decided against taking it. For some it may be a scheduling problem, others may be simply say they didn't like French I. If students indicate they don't like a class you're teaching, you will want to explore the reasons for that through the use of a survey or conversation with the student or parents. Such data will be useful in improving the delivery system, and also in recognizing trends where continuous improvement can be implemented.

Teachers of high school seniors will also want to include some method of securing data from employers and post-secondary institutions. This can be accomplished through a survey of employers, though it is somewhat more difficult to track the success rate of graduates at post-secondary institutions. One may wish to send a survey about the class directly to the student. If one is familiar with any university or college instructors, ask them about their expectations for entering freshmen. This provides one with information that may lead to curriculum revision, not to mention altering classroom activities. (See chapter 10 for more details.)

Break down barriers between departments

TQ teachers collaborate with faculty from other departments as well as from within their own department to allow for a free flow of information and to remove artificial barriers that currently exist, including any existing biases. Faculty will also use this as a means of making inter-disciplinary connections, as outlined in the cross-curricular examples in Chapter 7. It is impossible to commit to TQM and not collaborate with colleagues.

As suggested in Chapter 3 all teachers have a responsibility to leave the classroom and begin networking with fellow teachers. This is difficult for several reasons. One, due to time constraints, many teachers don't feel they have time to spend with their colleagues. Two, the classroom has traditionally been the sole domain of each teacher, and what happens within that classroom is viewed as personal. Many teachers believe in the sovereignty of their classrooms, and regard the presence of others as a personal affront, with the exception of the principal who annually evaluates them. In many school districts little or no time is allotted to departments to perform curricular reviews encompassing the K-12 curriculum.

We recognize the problems this poses for many teachers. In particular, as the research indicates, there is more need to interrelate subjects, sharing information across all subjects within the school district. No longer can we accept the idea that what one does in English, or Science, or Geography, does not relate to all other areas of the curriculum. This recognizes the need for educating with a global perspective, utilizing all possible cross-curricular approaches. It also recognizes that teachers need to interact with one another, attend conferences, receive staff development, and be willing to accept advice and share information with colleagues.

TQ teachers will be responsible for taking the necessary initiative to begin this process. Start by inviting others into your classroom, and actively seek input from colleagues. Work with the administration and your collective bargaining group to open the lines of communication. One can then become leader by encouraging colleagues to engage in meaningful dialogue. Work to institute some cross-curricular activities within the classroom and then share the results with others, encouraging them to do likewise.

We must all respect the work of our colleagues and not demean any one discipline, but recognize the worth of all. Become an advocate for the entire curriculum by speaking to students and parents about the importance of each aspect of the curriculum on one's total education. Encourage, where possible, linkages with other schools within the system to provide a continuous educational process for the students.

The following is a check sheet tool to help the reader baseline their **Quality Assurance or Products and Services** skills. There are four subcategories that we consider important. Please refer to the table and circle the "point" next to the "criteria" that most nearly describes your present classroom situation.

6.1   What methods do you use to evaluate your student's academic performance?

Points	Criteria
1	Traditional paper/pencil evaluation with teacher grading
2	Students grade each other's quizzes
3	Teachers grade all unit tests, and students are able to continue improving their grade until mastery is achieved.
4	Students turn in a portfolio of work at the end of each unit, along with a self-evaluation. The teacher then evaluates the level of achievement for mastery learning at the 80% level.
5	Students work together to evaluate each other's work and provide appropriate feedback for revision/discussion. A portfolio of work is included reflecting cross-curricular, critical thinking and writing or computational assignments. The teacher's assessment reflects mastery learning at the competition with "World Class" levels.

6.2   How do you define waste in your classroom and what preventive measures do you take to reduce waste?

Points	Criteria
1	No formal evaluation of "waste," such as the retention rate of students.
2	"Waste" is considered as students who do not pass and is determined solely by inspection such as paper/pencil tests or as "scrap" because the job has to be redone.
3	"Waste" includes measurable external failure costs such as the cost of drop-outs to society, illiteracy, teen pregnancy rates, drug and alcohol problems, juvenile delinquency, and truancy.
4	Process orientation regarding waste is considered such as time, steps, complexity, special projects, etc. to get ALL students to minimal standards.
5	"Waste" is recognized as a result of poor processes and systems and includes all aspects of the educational system; and as a result, an ongoing effort utilizing, K-12 curricular teams, cooperative learning, cross-curricular teams, and mastery learning is employed.

6.3   How do you bring about improvements in quality to those supplying good and services to you, including those students coming to you?

Points	Criteria
1	There is no effort made to improve the quality.
2	There is an informal agreement to discuss deficiencies student's have with former teachers and parents.
3	Suppliers (former teachers and parents) are provided with instruction in TQM and encouraged to incorporate the principles. Textbooks and instructional materials are continuously examined to meet improved curriculum and teaching techniques.
4	Through the teacher's efforts, former teachers within the district have process oriented quality improvement capabilities.
5	The teacher has an active partnership with all suppliers (including parents) to set and improve quality. There is cross training throughout the curriculum

6.4   How do you evaluate and integrate the quality of skills your students use that they've learned from other classes within your school?

Points	Criteria
1	No formal tracking system
2	No effort is made to meet with other teachers, but concern is vocalized about the skills of the students
3	Evaluation of skills from cross-curricular classes is done once a year
4	Active interaction between all teachers across the curriculum
5	Partnerships are formed, and assignments are constructed so that skills from across the curriculum will amass to achieve quality. Suppliers are expected to improve continuously.

Chapter Nine: Quality Results

..an orderly study of productivity, to enquire whether any given activity is consistent with the aim of the organization, and what it is costing, can be very helpful to the management.

W. Edwards Deming
Out of the Crisis

We suggest that the reader take the time to briefly answer the following questions prior to reading this chapter and answering the questions on the checksheet at the end.

7.0 **Quality Results**

This category examines quality improvement based upon objective measures derived from customer requirements/expectations analysis and from operations analysis. Also examined are current quality levels in relation to those of competing organizations.

7.1   Enclose in graph form some key improvement data in your students

7.2   Briefly describe one or two continuous improvement projects(s) which have led to the results in 7.1

7.3   Please describe how you compare your classroom with other classrooms within or outside of your product or service area (benchmarking)

Data determines how one can work towards continuous improvement. TQM is based upon the use of statistical data properly analyzed to show the level of one's achievements.

Data used to obtain information on one's current state of functioning is called baseline data. It is a starting point for the improvement process. Baseline data is used to prepare charts and graphs for each of the areas one wishes to improve. Display these data in the classroom and make it available to administrators and parents. This is a starting point, however, to be effective, one must also collect data after making some changes in the processes and systems within the classroom. Since the goal is continuous improvement, the only true way to measure that improvement is with data collected from one's internal and external customers before and after changes are made to the processes and systems.

As a TQ teacher, never lose sight of the importance of the customers. It is essential to know their perceptions about your students and your work. As important, are the self-measurements you will be undergoing in pursuit of a personal continuous improvement plan.

Most of us recognize the need for feedback about our work. However, feedback that is hearsay, or based on "hunch," intuition, or sporadic observation is neither sufficient nor adequate for determining processes requiring continuous improvement. **Feedback based on fact** is vital if one is to truly embark on a continuous improvement journey.

Crosby, in his book, *The Eternally Successful Organization* (1988, p. 191) says, *[p]erformance reviews probably do more to make employees antagonistic to their company than any other single item.* One of the problems with traditional teacher evaluative methods is that most are based on administrative classroom observation and not data. While observation can provide some classroom insights, it cannot ever replace an efficient, effective on-going data collection process. We have known many good teachers who have become very defensive and angry upon receipt of one or two suggestions for improvement from the principal. Clearly, this response suggests an evaluation system based on fear. Deming (1982, p. 109-110) says:

> *A common fallacy is the supposition that it is possible to rate people; to put them in rank order of performance for next year, based on performance last year.*
> *The performance of anybody is the result of a combination of many forces—the person*

himself, the people that he works with, the job, the materials that he works on, his equipment, his customer, his management, his supervision, environmental conditions (noise, confusion, poor food in the company's cafeteria). These forces will produce unbelievably large differences between people. In fact, ..., apparent differences between people arise almost entirely from action of the system that they work in, not from the people themselves. A man not promoted is unable to understand why his performance is lower than someone else's. No wonder; his rating was the result of a lottery. Unfortunately, he takes his rating seriously.

Data collection gives a much broader, more accurate picture of what is working and what systems and processes require improvement. Again, we want to emphasize the importance of breaking through the barrier of fear one might have of data. When this occurs you can enjoy the benefits that can come only from information. You will never again want to rely on hearsay or someone's observation of your work. You will gain in self-confidence because problem areas have been identified, thus making it easier to work out positive action plans to improve student achievement and at the same time make your job easier.

Students empowered through TQM methods will not only assist you in data collection and determining plans for continuous improvement, but they will also work harder and accomplish more. Everyone will have fun in the classroom.

Looking at the Quality Index Profile for **Results**, one can see clearly that subsection 8.1 speaks to the baseline data and the ways one has chosen to continue charting the data after making some changes within the classroom. These data will be collected on groups of students with whom one is working. An important thing to remember as one collects and graphs such data, trends may develop indicating another area where improvement can be made.

Continuous improvement projects will be directed towards one or two areas within the classroom. If everyone jointly determines there are many things that need "fixing," we recommend the action team, *i.e.* the teacher and students, agree to initially focus on only one or two. It is necessary to provide an opportunity to "see" results in the data due to any process change. Attempting to change too many things at once will make it impossible to be certain what is happening. Remember change is very difficult for any of us; most people resist change, therefore, permanent change in the classroom culture takes time.

To maintain the focus on continuous improvement and the TQM methods, limit the number of initial changes to one or two.

As you continue with data collection the action team may decide to make other changes based on new information. A systematic, slow approach will work better than a shotgun approach. Patience will be a key factor in spite of society's desire for a "quick fix." Continuously remind yourself, *[e]veryone makes changes, but very few take care to inject them into the bloodstream of the company* (Crosby 1988, p.120). This implies that you implement change to prevent the problem from being repeated only after assessing the data. In order to understand happenings within the classroom processes and systems, one must take a methodical approach. For example, if one suspected that one had food allergies, it would be prudent to systematically eliminate certain foods. Eliminating most foods at once clearly wouldn't provide the information necessary to determine which specific item(s) causes the allergy. The same can be said for modifying the processes and systems within the classroom.

Once the action team has agreed on the root cause of the problem and implemented an action plan, the project is continued until the desired results are either demonstrated or denied by the data.

There are endless ways in which a TQ teacher can get the class involved in any continuous improvement project. An important point to remember is that the class is a team working together to (1) determine the project, (2) include everyone in the transformation...no mysteries allowed, and (3) agree to continue systematically collecting and reporting the data so everyone knows the outcomes. Accurate, factual information will become a friend to everyone.

The other necessary element for the Total Quality Classroom is some evidence that the TQ teacher is working towards achieving excellence as compared to the **BEST** examples of similar classrooms throughout the state, region, or the nation. When we refer to "similar classrooms," we mean classrooms at the same grade level, or referring to the same subject matter being taught. (First grade classrooms compared with other first grade classrooms; English classrooms compared with other English classrooms, etc.) Simply stated we mean the BEST examples of classrooms wherever they may be. This kind of information will provide each TQ teacher with the very best opportunity for benchmarking.

You may be thinking, how can I find out about these classrooms? It is a valid question, and one that can only be addressed by networking with teachers from other districts and involvement in professional organizations at the local, state and national level. By watching television programs highlighting various schools across the nation it is possible to get some idea of where to begin the search for the BEST in any subject matter area. Professional organizations often are well acquainted excellent examples throughout the country, and armed with this information, one can write for names of exemplary schools and/or teachers. When you are good, the word of mouth will let everyone know!

Contact your state department of education for names of teachers who have received the Teacher of the Year Award. While seeking names, examine the criteria upon which they were selected. These are just a few of the ways one can obtain information about excellence in the classroom.

Once one has received the demographic information about the BEST examples in any subject matter, communicate with those teachers. Arrange a visit if it is at all possible. Site visitations often reveal important data that is overlooked when writing. Our experiences tells us this is so because these TQ teachers have assimilated so much into their classroom that it is second nature to them. They are not aware of the significance of seemingly minor classroom processes they practice daily that make a major impact on student outcomes.

Benchmarking one's class with a "world class" classroom will be the best indicator of any progress. It is possible to take the best of several classrooms and capitalize on the strengths of each, to make massive improvements in one's classroom. American students will need to be the most competitive possible upon graduation from high school to meet the demands of the 21st century. Whether one teaches kindergarten, or seventh or twelfth grade, it is each teacher's responsibility to be the best *TQ* teacher possible.

If your school is located in a low socio-economic area, or is one with many students of color, the urgency to become personally involved in the TQI process is as great or greater than if one works in a very affluent school district. Benchmarking against the very best will help one realize the potential for students as well as the challenges. By leading the students through the continuous improvement process, driving out fear, and empowering the students, you can realize greater achievement than ever before imagined. Maintain high expectations, then work toward improving the systems and processes within the classroom so everyone can achieve them. Continuous self-evaluation is not a luxury, it is vital to one's goal. It can be and is being done in some classrooms around the nation. You can do it too!

The following is a check sheet tool to help the reader baseline their **Quality Results** skills. There are three subcategories that we consider important. Please refer to the tables and circle the "point" next to the "criteria" that most nearly describes your present classroom situation.

7.1   Enclose in graph form some key improvement data in your students

Points	Criteria
1	Graphs are not generated.
2	Traditional quality indicator information is used (i.e. the grade).
3	Traditional information is evaluated regularly in the classroom using graphs that are understood by all students
4	Field intelligence data are gathered by the teacher and evaluated in graphical form, (i.e. the number or percent of those passing the AP test, number enrolling in college, number going on to a more difficult level of instruction, etc.)
5	Information related to strategic quality objectives is regularly used and is posted in graphical form throughout the classroom for all to see; reports are provided to the school board, administration, and are sent home to all parents.

7.2   Briefly describe one or two continuous improvement project(s) which have led to the results in 7.1

Points	Criteria
1	No project groups or no measurable results available
2	Project groups are put together quickly with effort put into the nature of the project and how it might lead to quality improvement.
3	Mastery learning is utilized and results are charted, but cooperative learning is only utilized occasionally.
4	Project groups are established with assignments that are cross-curricular and meaningful.
5	All students are engaged in project groups that study issues and result in cross-curricular meaningful work, and value added work is accomplished by the teacher remaining a supportive leader. The main work, using quality tools and methods, is done by the students.

7.3   Please describe how you compare your classroom with other classrooms within or outside of your product or service area (benchmarking)

Points	Criteria
1	No comparable data is available.
2	Standard accounting information such as: standardized test scores, students passing, etc.
3	Passive collection and analysis of data from outside sources such as parents and former students.
4	Benchmarking of competitors, (i.e. percent of your students going on to next highest level of schooling, those taking the most difficult classes, compared to other like classes).
5	Instituted an active program to obtain comparative "benchmarking" data on all functions and services from the BEST in those areas whether they are competitors or not (i.e. continuous search for the premier approaches to teaching/learning your subject matter).

Chapter Ten   Customer Satisfaction

Satisfy the Customer, first, last, and always.

Philip Crosby
Let's Talk Quality

We suggest that the reader take the time to briefly answer the following questions prior to reading this chapter and answering the questions on the checksheet at the end.

8.0 Customer Satisfaction

This category examines the organization's knowledge of the customer, overall customer service system, responsiveness, and ability to meet requirements and expectations.

8.1   How do you determine your customers, and their satisfaction level outside your classroom?

8.2   How do you determine your internal customers and their satisfaction level inside your classroom?

8.3   In what functional areas, processes, or systems do you have defined, measurable product and/or service quality criteria? Please list.

8.4   What methods do you use to determine customer satisfaction?

8.5   Summarize trends in customer satisfaction and list measurements you have in specific areas.

8.6   What happens in your classroom that significantly promotes continuous improvement to increase customer satisfaction?

Who are the customers?

Internal customers include students and teachers from all grades who teach the sequence courses in any subject matter area. Current students are internal customers. **External customers** are parents, post-secondary institutions, employers, and the community. Identifying the customer is important in order to know how to proceed in establishing a feedback mechanism. The process of identifying and modifying systems within the classroom begins with recognition of **all** customers.

At each level of formal schooling there are several customers that teachers must address. In the primary grades, customers are children, parents, and each subsequent grade level teacher. In other words, the first grade teacher is a customer of the kindergarten teacher, the second grade teacher is a customer of the first grade teacher. Additionally, the art, music, physical education teachers and the librarian are customers of classroom teachers. It isn't enough, for example, for a first grade teacher to satisfy students and parents and disregard the second grade teacher. Care must be taken to discover the competencies (both academic and social) required for continued growth from K-12. The significance of this is that teachers can begin identifying the systems within the classroom that aren't currently meeting the customer's needs.

Teachers of children who will be moving to another level in school (*e.g.* primary grades to middle school or junior high school, middle school to high school, high school to post secondary institutions) have the opportunity to practice continuous improvement through a process of surveying customer needs. Students with deficiencies moving from one's class into the next level will be hampered from the beginning. An assessment of classroom practices is helpful in recognizing ways in which to improve the classroom processes and systems to eliminate similar future waste. (Remember, waste is defined as the cost of non-conformance, *i.e.* the cost of not doing it right the first time.)

It is only through a systematic, factual collection of data from customers that one can truly know whether or not the job is being done right. Feedback methods permit one to amply measure what has occurred within the classroom such as through the use of statistical tools as control charts, run charts, and Pareto diagrams.

In fact, each system within the classroom is a pocket for data collection. You'll recall, we identified classroom systems in Chapter 1. While it would be unrealistic and unfair to both students and teachers to attempt to collect data on every system within the first year of implementing TQM, one will surely want to give some thought to how data might be collected for each. Failure to solicit such information from one's customers virtually is akin to being blindfolded and attempting to wash an elephant. At best, it is classroom management by intuition. At worst, it is band-aiding problems, with no regard to prevention.

It is important to establish methods to collect data on student satisfaction as quickly as possible after the first month of school. This then becomes a continuous process throughout the school year. As with any data collection, a formal, written procedure works best, although in the very early grades, this can be done orally. A word of caution. If one chooses to collect data from students orally—(K-2 only), please be aware that one's choice of words and responses can skew any data. Also, small children, in their desire to please the teacher or out of fear, may be reluctant to respond honestly. An alternative data collection method for grades 1 and 2 would be to invite a parent in to read a set of questions (prepared by teacher and parents) which students have only to put a check in a column representing "yes" or "no". Results should be able to be graphically represented and posted for all to see. These results become the catalyst for implementing the P-D-C-A cycle.

Other internal customers (colleagues) can also provide you with information on their satisfaction rate of students from the previous year. Care should be taken not to rely to hearsay as evidence of satisfaction. Nor, should one be tempted into using gossip as a basis for data. Instead, design an instrument that measures specific criteria based on the desired student competencies. Such an instrument should address academic and social outcomes. It is essential to resist assigning blame about low satisfaction levels. For instance, we've heard many teachers and administrators claim that certain groups of students can't learn because of their family background, living conditions, ethnic heritage, etc. TQM takes away all blame and focuses on continuous improvement plans, thus diminishing the aforementioned factors.

There is a certain amount of fear involved in discussions such as this, and we would be remiss if we didn't address those fears. Teacher and public school bashing seems to be fairly popular these days. It is rampant within government, industry, and many community groups. Yet teaching is an occupation that requires a great deal of energy and yields few monetary rewards; often within a system that keeps teachers out of the loop of making important decisions about school governance. Government is great at mandating additional programs and services (often without adequate funding) and requiring additional paperwork for teachers. School boards, with responsibility for directing the education of students within the district, often restrict funds, or refuse to allow teachers time to attend conferences, workshops and other events that would improve their instruction and perhaps rejuvenate them. Building and district administrators sometimes take action without consulting the teachers directly affected by such decisions. This leads to a general feeling of alienation, isolation, and anger. When a teacher internalizes such feelings the result is burn-out, depression and an "I don't care" attitude.

A lack of trust is demonstrated when teachers are defensive about having administrators, colleagues or parents come and observe in the classroom. Without trusting relationships, it is doubtful that many teachers will be able to fully develop their potential as TQ leaders. Each teacher can begin today building trust between teacher and administrators, teacher and students, student and student, and teacher and parents.

Building trust can be accomplished in many ways, including frank and open discussions about trust and what it means. Even the youngest student will respond to teachers who are open, friendly and willing to listen. This dramatically affects the learning climate of the classroom. Listening without intimidating, manipulating or becoming defensive is the key. When a teacher can listen to **all** children without being judgmental, the students will begin to trust the teacher and the resulting feedback cycle will provide insights for implementing continuous improvement projects consequently, the students will begin to take a more active role in their own education.

Likewise, when teachers, administrators, parents, and community leaders can listen nonjudgmentally to each other, everyone can become partners in the continuous improvement process. Unfortunately bad publicity has created a wide chasm at a time when these groups need to work together to improve education for all. Some of this comes from misuse and incorrect reporting of data. We believe many readers may be feeling trapped, feeling that data collection and reporting are out of their hands, and out of their control. In some school districts this has been an issue leading to intimidation and coercive tactics used towards teachers by school boards, administrators and by some communities. The finger of blame is always easy to point at others and each of the above groups share responsibility for this problem. It is our belief that **unless data is used responsibly (to resolve problems) there is no valid reason for collecting it.**

Blaming others never solves problems. Blame is wasted energy; energy that is better used in problem resolution. In our minds, there are no groups that can escape some responsibility for the problems faced in education today. We believe each citizen in this country must share part of the responsibility for the condition of our educational system today. Our schools are a true reflection of our society. The ills of our schools will never be resolved unless we all become partners, working together for the education of our children. One way to begin is to cease blaming others and accept this as a major societal problem that must change. Changes made with a shotgun approach will never work because they are not based on supportive data that identifies problems. This is exactly what has been happening in schools since their inception. Has it been effective? One look at the alarming statistics on at-risk youth shouts "NO!"

It is prudent then to have the courage to take a closer look at the potential for positive change that comes with data collection, analysis and working with a team towards continuous improvement. In the beginning, we confess (Byrnes') that our educational background and commitment to teaching made us skeptics about the need, indeed the feasibility, of using statistical data for improving the classroom systems and processes. Fortunately for us, our esteemed colleague, Dr. Cornesky (a scientific sort) provided the opportunity for us to become educated about how valuable this process is. After searching the literature for proof that this would not work, we are now convinced and firmly committed to this approach to restructuring schools and each classroom.

Data collection takes courage at first, since it is a signal that one is serious about not doing business as usual. In his book, *Peak Performance Principles for High Achievement*, John Noe (1986, p. 110) says:

> *The great enemy of courage is not cowardice, but*
> *conformity. The vast majority of people yield to*
> *the pressures of conformity because it is safe. It*
> *is unconventional to set your sights high, to*
> *climb out of ruts. That takes courage.*

Data collection however, without proper use will anger and frustrate anyone. Collect data with the same zeal and enthusiasm as if embarking on a great adventure. Be ready to accept the results without blame and shame, but with a sense of responsibility for establishing teams to find ways to improve. Allow your heart and ears to remain open as the customers respond. One's sincerity will allow all the customers be more honest in their responses. Anything less than honest responses will not provide the necessary information. Be prepared for the customers to point out areas that need improvement. In fact, be joyful for the assistance. View the process as if heading a great team of scientists, seeking a solution to one of life's major problems, and in the process to prevent it from happening again.

Lastly, receive the data impersonally. Data and information collection is never for the purpose of blaming or casting stones. TQM requires that the information be gathered and used solely for purposes of continuous improvement.

We recognize these issues and empathize with teachers and would like to issue an opportunity to all educators. Change begins with an idea. One thought can begin a chain reaction of mobilization towards problem resolution provided that thought is nurtured and allowed to grow. One individual **can** make a difference in the lives of many children by taking the challenge we are putting forth here. When colleagues see the increase in learning and the excitement with which students come to class, their curiosity will be aroused and many will come seeking information about your successes. Thus, one becomes a TQ leader within the classroom and eventually within the school and district.

Secondary teachers also have the challenge and opportunity to survey any post-secondary institution and/or business their students enter after leaving high school. This means, establishing some sort of questionnaire and tracking the graduates. In the twenty-first century it will become even more crucial to gain information (in a systematic way) on customer satisfaction.

If we are to meet the America 2000 goals, and if we are going to prepare students to meet the challenges of the workplace in the next century, then we must have a mechanism to tell us whether or not we are doing the job. If we don't have such a systematic, measurable mechanism in place, we too often rely on word of mouth, or imagine that no news is good news. The obvious problem with that attitude is that the most dissatisfied employer won't report concerns, but will simply stop hiring your students. Colleges and universities may be reluctant to admit your students if they become aware of high failure or drop out rates. Each will, however, probably tell others how dissatisfied they are with those students.

We can no longer rely on haphazard methods of feedback. Once a system to measure customer satisfaction is established, the teacher becomes empowered because results will demonstrate concrete evidence of areas needing improvement. Armed with this information, one can alter (with teams of students, and/or parents) whatever classroom systems and processes that are necessary to increase students' achievement. Thus, the P-D-C-A cycle is established making the continuous improvement process the focal point until all customers are satisfied. Using this approach there can be no doubt that yearly evaluations will be positive.

We urge teachers not to be afraid of this process. Often we become overwhelmed with fear of the unknown. As a first step, face the fear that comes from new beginnings, push through the fear, and do it anyway. This is the only way to reap massive, positive results over the long term.

What is the cost of not satisfying customers?

The kinds of negative press educators receive on a daily basis is evidence of the price of not satisfying customers. Now, government, business and industry have combined to insist on school reform as each segment of our society realizes too many students are leaving school without the requisite skills to become responsible, concerned, self-sufficient citizens. Crosby says, *[w]hen the corporations of this country tell the schools that they are not satisfied with the way quality and other things are being taught, things will change* (1989, p. 32). This has now become a reality. Many large and small corporations are faced with a diminishing supply of workers possessing the skills required for entry-level jobs. Unless teachers do something dramatic, the government will impose major restructuring of schools and curriculum. In the past, mandates like this from government have not helped, and they are scarcely the answer today, however, they do represent a level of frustration and anger over the current status of our public schools that educators can no longer afford to ignore.

From whom do these perceptions come from?— **THE CUSTOMERS!** The teachers, parents, students, business/industry, community, and post-secondary institutions determine the satisfaction level. In the past, this was not an issue for public school teachers simply because there were few options for those unhappy with the local system. Now many states have adopted a plan where students have free choice of the public —or in some cases, private— school they wish to attend. In Minnesota, for instance, students can attend any public school within the state, regardless of their place of residence. School choice has been bantered about for many years and is now a national issue. Some states are considering a bill to provide money for parents desiring to enroll their child in any private, parochial, or public school within or without the local school district. In most cases, the sum isn't enough to cover tuition, however, the public schools will lose their entire government allotment for each student whose parents accept the voucher. This represents potentially a major financial loss to some public schools.

Knowing this provides a strong impetus for all teachers to examine their fears of gathering data. Perhaps fear of the data is outweighed by concerns about who will gather the data, what data will be collected and what will be the outcome for individual teachers as a result. We suggest, however, that a proactive stance on customer satisfaction will provide one with necessary and sufficient information to make alterations within the classroom to increase student achievement rates, therefore, reducing the risks of low enrollment. Results of increased achievement will, in the long run, provide more trust and better relationships between teachers and customers. It will also improve the children's rate of learning and, isn't that what education is all about?

Crosby states, in *Let's Talk Quality* (1989, p. 49):

> *If we make our profit goals, but don't pay our bills, then we have not met our profit goals. If we deliver on time, but the product has defects, we have not delivered on time. If we meet our safety objectives, but damage somebody, we have not met our safety objectives.*

A wonderful analogy can be drawn from Crosby's statement with education. If we say everyone is entitled to a free, public education, and students drop out because they are not receiving an education, we have not met our goal. If we promise to prepare children for the future, yet upon graduation they cannot read, do not possess job readiness skills, or are unprepared for college, they are defective, and our goal is not met. If we say children are going to be provided a safe learning environment, and even one student is harmed by verbal or physical abuse from educators or fellow students, we have not met our goal. (This does not even begin to measure the goal of removing all weapons from schools.)

One clear way to determine one's commitment to the TQM approach is to think about this issue while focusing on the classroom mission statement. How can one really measure success unless one has gathered the necessary data? Perhaps a more pertinent question to ask is, *how will I know where to start unless I gather the necessary data?* Customer satisfaction is the real measure of whether or not goals are being met. This hinges on a complete understanding of all one's customers, and on methods used for data collection.

What does P-D-C-A mean?

Plan, Do, Check, Act (P-D-C-A) are part of the Deming Cycle. Essentially, this represents an action plan for implementing continuous improvement within any organization. We recommend when beginning TQM it is best to work with one class, rather than attempt to alter all classes at once. Begin slowly, with careful and thorough attention to each step. The goal is to improve the classroom for **all** students and as one gains experience and confidence in TQM it will be easier to practice it with all classes. The P-D-C-A cycle is shown graphically below.

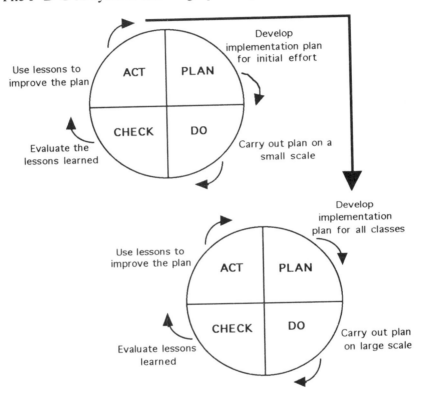

The first step **Plan,** requires you to carefully review classroom goals and the mission statement. With these as a focal point, gather a quality team to ascertain the exact nature of the problem (based on data) and seek possible solutions. It is important to gain agreement on the best plan, otherwise, you run the risk of having less than total commitment to completion of the plan. The TQI tools that are necessary to accomplish this are presented in the Appendix and include such tools as the Nominal Group Process, the Affinity Diagram, the Cause-and-Effect Diagrams, the Force Field Analysis, the Pareto Diagram, the Run Chart, the Systematic Diagram, the Scenario Builder, the Histogram, Flow Charts, and Control Charts.

The next step is **Do.** Simply stated, this means everyone is dedicated to carrying out the plan. A flow chart is drawn showing everyone where changes will be made and what the loops are. This should be posted, alongside the old flow chart, demonstrating to everyone what the changes in the process are. Once you have followed through on the plan long enough to allow it to work, there is an assessment phase.

This is called: **Check**. The purpose of this stage is to discover whether or not the implemented changes have produced the desired results. Remember, "checking" does not simply mean the evaluative efforts of the teacher, but also includes empowering the students to assess their work and the work of their classmates.

The last cog in Deming's wheel is **Act**. This assumes you will take the evaluative data and use that information to alter and improve the process. All actions are now based on the use of data received from previous continuous improvement projects. Changes are made when the data provides evidence of other problems, or when it is clear that the original changes were not sufficient to effect positive change. Each turn of the wheel leads to the beginning of the next wheel, and, therefore, the P-D-C-A cycle is repeated continuously throughout the year until successfully implemented in all classes.

What is Quality Function Deployment and how does that relate to the classroom?
Quality Function Deployment goes beyond TQM. It was begun by the Japanese when they discovered that everyone within the company was dedicated to the Quality mission, but that sometimes the efforts within departments were uncoordinated. As a result, sometimes things did not get accomplished because groups believed the responsibility belonged to others. Within these same Japanese companies there existed a frustration regarding the amount of time required to accomplish some improvements.

Thus, a teacher committed to world-class goals for the class will need to diligently work with students, and other customers to **anticipate** what will be required of customers in the future. By anticipating the requirements, a process of planning can be implemented that has a backward flow to it. As an example, a teacher determines that in five years, his/her students will need "X" skills that are not currently being addressed in the curriculum. Using the five year time line as the goal, the teacher and students, with colleagues and administration, work backwards to determine what experiences student's will need in order to meet the goal. This is Quality Function Deployment.

Information about what skills students may need in the future can be gotten from several sources. First, by reading futuristic materials and magazines. Second, from watching the world news for trends and listening to the business news. Thirdly, reading books and magazines written by futurists. The half-life of scientific knowledge today is approximately five years. Therefore, it makes less sense to focus on teaching factual scientific information than it does on problem solving, research skills, and critical thinking. In history classes for example, a comparative study of causes of war would make more sense than focusing on certain battles, generals, or other details. Details pale in significance when compared to critical thinking skills. There is more value in teaching students how and where to seek information (and provide many opportunities to use such resources) so they become life long learners. A more accurate reflection of a student's competency may be assessing knowledge of the causes of wars, and how current world events may be similar or different to those prior to previous world/regional conflicts. It might also be important to have students reflect on more peaceful ways to live within one's community, state, or region. Based on their reflections, students can engage in community volunteer service projects designed to eradicate one of the problems reflected on.   This would allow students the opportunity to test their critical thinking skills and contemplate ways to avoid future nation, regional, or world conflict at the same time it empowers them to "make a difference." This is just one example of altering the classroom goals to meet the needs of students in the future.

Promote continuous improvement.

Continuous improvement comes from empowering students to be self-motivated. The carrot and stick approach simply hasn't proven effective over the years. In one glaring example of this, years ago we visited a vocational school operated by private business for native Americans. Observing classes in reading, we noted that the teacher had a cup of M&M ™ candies on her desk. Each time the student got a sentence correct, several candies were given. Students were very lethargic, seemingly depressed, and totally indifferent to what was happening in the class. The candy provided caffeine and sugar, but did little to motivate the students to become better readers or life long learners. There was a sad sense of boredom in the class and the energy level was extremely low. We left wondering how anyone could have pride in that classroom (either student or teacher). We also mused about what might happen if the teacher were to ask students to read books in English about their culture and tribal traditions.

Fortunately, there are few classrooms still operating in this manner today. However, upon talking to many high school students from across the nation a standard complaint can be heard: **school is boring!** Fortunately, this does not seem to be the case in as many elementary school classrooms. The fact that school is perceived as boring is a major problem for educators, and one that each educator must recognize and address. The continuous improvement process will be helpful to both teachers and students.

However, motivation to learn and continuous improvement must come from within. It cannot be mandated from teachers, parents or others. In fact, we believe that everyone has a desire to learn. The discrepancy comes when students do not want to learn material in the way the teacher has planned. TQM offers an answer. It values teamwork and suggestions for improving the processes and systems within the classroom leading to attitudinal, behavioral, and finally change in quality results. All students must have opportunities to participate on quality teams. Leaving anyone or any one group out can be destructive to the entire process.

Teams and individuals can be rewarded in a variety of ways. Quality Council teams can be formally recognized through a ceremony which formally recognize the contributions each has made to the classroom. Awards, which can be certificates, plaques, lapel pins, etc., should represent the **quality** movement. This separates their work on **Quality Control** (QC) **Teams** from that of individual accomplishment in terms of academic honors.

The significance of the QC teams may well mean vastly improved processes and systems enhancing every student's ability to improve their learning. Hence, these awards represent a significant honor for recipients from teachers, students, and all customers.

The following is a check sheet tool to help the reader baseline their **Customer   Satisfaction** skills. There are six subcategories that we consider important. Please refer to the tables and circle the "point" next to the "criteria" that most nearly describes your present classroom situation.

8.1   How do you determine your customers and their satisfaction level outside your classroom?

Points	Criteria
1	There is no formal collection system to measure customer satisfaction.
2	A complaint follow-up process is in place but the information provided is infrequently used.
3	A formal complaint handling system is in place and provides feedback to the teacher. Complaints are treated as "special cases"
4	A **P-D-C-A** process is used with the information gathered from customer (i.e. alumni, students, parents, employers, post secondary institutions) satisfaction surveys. Processes are in place to monitor key indicators of customer satisfaction.
5	The teacher maintains a comprehensive data collection system that leads to **Quality Function Deployment** within the classroom relating to processes and assignments

8.2   How do you determine your internal customers and their satisfaction level inside your classroom?

Points	Criteria
1	No formal program exists.
2	Communication of satisfaction is mainly "hearsay".
3	Satisfaction is determined routinely through surveys.
4	Satisfaction is determined routinely though surveys and a P-D-C-A process is used to improve the relationship between students and other teachers within the building or district.
5	All functions are engaged in quality for internal customer (student, other teachers); satisfaction and communications are horizontal

8.3   In what functional areas, process, or systems do you have defined, measurable product and/or service quality criteria? Please list.

Points	Criteria
1	None
2	Teacher measures certain products
3	Teachers measures at least 50% of the products or services
4	Teacher and students measure at least 50% of the products or services
5	There is a total quality system oriented towards data gathering

8.4   What methods do you use to determine customer satisfaction?

Points	Criteria
1	No analysis is done.
2	There is some tracking of passively gathered data (keeping a mental count of reports of satisfaction).
3	There is regular tracking of passively gathered data (maintain records with information and source on a yearly basis).
4	Active accumulation and analysis of data in areas of customer satisfaction.
5	Management (teacher) is actively involved with all internal and external customer satisfaction measures and actually gathers information from employers, parents, graduates, and post-secondary institutions.

8.5   Summarize trends in customer satisfaction and list measurements you have in specific areas.

Points	Criteria
1	There is no information.
2	Information is just hearsay such as "enrollment in this class is up, therefore I must be doing something right".
3	Specific measurable data are available through external sources such as employers or post secondary schools showing increasing customer satisfaction with the results of the student's work in class.
4	Valid questionnaires are regularly sent to other teachers, parents, post secondary institutions, and employers to identify trends.
5	The teacher generates and monitors the data which evaluates key quality criteria showing constant year-to-year improvements.

8.6   What do you do that significantly promotes continuous improvement to increase customer satisfaction?

Points	Criteria
1	Nothing
2	Quality successes are recognized through awards, certificates, etc.
3	In addition to recognition awards, the teacher sends kudos personally to students and parents.
4	The teacher has applied for the classroom quality award and has demonstrated measurable improvement.
5	The teacher has become actively involved in the Quality Movement not only locally, but also nationally. The teacher has published papers and/or made speeches about the quality processes and systems.

Chapter Eleven: Conditions Necessary for Implementing TQM

Lead, Kindly Light, amid the encircling gloom, Lead Thou me on!

John Henry Newman
Pillar of the Cloud

This section describes the conditions necessary for establishing a total quality culture classroom. Although we have borrowed extensively from quality leaders, we have not promoted a single philosophy such as Deming's or Crosby's, as we believe that individual teachers may wish to use key points from all the theorists or develop their own TQM philosophy. We believe, however, that teachers wishing to adopt a new approach that emphasizes total quality management can do so by adopting a clear focus on these conditions which are necessary for change.

The following six conditions for implementing TQM and TQI should be established sequentially, rather than at random:

Condition #1: Education and Commitment of the Teacher
Condition #2: Education and Commitment of Students
Condition #3: Education and Commitment of Parents
Condition #4: Establish Trust
Condition #5: Establish Pride In Workmanship
Condition #6: Change the Classroom Culture

Condition One: Education and Commitment of the Teacher

All of the quality leaders say that, before lasting change towards quality can be realized, management must 1) be trained in quality processes and systems, and 2) make it clear that they are going to support the commitment to quality.

Since implementing TQM and TQI in the classroom requires an enormous deviation from typical supervisory techniques, teachers should undergo a training program on the principles of TQM and TQI.

The teacher must make it clear to the students that TQM and TQI are not being tested as concepts, but that the commitment to proceed with them is genuine! In fact, teachers must consistently "walk the talk" on TQM/TQI and let it be known that the only thing debatable is how best to implement them in his/her classroom.

Condition Two: Education and Commitment of the Students

Critical to the success of TQM and TQI is the education not only of the teachers, but also of the students. Once the students understand the principles of TQM and TQI, they will commit to this approach even if only in incremental amounts. The education of students should include an understanding of quality philosophies and processes as well as training on the tools and techniques they will use in TQI implementation.

The obvious reason for educating students on TQM and TQI is to inform them that their participation is essential for the processes to work. After they realize that TQI is not just another tool for increasing productivity, but that their contributions are respected and their responsibilities for improving the quality are essential, most students will make a commitment.

**Condition Three: Education and Commitment of
                      Parents**

Implementing TQ within the classroom requires educating parents as to their role as customer and supplier. It presupposes that they will become true partners with teachers to assist the child as s/he proceeds along the TQI path. Educating parents about the Quality Goals and the dramatic role they and their child will play in the Quality Classroom is essential to full implementation. Their involvement in the continuous improvement projects, via participation on Task Forces represents major deviations from traditional classrooms.

Condition Four: Establish Trust

Since one of the main functions of TQM and TQI is to show constant improvement in increasing the quality of education, measurements must be taken to gather baseline data. The teacher and the students must take measurements on various operations over time to show that the changes have resulted in improvements. The improvement process of gathering data and pointing out defects will be considered initially as a threat by students. The only way to overcome the perceived threat is to establish trust. This may take time. Note, however, that only the teacher can extend the offering of empowerment and trust since they control 85-95 percent of the processes and systems which the students work.

The first action in establishing trust is to explain in detail the reasons why comprehensive measurements have to be taken. Explanations should show how data can 1) demonstrate trends in student satisfaction levels, including their satisfaction with the teacher and other students; 2) determine if the teacher is meeting his/her mission and quality goals; 3) reveal to the school board that the institution is improving in efficiency and productivity; and 4) let the students know how well they and their classmates are performing.

Second, the students should also be informed that most of the measurements will be made by them and will be relevant to their needs. They should also be informed that the measurements will be simple, understandable, and few in number. The measurements will be done by all because baseline data is valuable as a means of taking a picture of the system in order to measure improvement.

Third, teachers must be involved in measuring their own effectiveness and making honest judgments from the data.

Instead of control, trust is the main ingredient that must be established in order to make the classroom a place where working relationships can flourish. People cannot feel like robots; they must flourish and have fun in their work. Of course, the act of trust involves a gamble. According to Levering (1988, p.188) *[t]rust is, ... , a calculated risk made with one's eyes open to the possibilities of failure, but it is extended with the expectation of success.* When poor teacher-student relationships occur, a lack of trust is usually the main cause.

When trust exists students will realize that the teacher really respects their opinion. As a result of this, students will feel empowered to take corrective action on poor processes and will feel free to express their true feelings about the tasks, processes, and systems that are out of control and need attention for the class to demonstrate constant improvement.

If trust and empowerment are foci of initial TQI projects, students will participate actively in the actual implementation of TQI. For this to occur, teachers must treat trust and empowerment as an evolutionary process by getting the students involved initially in processes that show respect and trust for their knowledge and judgment such as using the nominal group process to direct course planning. As students become more involved—by virtue of feeling trusted and empowered—in changing the processes and the systems, teachers must focus their attention on trust and empowerment. This involves getting the students educated in TQM and TQI as mentioned in Condition Two, and then applying the **adhocracy** procedures as discussed by Waterman (1990). Among his suggestions for instituting participative management are 1) get the right start, 2) action, and 3) get results.

Let us look at these procedures.

Get the right start includes getting teachers and students involved immediately after they have been educated in TQM and TQI. This is best accomplished by selecting a project team and project which requires "fixing" processes and systems so that an increase in quality can be measured effectively. The chairperson of the cross-functional team should not be the perceived "expert" (Waterman 1990, p. 23), nor should the chairperson be a teacher. The team should consist of ten or fewer people and should represent as many social units as are in the class. After the project team is formed, it must have

- Consistent support of the teacher.

- Baseline data to demonstrate improvements.
- Time for regular meetings.
- Recognition of team success and efforts.

Action means "do it!" Examine the baseline data and measure the cost of nonconformance. It means defining the problems and examining alternatives. Eventually it may mean making suggestions that are innovative—suggestions that may make the teacher uncomfortable as no one likes potential failure(s). Action means that the teacher implements, to the extent possible, almost every suggestion made by the team. Action means measuring the results of the modified process and/or system and rewarding the team if improvement occurs, but not punishing the team if there is no improvement. After all, it is far better to have tried and failed, than is not to have tried anything.

Getting results, according to Waterman (p. 55), is implementing change. Like most American institutions, our schools plan well, but are deficient at implementing those plans. It is no wonder, therefore, that most teachers have difficulty implementing even the most basic action plan that requires significant change.

These three steps, along with establishing trust and empowering students, will crystallize the implementation of TQM. If properly nurtured with continuous educational experiences, TQM should result in students making correct identification of poor processes and systems as well as in making better decisions and/or recommendations of how not only to solve the problem, but also methods to improve it. In addition, empowered students feel better about themselves as they develop their skills to a fuller extent. This will result in greater learning satisfaction and better morale as well as in improved productivity and quality.

Condition Five: Establish Pride in Workmanship
One outcome of dedicated efforts towards improving the processes and systems for quality results is that the students are trusted. Empowered students begin to improve the processes and systems, and they begin to contribute significantly to improving the quality. When they are rewarded and recognized for their efforts, they have greater pride in workmanship. A good reward and recognition program is an essential catalyst for involving everyone in TQI and for changing the classroom culture.

Condition Six: Change the Classroom Culture

In the previous sections, we elaborated on the necessity to empower teachers and students in order to establish trust, pride-in-workmanship, and quality. Much of what we promoted can be described as establishing self-leadership skills in the student body, including teachers. Maximum autonomy and self-leadership are necessary in educational institutions if a culture of excellence is to result. Whereas minimum autonomy will surely result in a quality crisis, maximum autonomy that recognizes the unique talents and contributions of each individual, including the students, will lead to positive subcultures based on quality. When quality results are recognized and rewarded, all will have an increased pride-in-workmanship which will result in additional increases in quality and teaming. This cycle can be so strong that the entire classroom/school culture may change within five or six years.

Until **trust** and **empowerment** are established as routine, students will not readily move towards TQM and TQI. They will resist change in attempts to protect themselves. Such behavior reinforces the old classroom culture. It is apparent, therefore, that even if the entire institution is educated and trained in TQM and TQI processes and systems, little or no change will occur until the trust and empowerment factors are generously woven into the very fabric of the classroom. When this occurs, everyone will be highly supportive of each other's efforts for TQI. As a result, pride-in-workmanship increases and the cycle breeds on itself.

The basic philosophy of every quality leader is based on principles of managing the institutional culture, and not the people. Managing does not necessarily mean control. If control is the main agenda of the teacher, quality will be difficult to achieve because students do not and will not relinquish to a cookie-cutter approach their rights to individual innovation.

Leadership, according to Gardner (1990, p.1). . . *is the process of persuasion or example by which an individual (or leadership team) induces a group to pursue objectives held by the leader or shared by the leader and his or her followers.*

Gardner says that leadership must not be confused with status, power, or official authority. Leaders are part of a system and they are affected by the system in which they work. Leaders perform tasks that are essential for others to accomplish their purpose, which in the case of TQM would be to increase the quality of services and/or product. As quality increases so will the pride-in-workmanship. The end result will be that a new classroom culture will emerge, one in which working becomes fun.

During a recent teleconference, W. Edwards Deming stated that the main reason for working is to have fun. In his book *Joy in Work*, Henri de Man (1939) concluded, after interviewing industrial workers in Germany during the mid-1920's, " . . . every *worker aims at joy in work, just as every human being aims at happiness*" (p. 11).

References

American Association of School Administrators. *Students at risk: Problems and Solutions.* Arlington, VA: AASA Critical Issues Report, 1989.

Bennis, Warren, *Managing the Dream: Leadership in the 21st Century.* Training, May 1990.

Canter, Lee and Marlene Canter, *Assertive Discipline.* Los Angeles: Canter and Associates, 1976.

Carnegie Council on Adolescent Development, *Turning Points: Preparing American Youth for the 21st Century.* Washington, D.C.: Carnegie Foundation, 1989.

Cornesky, Robert A. et al. *Using Deming to Improve Quality in Colleges and Universities.* Madison, WI: Magna Publications, Inc., 1990.

Cornesky, Robert, Sam McCool, Larry Byrnes, and Robert Weber. *Implementing Total Quality Management in Higher Education.* Madison, WI: Magna Publications, Inc., 1991.

Crosby, Philip. *Let's Talk Quality.* New York: McGraw-Hill Book Co. 1989.

Crosby, Philip. *Quality Without Tears: The Art of Hassle-Free Management.* New York: McGraw-Hill Book Co., 1984.

Crosby, Philip. *The Eternally Successful Organization: The Art of Corporate Wellness.* New York: McGraw-Hill Book Co., 1988.

Deal, T.E. and A.A. Kennedy, *Corporate Culture.* Reading, MA: Addison-Wesley, 1982.

De Man, Henri. *Joy in Work.* Trans. Eden and Cedar Paul (from the German). London: George Allen & Unwin, 1939.

Deming, W. Edwards. *Out of the Crisis.* Cambridge, MA: Productivity Press or Washington, DC: The George Washington University, MIT-CAES, 1982.

Gardner, John W. *On Leadership*, New York: The Free Press, 1990.

Glasser, William. *Control Theory in the Classroom.* New York: Harper & Row, Publishers, 1986.

Glasser, William. *The Quality School,* New York: Harper & Row, Publishers, 1990.

GOAL/QPC. *The Memory Jogger: A Pocket Guide of Tools for Continuous Improvement,* Methuen, MA: GOAL/QPC, 1988.

Hopkins, Susan and Jeffrey Winters, Editors. *Discover the World: Empowering Children to Value Themselves, Others and the Earth.* Philadelphia: New Society Publishers, 1990.

Imai, Masaaki. *Kaizen: The Key to Japan's Competitive Success.* Cambridge, MA: Productivity Press, 1986.

Juran, J.M. *Juran On Planning For Quality.* Cambridge, MA: Productivity Press, 1988.

Kotter, John P., *What Leaders Really Do.* Harvard Business Review, May-June, 1990.

Levering, Robert. *A Great Place to Work.* New York: Random House, Inc., 1988.

Manz, Charles C., and Henry P. Sims, Jr. *Super-Leadership.* New York: The Berkley Publishing Group, 1990.

McKay, Matthew, Peter D. Rogers, and Judity McKay. *When Anger Hurts: Quieting the Storm Within.* Oakland, Ca: New Harbinger Publications, Inc., 1989.

Noe, John R., *Peak Performance Principles for High Achievers.* New York: The Berkley Publishing Group, 1986.

Peters, Tom. *Thriving on Chaos.* New York: Harper & Row, 1988.

Quehl, Gary H. 1988. *Higher Education and the Public Interest: A Report to the Campus*, Washington, D.C.: Council for Advancement and Support of Education.

Tichy, Noel M. and Mary Anne Devanna, *The Transformational Leader,* Training and Development Journal, July, 1986.

Tribus, Myron. *Deployment Flow Charting.* Los Angeles: Quality and Productivity, Inc., 1989

United States Department of Education, *America 2000: An Education Strategy.* Washington, D.C.:   U.S. Department of Education, 1991.

United States Office of Personnel Management, *How to Get Started Implementing Total Quality Management.* Washington, D.C.: U.S. Government Printing Office, 1990.

Waterman, Robert H. *Adhocracy: The Power to Change.* Knoxville, TN: Whittle Direct Books, 1990.

APPENDIX

Page

Section I. Total Quality Improvement Tools
Affinity Diagram 205
Cause and Effect Diagram (Fishbones,
Ishikawa Diagram) 211
Control Charts 215
Flow Charts 223
Force Field Analysis 247
Histogram 251
Nominal Group Process 257
Operational Definition 267
Pareto Diagram 269
Relations Diagram 275
Run Chart 279
Scatter Diagram 285
Scenario Builder 287
Systematic Diagram 301

**Section II. Formula for Determining the Cost
of Waste in School Districts** 303

**Section III. Customer-Supplier and
Professional Work Contracts** 305

Section IV. Quality Index Profile 309

AFFINITY DIAGRAM

The **Affinity Diagram** was invented by Kawakita Jiro and is used as a planning tool. Unlike the Scenario Builder which roughly quantifies the outcomes resulting from a change in a system, the affinity diagram is more of a creative procedure that tries to organize the issues concerning a process or a problem without quantification.

An **Affinity Diagram** is especially useful in elucidating a problem or issue that is difficult to understand, or a problem or issue that appears to be enormous and in disarray. One benefit of using the **Affinity Diagram** at the very beginning of a TQI process is that it helps build consensus among the task force members studying the problem.

An **Affinity Diagram** is rarely used alone. However, when used with the **Scenario Builder**, and/or with a **Relations Diagram**, and/or with the **Nominal Group Process**, it can help an action team and/or task force to identify the major root causes of a problem or issue. When the major root causes of a problem or issue are identified, the group can direct its efforts more efficiently.

Procedure
1. Statement of the Problem

Under the direction of a team leader the members of the team should arrive at a statement of the problem or issue being addressed. For example: The Mr. Jones' tenth grade social studies classes wanted to include a community service project as part of the curriculum. The students wanted to volunteer to improve their community in some capacity. A task force of students and Mr. Jones, along with two parents agreed to work on the problem. The question they asked was: What are the obstacles to including a community service project requirement in Mr. Jones' tenth grade social studies classes?

2. Recording the Perceptions

Working alone, each person writes his/her comment on sticky note paper or on an index card after announcing his/her idea to the group. The purpose of announcing the perception is to permit others to piggy back any related ideas. Only a single idea should be entered on one note paper/index card. This proceeds until all of the people have exhausted their perceptions. Remember, as in any brainstorming session, there is no verbal exchange between the members. All of the notes are placed on the wall or in the center of a large conference table. Let's assume the following perceptions were generated and posted.

| The school board won't permit it. |

| Students lack transportation |

| Class periods are too short. |

| The principal won't support it. |

| The superintendent won't support it. |

| There is no need. |

| Other teachers won't support the idea and cooperate in flexible scheduling. |

| The liability of having students out of the building is too great. |

| The community doesn't want students out of school unsupervised (too difficult to supervise). |

| Community service isn't perceived to be a school function. |

| Parents don't want students out of school. |

| Students lack commitment. |

3. Group Similar and/or Related Perceptions
   The members of the group place similar cards (or sticky

notes) into related groups. These are said to have an "affinity" for each other. It is important that the members of the task force do this is silence. The note pads (or cards) can be moved any number of times. It is not uncommon to have ten related groups, although one may have a few as three.

The grouping that resulted from the aforementioned example are shown below.

GROUP 1

> The school board will not permit it.

> The Superintendent won't permit it.

> The Principal won't support it.

> Community service is not perceived a function of the schools.

> The liability of having students out of the building is too great.

GROUP 2

> There is no need.

> Students aren't interested.

> Students lack transportation.

> Students lack commitment.

GROUP 3

> Parents don't want students
> out of school.

GROUP 4

> Impossible to supervise.

> Parents don't want students
> out of school.

> Other teachers
> won't support
> the idea and
> cooperate in
> flexible
> scheduling.

> Class periods are too short.

4. Assign a Name to Each Group with a Header Designation

The team leader should read all of the cards in each group and the members should agree to a name that can be assigned to each of the groups. The team leader then writes a header card for each group. If there is a miscellaneous group, the task force should exam each perception and, if possible, place each note or card into one of the groups. If not, it is acceptable to have a group named "miscellaneous." In the above example, the four header groups are shown below.

GROUP 1: THE ADMINISTRATION

> The school board will not permit it.

> The Superintendent won't permit it.

> The Principal won't support it.

> Community service is not perceived a
> function of the schools.

> The liability of having students out of
> the building is too great.

GROUP 2: THE STUDENTS

There is no need.

Students aren't interested.

Students lack transportation.

Students lack commitment.

GROUP 3: THE PARENTS

Parents don't want students out of school.

GROUP 4: THE TEACHERS

Impossible to supervise.

Parents don't want students out of school.

Other teachers won't support the idea and cooperate in flexible scheduling.

Class periods are too short.

5. Draw the Affinity Diagram

The task force members should tape the cards/sticky notes in each group either onto a board or a large flip chart. With the header cards at the top the leader should draw borders around each group. In the figure below the completed **Affinity Diagram** is shown for the above example.

6. Discuss Each Group

The task force members should discuss each of the groups and how they relate to the problem. This will result in a better understanding of the issues and/or processes making up the problem.

In order to arrive at deeper understandings of each of the root causes, the task force may want to use a **Relations Diagram** for each of the groups. Depending upon the problem or issue, the **Scenario Builder, Systematic Diagram,** and **Cause & Effect Diagram** may be of value.

AFFINITY   DIAGRAM
OBSTACLES   TO   ESTABLISHING   A   COMMUNITY
SERVICE   PROJECT   REQUIREMENT

The   Administration

School Board will not permit it.	Liability is too great
Superintendent Won't permit it.	Community service is not perceived as a function of the schools
Principal won't support it.	

The   Students

There is no need.	Student's aren't interested.
Students lack commitment.	Students lack transportation

The   Parents

Parents don't want students out of school.

The   Teachers

Impossible to supervise

Class periods are too short.

Parent's don't want students out of school.

Other teachers won't support the idea and cooperate in flexible scheduling.

CAUSE AND EFFECT DIAGRAM

The **Cause and Effect Diagram** was developed by Kaoru Ishikawa. It is also referred to as a "fishbone" diagram since it looks like a fish skeleton, or an Ishikawa diagram after its inventor.

A **Cause and Effect Diagram** (CED) is extremely useful for getting input regarding the root causes of a specific problem. It can be used in brain storming sessions within a task force or committee or action team; or as a method to get input from an entire class, school, or district since the CED can be posted at various sites.

The CED is rarely used alone. However, when used with a **Relations Diagram**, an **Affinity Diagram**, and/or a **Nominal Group Process**, it can help an action team and/or a task force to look at the root causes of a problem in many different ways.

Procedure
1. Statement of the Problem
    A specific, identified problem contributing to a non-quality result is identified. It is placed on the far right hand side of an overhead, paper, flip chart or butchers paper.

2. Recording the Perceptions
    After the backbone and the box with the either the identified problem or the effect is drawn, add the primary causal category boxes (people, equipment, materials and procedures [some also add "environment"]) and draw arrows to the backbone. This is the beginning of the CED. Some institutions have reusable 3' x 2' boards with the skeleton and primary causal categories painted on permanently. They have Highland ™ note pads attached so that written remarks could be added by those participating in the analysis.

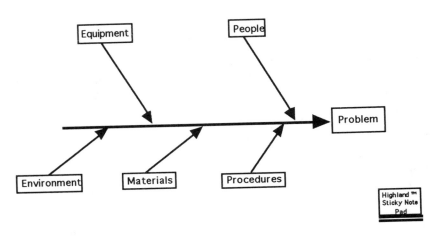

The **Causes** and **Sub Causes** are written on the sticky note pads and are placed in one of the primary causal categories.

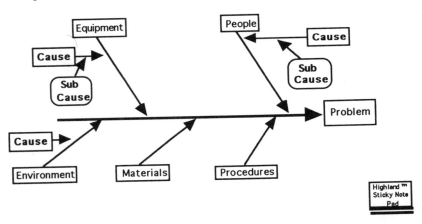

In some instances additional levels can and should be added to **Sub Causes**.

3. Complete the Cause and Effect Diagram

Shown below is the CED showing the perceptions of Mr. Lake's students as to why they are doing poorly in Chemistry.

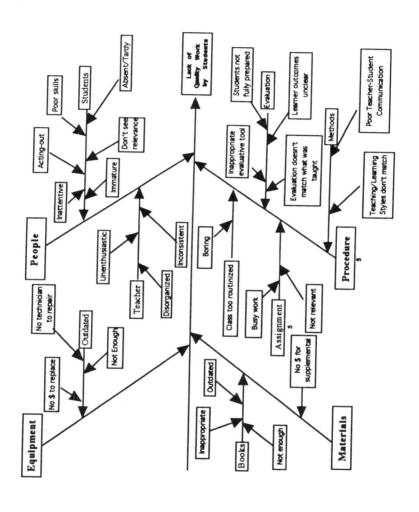

4. Record and Discuss the Results

The results are recorded and discussed in order to determine the root causes of the undesired effect or problem. Remember the purpose is to generate ideas as to the probable causes of the problem and to get everyone involved in submitting suggestions. Therefore, criticism of any idea or comment should not be tolerated by the group. Instead people should be encouraged to build upon the causes and sub causes posted by others.

5. Other Suggestions

If a major root cause for a problem is identified it could become a likely candidate for a fishbone problem.

CONTROL CHARTS

Control Charts are used to test the stability of a system. They measure the number or proportion of nonconforming items. They all have a common centerline which represents a process average and lines that display upper and lower control limits that provide information on the variation. They are used to identify either "common" or "special" causes of variation and to prevent over- or under-control of the processes within a system.

The charts are drawn by gathering samples, called subgroups, from a process, product, or service characteristic. Control limits are based on the variation that occurs within the subgroups. The centerline of the chart is taken to be the estimated mean of the sampling distribution while the upper control limit (UCL) is the mean plus 3 times the estimated standard error and the lower control limit (LCL) is the estimated mean minus 3 times the estimated standard error.

We will describe two control charts in detail, namely the np-chart and the p-chart. Both charts are **attribute** (characteristic) charts in that the characteristic under study gives an yes/no, good/bad, pass/fail, or present/absent answer. Two additional charts, the c-chart and the u-chart, will also be described briefly. They are used when the characteristic under study is too complex for a simple answer.

The np-chart is used to plot the **number** of nonconformances and the subgroup size is constant. The p-chart is used plot the **proportion** of nonconformances and the subgroup size is either **constant** or **variable**.

np-Chart

A np-chart, an attributes control chart, is used when the stability of a system is to be measured. The attributes control chart is used when the characteristic under study has a definite yes/no answer, the subgroups are of equal size, the sampling time is consistent, and the data is plotted in the order it was taken.

1. Select the Data to be Analyzed

We have assumed that the Task Force or the individual studying a system has collected the attribute (counts) data. In the case study below the number of incomplete homework assignments in Miss Wright's basic math classes for six weeks (30 days) were examined. Miss Wright had a total of 60 students in her math classes and she gave a homework problem after every class period. The homework problem was to be returned at the beginning of the following class period.

2. Record the Data
Record the data in the order which it was collected.

Day #	Day	# Students Sample Size	Homework Assignments Not Completed	Proportion
1	M	60	3	0.05
2	T	60	6	0.10
3	W	60	14	0.23
4	H	60	12	0.20
5	F	60	15	0.25
6	M	60	2	0.03
7	T	60	6	0.10
8	W	60	14	0.23
9	H	60	17	0.28
10	F	60	16	0.26
11	M	60	1	0.01
12	T	60	8	0.13
13	W	60	11	0.18
14	H	60	18	0.30
15	F	60	20	0.33
16	M	60	5	0.08
17	T	60	6	0.10
18	W	60	25	0.41
19	H	60	12	0.20
20	F	60	26	0.43
21	M	60	6	0.10
22	T	60	21	0.35
23	W	60	18	0.30
24	H	60	17	0.28
25	F	60	17	0.28
26	M	60	11	0.18
27	T	60	26	0.43
28	W	60	27	0.45
29	H	60	29	0.48
30	F	60	33	0.55
Totals		1,800	442	0.25

3. <u>Do the Calculations</u>
The **Average**, the **Upper Control Limit** (UCL) , and the **Lower Control Limit** (LCL) have to be calculated in order to determine the stability of the "system." Note, however, that a minimum of 25 to 30 subgroups are required to calculate the control limits.

3.1   **The average** =   total number / number of subgroups
$$= \ \Sigma np \div \ 30$$
$$= \ 3 + 6 + 14 + 12 + ...+33 \ \div 30$$
$$= \ 442 \div 30$$
$$= \ 14.73$$

This number (14.73) should be recorded with the space labeled "Avg" in the control chart.

3.2   **The Upper Control Limit** (UCL) is calculated using the formula:

$$UCL = Average + 3 \sqrt{Average (1 - Average \div n)}$$

$$= \ 14.73 + 3 \sqrt{14.73 (1 - 14.73 \div 60)}$$

$$= \ 14.73 + 3 \sqrt{14.73 (1 - 0.2455)}$$

$$= \ 14.73 + 3 \sqrt{14.73 \times 0.7545}$$

$$= \ 14.73 + 3 \sqrt{11.1138}$$

$$= \ 14.73 + 3 (3.333)$$

$$= \ 14.73 + 10.00$$

$$UCL = \ 24.73$$

This number (13.3) should be recorded with the space labeled "UCL" in the control chart.

3.3   **The Lower Control Limit** (LCL) is calculated using the formula:

$$LCL = \text{Average} - 3 \sqrt{\text{Average} (1 - \text{Average} \div n)}$$

$$= 14.73 - 3 \sqrt{14.73 (1 - 14.73 \div 60)}$$

$$= 14.73 - 3 \sqrt{14.73 (0.7545)}$$

$$= 14.73 - 3 \sqrt{11.1138}$$

$$= 14.73 - 3 (3.333)$$

$$= 14.73 - 10.00$$

$$LCL = 4.73$$

This number (4.73) should be recorded with the space labeled "LCL" in the control chart.

4. Draw the Chart

The first thing one has to do is to scale the chart. Begin by determining the largest number in your data and compare this with the UCL number. In our example the largest number is 33 and the UCL number is 24.73.

A rule of thumb is to count the lines on your chart paper and multiply it by 0.66. The chart paper in our example is shown below. It has 30 lines, therefore, 30 x 0.66 = 19.8, or ≈ 20.

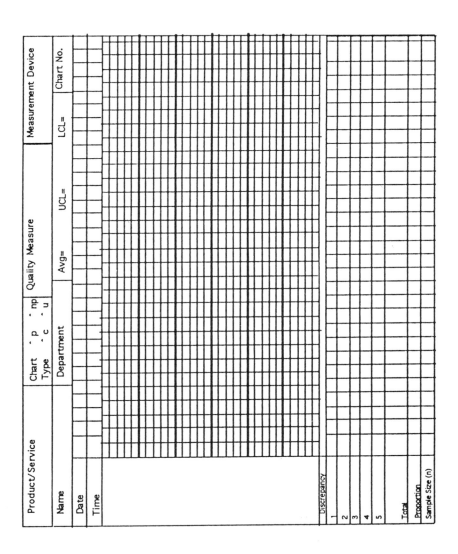

Divide the largest number in your example by 20 to obtain your increment value: 33 ÷ 20 = 1.65. Always rounding the figure upwards, every line in this case will represent 2.

The lines are usually numbered from the bottom up. The bottom line is 0 and every line will represent two incomplete homework assignments. (In other cases it may be necessary to label the lines with other multiples such as 5, 10, 25 etc.) The attributes control chart completely labeled with our example is shown below.

Product/Service	Chart Type	Quality Measure	Measurement Device
Homework	˙p ˙c x np ˙u	# Incomplete Assignments	Check Off Chart No. 16996

Class: Basic Math   Avg= 14.73   UCL= 24.73   LCL= 4,73

Name Miss Wright

| Date | 1 | 2 | 3 | 4 | 5 | 6 | 7 | 8 | 9 | 10 | 11 | 12 | 13 | 14 | 15 | 16 | 17 | 18 | 19 | 20 | 21 | 22 | 23 | 24 | 25 | 26 | 27 | 28 | 29 | 30 |
| Time | 5 pm | | | | | | | | | | | | | | | | | | | | | | | | | | | | | |

50
40
30
20
10

Discrepancy 0
1
2
3
4
5

	3	6	14	12	15	2	6	14	17	16	1	8	11	18	20	5	25	12	26	6	21	18	17	17	11	26	27	29
Total																												
Proportion																												
Sample Size (n)	60																											

Now draw the center line and the control limits then plot the values and connect the points. The completed chart is shown below:

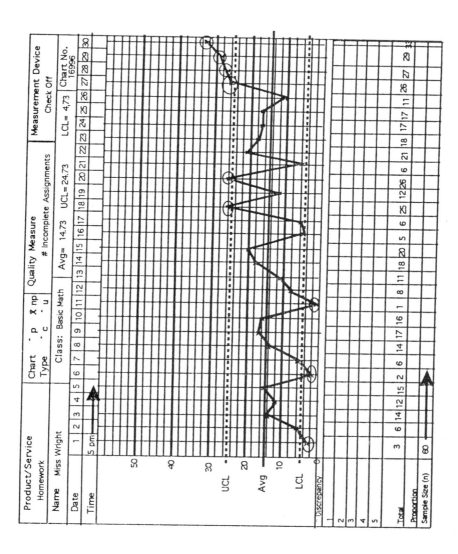

5. Analyze the Chart
   All control charts are analyzed using basic rules:
   > Look for points above or below the control limits.
   > Look for a run of seven or more points above or below the average (center line).
   > Look for a run of seven or more points either going up or down.
   > Look for cyclical patterns.

In our example the "homework" system in Miss Wright's class appears to be unstable. On days 1, 6 and 11 the number of incomplete homework assignments is below the lower control limit line. On days 18, 20, 27, 28, 29, and 30 the number of incomplete homework assignments are above the upper control limit line. However, there are neither a run of seven points above or below the center line, nor is there a run of seven points either going up or going down. A cyclical pattern appears to be present: the number of incomplete assignments appears to be lowest on Monday and Tuesday and highest towards the end of the week. Perhaps, the students have time to do the assignments over the weekends, but get too involved in school activities during the week.

The above system has "special causes" as a defect and improvement in the number of completed homework assignments could not be undertaken until these special causes were analyzed, addressed and the system stabilized.

After Miss Wright examined the circumstances behind the apparent lack of completing the home work assignments on days 18, 20, 27, 28, 29, and 30, she discovered that on days 18 and 20 the basketball team made the finals for the state tournament; likewise, during the days 27—30, the basketball team was involved in the actual tournament. Apparently, many of the students were caught up in the excitement of the championship tournament and that might be why they did not complete their homework. Miss Wright's solution: give five homework problems after Monday's class and have them returned by the following Monday. It worked!

When first using np-charts you may want to assess the stability of a system and then analyze the factors that contribute to variations. However, after improvements are generated and the system under study is determined to be stable, you may want to begin to collect data in a different way and to stratify your data by day of the week, time, location and redo the np-charts. Of course recalculations of new control limits will eventually be needed but this should be delayed until enough data are gathered to make the new chart statistically valid.

p-Chart

A p-Chart is used when one wants to plot the **proportion** of nonconformances and the subgroup size is either **constant** or **variable**. Like the np-chart, the p-chart is an attribute control chart that studies a characteristic that has an either/or, pass/fail/, yes/no answer. For example:

> A teacher may want to plot the proportion of students failing his/her class over the term.

> A teacher may want to plot the proportion of students not completing homework assignments over the semester.

> A principal may want to plot the proportion of graduating seniors who have a SAT score above 1000 over a period of time.

The p-chart, like any control chart, helps determine "special" and/or "common" cause variations in a system so that proper action can be taken for improvement without exerting over- or under-control. It is used by task forces to help determine the stability of a system and to monitor the improvement of the system after action is taken.

1. Select the Data to be Analyzed

In the case study below we will examine the proportion of students that failed "Introduction to Accounting" per term over a 7.5 year period. Since number of students who took the course varied over the seven year period, the sample size is variable. As a result the p-chart had to be used.

2. Record the Data

k #	Term-Yr	n Subgroup Size	np Number of Failures	np ÷ n Proportion
1	1-84	100	15	0.150
2	2-84	100	6	0.060
3	3-84	100	11	0.110
4	4-84	100	4	0.040
5	1-85	94	9	0.096
6	2-85	94	7	0.074
7	3-85	94	4	0.043
8	4-85	94	8	0.085
9	1-86	91	3	0.033
10	2-86	91	2	0.022
11	3-86	91	1	0.011
12	4-86	91	10	0.109
13	1-87	91	7	0.077
14	2-87	91	25	0.275
15	3-87	91	5	0.055
16	4-87	79	3	0.038
17	1-88	79	8	0.101
18	2-88	79	4	0.051
19	3-88	79	2	0.025
20	4-88	79	5	0.063
21	1-89	79	5	0.063
22	2-89	72	7	0.097
23	3-89	72	9	0.125
24	4-89	72	1	0.014
25	1-90	72	3	0.042
26	2-90	72	12	0.167
27	3-90	72	9	0.125
28	4-90	72	3	0.042
29	1-91	72	6	0.083
30	2-91	72	9	0.125
	Totals	2,535	203	0.0801

3. Do the Calculations

3.1   The **Proportion** for each subgroup has to be calculated. As shown in the table above, this is accomplished by dividing total number (np) by the subgroup size (n). In our first entry above 15 (number of failures during the first term of 1984) is divided by the 100 (sample size). Carry the calculations out to three places.

3.2   The **Average Proportion** is calculated by taking the total number in the sample size row (2,535) and dividing it by the total number in the subgroup row (203).

Average Proportion $(\overline{p})$
$$
\begin{aligned}
&= \text{total number / number of subgroups} \\
&= \Sigma np \div \Sigma n \\
&= 203 \div 2{,}535 \\
&= 0.0801
\end{aligned}
$$

This number (.0801) should be recorded with the space labeled "Avg" in the control chart.

3.3   The **Average Subgroup Size** $(\overline{n})$ is calculated by dividing the total number of the subgroup size (2,535) by the number of the subgroups taken (k).

Average Subgroup Size $(\overline{n})$
$$
\begin{aligned}
&= \Sigma n \div k \\
&= 2{,}535 \div 30 \\
&= 84.5
\end{aligned}
$$

3.4   Make certain that none of the subgroup size varies more than ± 25% of Average Subgroup Size (84.5). This is done by multiplying 84.5 by 1.25 for the number greater than 25%; and 84.5 by 0.75 for the number less than 25%.

>25% = 84.5   x   1.25   =   105.6
<25% = 84.5   x   0.75   =   63.4

Since none of our sample sizes (n) were higher than 105.6 or less than 63.4, separate calculations for the control limits do not have to be done. If, however, you have subgroup sizes 25% above or below 84.5, you will have to calculate separate UCL's and LCL's on **EACH** of the points by substituting the appropriate number (n) in the formula shown below. These points with their separate UCL and LCL are plotted on the same graph. (Refer to the example in the u-chart at the end of this section.)

3.5   Do the calculations for the **Control Limits.**

$$UCL = \bar{p} + 3 \sqrt{\frac{\bar{p}(1-\bar{p})}{n}}$$

$$= 0.0801 + 3\sqrt{0.0801\ (\ 1 - 0.0801) \div 84.5}$$

$$= 0.0801 + 3\sqrt{0.0801\ (0.9199) \div 84.5}$$

$$= 0.0801 + 3\sqrt{0.0737 \div 84.5}$$

$$= 0.0801 + 3\ (0.02953)$$

$$UCL = 0.1687$$

Now calculate the lower control limit:

$$LCL = \bar{p} - 3 \sqrt{\frac{\bar{p}(1-\bar{p})}{n}}$$

$$= 0.0801 - 0.0886$$

$$LCL = 0$$

4. Draw the Chart

The scaling and plotting are done in exactly the same manner as in the np chart. The largest proportion of failures in our example is 0.275 and 66% of the number of lines in our graph is 20, therefore, each line has to be 0.275 ÷ 20 = 0.014, and since adjusting is always done upwards, each line represents 0.020.

The completed chart is shown below.

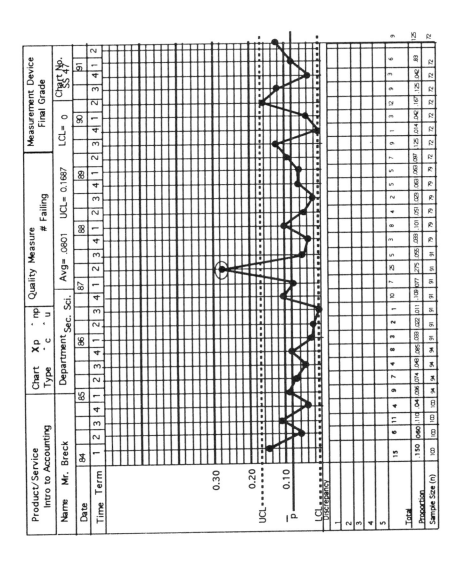

5. Analyze the Chart
   All control charts are analyzed using basic rules:
   > Look for points above or below the control limits.
   > Look for a run of seven or more points above or below the average (center line).
   > Look for a run of seven or more points either going up or down.
   > Look for cyclical patterns.

In our example the system appears to be unstable since one of the points lay outside the UCL, *i.e.* the second term of 1987. During that time the number of failures was above the upper control limit line. However, there are no run of seven points above or below the center line, nor is there a run of seven points either going up or going down, nor are there any cyclical patterns.

The above system appears to have "special cause" as a defect and implementing TQI processes to improve the number of students who would pass could not be undertaken until these special causes were analyzed, addressed and the system was stabilized.

After the teacher examined what occurred during that time, he informed us that the local textile plant announced massive layoffs and that it would be phasing out its operations in that area over the next several years. As a result, many students were more concerned about having to relocate and losing their friends than their final grades. A check of the high school records indicated that an unusually high rate of failing grades were given in the entire school that particular term. When this special cause is removed the system could be considered to be stable and the Mr. Breck may begin to add changes in order to increase the passing rate. Remember, however, that new control limits have to be calculated when changes are made on the system.

OTHER CONTROL CHARTS

There are two other control charts that should be described, both of which can be useful in the academic setting. They are the **c-chart** and the **u-chart**. Like the np-chart and the p-chart, the c-chart and the u-chart are used to test the stability of the system and both are attribute control charts.

The c-chart and the u-chart measure the number of nonconforming items. The c-chart is used when the number of nonconformities are measured and the subgroup size is the constant, while the u-chart is used when the number of nonconformities are measured and the subgroup size is either constant or variable.

Since the preparation of the c-chart and the u-chart are very similar to the np-chart and the p-chart described previously, we will present briefly when they may be appropriately used as well as the formulae.

c-Chart

A c-chart is used when the stability of a system is to be measured. It is an attribute control chart that is useful when the characteristic under study is too complex for either a simple yes/no, or a positive/negative answer. In other words, the data may have a number of discrepancies per subgroup. An example might include the type of errors while composing a letter in a word-processing class. The errors might include: 1) format, 2) grammar, 3) punctuation, 4) spacing, 5) date, and 6) spelling. (If you wanted to calculate the number of mistakes in composing a letter regardless of the type, you would use the np-chart; if you desired to calculate the proportion of nonconformances regardless of the type of mistake, you would use the p-chart.)

As with the other control charts, one should 1) Select the Data to be Analyzed, 2) Record the Data, 3) Do the Calculations, 4) Draw the Chart, and 5) Analyze the Chart.

1. Select the Data to be Analyzed

Before using any control chart, it is essential that the operational definition of the nonconforming characteristics be carefully identified in order to insure consistency in the collection process. In our example, a teacher and the students identified four major problems in the five sections of the word-processing classes, namely: 1) format, 2) grammar, 3) punctuation, and 4) spacing. These were perceived to be the major problems of the students not being able to produce an error free letter the first time. They decided to randomly sample two letters at the end of the five classes for one week (*i.e.* 5 straight days).

2. Record the Data

The data are recorded as shown in the table and in the completed c-Chart below.

The date, class period, type and number of mistake, and the total number of mistakes in Mrs. Herbst's word-processing classes.

Type of Mistake

Date	Class Period	Format	Grammar	Punctua-tion	Spacing	Total
Jan. 7	1	2	0	1	1	4
	2	2	3	2	1	8
	3	1	1	2	2	6
	4	1	0	1	0	2
	5	0	0	0	0	0
Jan. 8	1	3	1	2	0	6
	2	1	0	0	1	2
	3	3	3	0	2	8
	4	0	0	0	0	0
	5	1	1	1	1	4
Jan. 9	1	2	1	1	0	4
	2	2	1	2	1	6
	3	0	0	0	0	0
	4	1	1	1	1	4
	5	3	2	2	1	8
Jan. 10	1	0	0	0	0	0
	2	3	1	1	1	6
	3	1	1	1	1	4
	4	3	3	2	0	8
	5	0	0	0	2	2
Jan. 11	1	3	1	1	1	6
	2	0	0	0	0	0
	3	2	0	0	0	2
	4	2	1	0	1	4
	5	0	1	1	0	2
	Totals	36	22	21	17	96

3. Do the Calculations

3.1   The **Average Number** is calculated according to the formula:

$$\overline{c} \; = \; \text{total number} \div \text{number of subgroups}$$
$$= \; C1 + C2 + C3 + ...+Ck \div k$$
$$= \; 4 + 8 + 6 +...+2 \div 25$$
$$= \; 96 \div 25$$
$$= \; 3.8$$

This number is placed in the placed marked "Avg."

3.2   The **Control Limits** are calculated according to the formulae:

$$UCLc \; = \; \overline{c} + 3\sqrt{\overline{c}}$$
$$= \; 3.8 + 3\sqrt{3.8}$$
$$= \; 3.8 + 5.8$$
$$UCLc \; = \; 9.6$$

$$LCLc \; = \; \overline{c} - 3\sqrt{\overline{c}}$$
$$= \; 3.8 - 3\sqrt{3.8}$$
$$= \; 3.8 - 5.8$$
$$= \; -2$$
$$LCLc \; \approx \; 0$$

4. Draw the Chart

Do the scaling as described previously. In this case the largest c number is 8 and the UCLc is 9.6, therefore, take the 9.6 value and multiply it by 0.66 of the number of lines on your graph. In our case the number of lines is 30 and 0.66 of 30 is ≈ 20. Each line, in our case, has an incremental value of 9.6 ÷ 20 = 0.48. Adjusting upward we have an incremental value of 0.5.

The completed c-control chart is shown below.

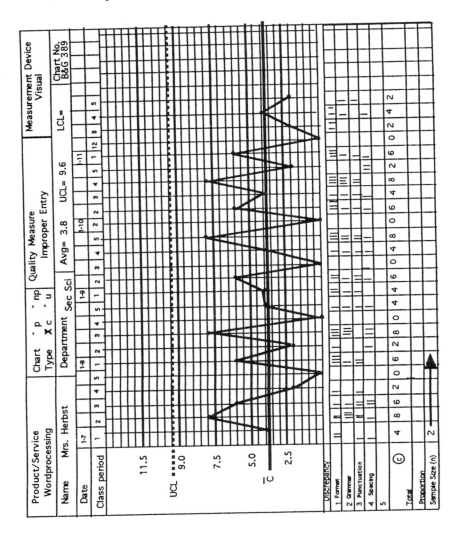

5. Analyze the Chart

The above chart does not demonstrate any special cause variation, therefore, the variability in the system appears to be due to common causes which can be reduced by improving the processes within the system. Both the teacher and the students in all five classes were happy to hear that they did not have to consider any special causes and that they could now begin to work as a team to improve the learning experiences for all!

u-Chart

A u-chart is used when the stability of a system is to be measured. It is an attribute control chart that is useful when the characteristic under study is too complex for either a simple yes/no, or positive/negative answer. In other words, the data may have a number of discrepancies per subgroup. An example might include laboratory reports that are incorrectly completed because of errors in filling out one of many entries. (If one desired to calculate the number of incorrectly completed reports regardless of which information item was incorrectly completed, they would use the np-chart; if they desired to calculate the proportion of nonconformances regardless of which information item was incorrectly completed, they would use the p-chart.) However, unlike the c-chart mentioned above, the u-chart can be used with either a constant or **variable** subgroup size. If the subgroup sizes vary more than 25% as demonstrated in our example below, individual control limits have to be calculated.

As with the other control charts, one should 1) Select the Data to be Analyzed, 2) Record the Data, 3) Do the Calculations, 4) Draw the Chart, and 5) Analyze the Chart.

1. Select the Data to be Analyzed

Before using any control chart, it is essential that the operational definition of the nonconforming characteristics be carefully identified in order to insure consistency in the collection process. In the example below, a high school chemistry teacher, working with her students, identified five principal discrepancies that resulted in incorrect laboratory reports being submitted. For this study we simply designated them "type 1" through "type 5." The discrepancies are scored in the same manner as shown for the c-chart above. Redoing the reports were not only a major cause of rework, but also for not submitting the reports in a timely fashion, both of which caused unhappy customers, namely, students, teacher, and parents. A group of students, several parents, and the teacher formed a task force to examine the root causes and what could be done to improve the quality of the initial submission of the reports. They decided to examine a random number of reports for 25 straight school days.

2. Record the Data
   The data are recorded as shown in the completed u-chart
below.
3. Do the Calculations
   3.1   The **Average Number per Unit** is calculated
          according to the formula:

$$\bar{u} = \Sigma c \div \Sigma n$$

$$= 192 \div 103$$

$$= 1.86$$

This value is placed in the placed maker "Avg."

   3.2   The **Average Subgroup Size** is calculated
          according to the formula:

$$\bar{n} = \Sigma n \div k$$

$$= 103 \div 25$$

$$= 4.12$$

   3.3   The **Subgroup Size Limits** are calculated:
          $>25\% = 4.12 \times 1.25 = 5.15$
          $<25\% = 4.12 \times 0.75 = 3.09$
          Therefore, any proportion number in any subgroup
          that is less than 3.19 or greater than 5.15 will have to
          have their UCL and LCL's calculated separately. In
          our example shown below, please refer to subgroups
          #1, #7, #8, #11, #15, #16, #17, and #20.

   3.4   The **Proportions** (u) for each subgroup are
          calculated according to the formula:
          u = number in subgroup (c) ÷ subgroup size (n)

These figures are added to the chart as shown below.

3.5   The **Control Limits** are calculated according to the formulae:

$$UCLu = \bar{u} + 3\sqrt{\bar{u} \div \bar{n}}$$

$$= 1.86 + 3\sqrt{1.86 \div 4.12}$$

$$= 1.86 + 3\sqrt{0.4514}$$

$$= 1.86 + 3\,(0.6719)$$

$$= 1.86 + 2.02$$

$$= 3.88$$

$$LCLu = \bar{u} - 3\sqrt{\bar{u} \div \bar{n}}$$

$$= 1.86 - 2.02$$

$$= -0.16$$

$$\approx 0$$

3.6   The control limits for these subgroups that vary ± 25% are calculated separately. In our case this includes #1, #7, #8, #11, #15, #16, #17, and #20. For subgroups #1, #7, #15, and #17:

$$UCLu = 1.86 + 3 \quad u \div n$$

$$= 1.86 + 3 \quad 1.86 \div 3 \quad = 4.22$$

$$LCLu = 1.86 - 3 \quad u \div n$$

$$= 1.86 - 3 \quad 1.86 \div 3 \quad \approx 0$$

For subgroups #8 and #16:

$$UCLu = 1.86 + 3\sqrt{\bar{u} \div n}$$

$$= 1.86 + 3\sqrt{1.86 \div 2} = 4.75$$

$$LCLu = 1.86 - 3\sqrt{\bar{u} \div n}$$

$$= 1.86 - 3\sqrt{1.86 \div 2} \approx 0$$

For subgroups #11 and #20:

$$UCLu = 1.86 + 3\sqrt{\bar{u} \div n}$$

$$= 1.86 + 3\sqrt{1.86 \div 7} = 3.41$$

$$LCLu = 1.86 - 3\sqrt{\bar{u} \div n}$$

$$= 1.86 - 3\sqrt{1.86 \div 7} = 0.32$$

4. Draw the Chart

Do the scaling as described previously. In this case the largest proportion (u) is 8 and the ULCu is 1.86, therefore, take the 8 value and multiply it by 0.66 of the number of lines on your graph. In our case the number of lines is 30 and 0.66 of 30 is ≈ 20, therefore, 8 ÷ 20 = 0.4 or ≈ 0.5. Adjusting upward is done so that the dark lines have numbers whose multiples are easy to work with, *i.e.* 1, 2, 5, 10 etc. The completed chart is shown below:

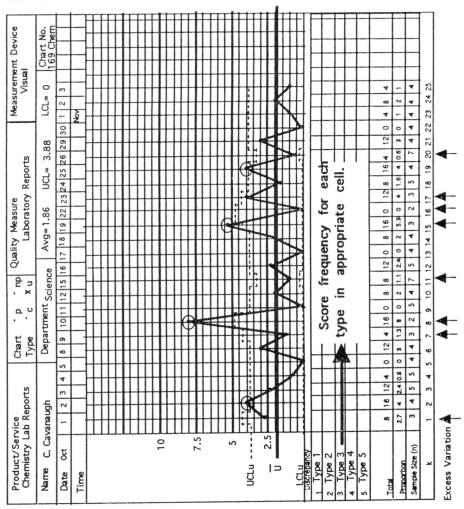

5. Analyze the Chart

The above chart indicates that the laboratory reporting system is not in control. On October 2, 10, 19 and 25 the number of errors exceeded the UCL which indicates special cause variation. The task force can begin to examine the reasons as to the variations.

FLOW CHART

Although flow charting is one of the most useful tools in total quality management (TQM), it is probably the most under utilized in education. Flow charting is a way in which one can get a snapshot of each process within a system. As a result, a flow chart can demonstrate where non-value added work is performed. Of course, non-value added work adds to the cost of doing business, and in the case of higher education, this cost can be substantial.

When a flow chart is drawn and redundant processes are identified, a task force can easily generate a different flow chart showing how the processes within the system should be done. It is essential that when a flow chart of a system is drawn that everyone working within the system be involved in drawing it. There are many different types of flow charts, but we will describe two which we found to be useful in the academic units, namely, the **Deployment Flow Chart** and the **Process Flow Chart**.

Deployment Flow Chart

Procedure

1. Definition of the System

Each system consists of a series of processes. However, it is not always clear where one system ends and another begins since many systems involve more than one process. Therefore, the task force should agree as to the starting and ending points they wish to study.

As with any universal visual tool, flow charting has a set of standardized symbols (Myron Tribus, 1989). They are as follows:

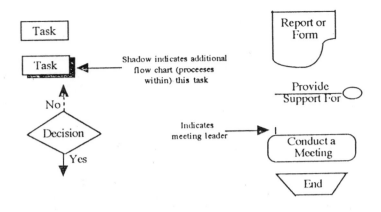

2. Drawing the Deployment Flow Chart

A deployment flow chart is useful when one wants to show the inter-relationships between the people and the tasks they actually perform while working within a system in order to generate either a service or a product.

The members of a task force should take it upon themselves to actually walk through each step in the system they are studying. As they do, they should inquire from the people performing each task what is actually involved. Copious notes should be taken along with sketches. Only after this is done should the members draw a deployment flow chart.

It should be mentioned that flow charts should not be drawn only when there are problems within a system. Instead, charts should be drawn for every task and process within all systems in order to root out non-value added work. In addition, if there are any changes within a system, its flow chart should be updated immediately for all to see.

The first thing that should be done in preparing the deployment flow chart is to enter the "people" coordinate horizontally. The boxes can contain either the particular person or his/her position or the particular department/unit that is performing a task. In the example below we will follow an actual deployment flow chart of class assignment in a social studies class.

| Teacher | Group/Team | Student |

Next the actual tasks and/or major steps are listed:

1. Prepare Assignment (Teacher)

2. Determine Options (Teacher and Group)

3. Analyze Options and Select Preferred One (Group)

4. Approve Group Option (Teacher)

5. Research Assignment (Individual Students)

6. Compile Research (Group)

7. Outline Research Paper & Submit for Approval

    (Group)

8. Approve Outline (Teacher)

9. Write Subsections or Implement Project (Individual

    Students)

10. Approve Subsections (Group)

11. Combine Paper or Project Results (Group)

12. Approve Combined Effort (Group)

13. Submit Final Results (Group)

14. Approve (Teacher)

15. Evaluate (Teacher and Groups)

Using the symbols described above, draw the flow chart.

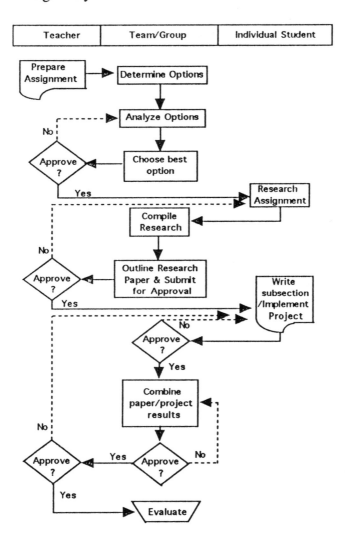

3. Record and Discuss the Results

Because the horizontal lines represent a customer-supplier relationship, the flow chart reveals the nature of the interactions. Examine the lines and try to determine if there is any non-value added work that can be reduced or eliminated. If there appears to be a breakdown in the system where someone is not supplying his customer with quality work try to examine the reason(s) why. Are there barriers or decision making delays that slow the flow?

A task force, after examining the system, recommended the revision shown below which reduced the inspection time and empowered groups of students to make decisions about the member's work quality. As a result, the students worked harder, assignments were completed faster and results were excellent.

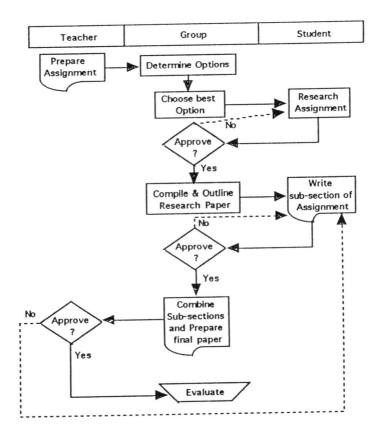

Process Flow Chart

Procedure

1. Statement of the Problem

The process flow chart simply shows the major steps within a system and does not attempt to demonstrate the inter relationships between the people doing the tasks. Like using any flow chart, the task force should agree to the starting and ending points of the system they wish to study.

2. Drawing the Process Flow Chart

The members of a task force should take it upon themselves to actually walk through each step in the system they are studying. As they do, they should inquire from the people performing each task what is actually involved. Copious notes should be taken along with sketches. Only after this is done should the members draw a process flow chart.

The first thing that should be done in preparing the process flow chart is to list the major steps in the system. Then using the standardized symbols shown below one should draw the flow chart.

Start / End   Task   Decision ?

Using the example in the aforementioned Deployment Flow Chart, one may have listed the major steps as follows:

1. Prepare assignment

2. Determine options

3. Choose best option

4. Research assignment

5. Outline paper

6. Write subsections

7. Prepare final paper

8. Submit results

9. Get approval

10. Evaluate

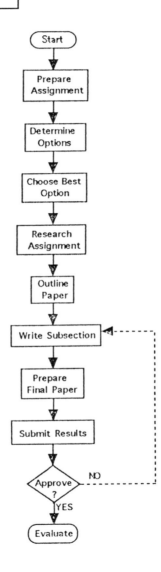

3. Record and Discuss the Results

By studying the flow chart the task force members may be able to recommend ways to better reduce redundant steps and improve the processes of the system.

FORCE FIELD ANALYSIS

The **Force Field Analysis** tool was the product of federally funded research to change the meat buying habits of American housewives during the second world war. It was invented by Professor Kurt Lewin of the University of Iowa.

Force Field Analysis helps a task force to identify the perceived driving and restraining forces towards effecting a recommended change. Then, by increasing the forces driving the change, or by decreasing the forces inhibiting the change, or both, a task force can recommend actions to bring about the change successfully.

Actually the **Force Field Analysis** is much more useful when used with other TQI tools, *e.g.* the nominal group process, affinity diagram, and/or scenario builder. This is especially true if the recommended change is counter to the "tradition" of the classroom. Like the nominal group process, affinity diagram, and/or scenario builder, the **Force Field Analysis** involves the use of proper brainstorming procedures: a facilitator is selected, team members have an equal opportunity to express their ideas without criticism, and building upon the ideas of others is encouraged.

Procedure
1. Statement of the Problem

Under the direction of the team leader (or the facilitator) the members of the task force should arrive at a statement of the precise desired change that will be made to management. To arrive at this statement it may be necessary to use other TQI tools such as the nominal group process (NGP) and the affinity diagram as previously explained.

For example, Mrs. Moore teaches second grade in a traditional school. Since she had heard from a teacher in another school that thematic units represented an effective teaching technique, she wanted to use it in her class. She realized there were some potential problems and established a task force to analyze the feasibility of such a change.

247

2. Recording the Suggestions

After brainstorming on the driving and restraining forces much like the procedure for the NGP, the task force, consisting of including herself, parents, the instructional support teacher and the principal recorded the following perceived driving and restraining forces.

FORCE FIELD ANALYSIS	
Recommended Change: Infuse Thematic Units into Classroom	
Driving Forces (+)	**Restraining Forces (−)**
	Alters the curriculum
Students respond enthusiastically to this approach	Teacher isn't knowledgeable about thematic units
	Requires the teacher to think about the curriculum differently and plan alternative activities
Interrelates many aspects of the curriculum	Teacher lacks the skill to create instructional materials for thematic units
	No incentive for teachers to try new ideas in their classes
Accommodates many different learning styles	School lacks resources for teachers to create materials

3. <u>Discuss and Prioritize the Driving and Restraining Forces</u>
We recommend that the person who generated the idea give his/her rationale as to why s/he felt it was important. Then an open discussion should be conducted on each point, and, if possible, certain points could be combined under a single heading if the task force agrees.

After discussion and grouping of the driving and restraining forces, the task force should assign a value of relative importance to each point. The values could be determined much like the way we recommended in the nominal group process (NGP) where either a rank value or total points could be determined using a n-1 numbering system. (For example, in the restraining forces there are 6 separate items listed. Therefore, the group may wish to use the NGP technique and assign #5 to the most important perceived restraining force, #4 for the second most important, etc.)

In this case, the task force decided to use the NGP and the final ranking value, *i.e.,* #1 was considered the most significant driving/restraining force, #2 the second most important, etc. These values are placed along side of the comments and are shown below.

FORCE FIELD ANALYSIS

Recommended Change: Infuse Thematic Units into Classroom

Driving Forces (+)	Restraining Forces (−)
	Alters the curriculum (-5)
Students respond enthusiastically to this approach (+1)	Teacher isn't knowledgeable about thematic units (-1)
	Requires the teacher to think about the curriculum differently and plan alternative activities (-4)
Interrelates many aspects of the curriculum (+3)	Teacher lacks the skill to create instructional materials for thematic units (-6)
	No incentive for teachers to try new ideas in their classes (-2)
Accommodates many different learning styles (+2)	School lacks resources for teachers to create materials (-3)

4. Recommending Steps to be Taken

After the driving and restraining forces are recorded, discussed, and prioritized the task force should begin to recommend steps that should be taken in order to effect the desired change. This should be done on the bottom of the form as shown below.

FORCE FIELD ANALYSIS

Recommended Change: Infuse Thematic Units into Classroom

Driving Forces (+)	Restraining Forces (−)
	Alters the curriculum (-5)
Students respond enthusiastically to this approach (+1)	Teacher isn't knowledgeable about thematic units (-1)
	Requires the teacher to think about the curriculum differently and plan alternative activities (-4)
Interrelates many aspects of the curriculum (+3)	Teacher lacks the skill to create instructional materials for thematic units (-6)
	No incentive for teachers to try new ideas in their classes (-2)
Accommodates many different learning styles (+2)	School lacks resources for teachers to create materials (-3)

RECOMMENDED ACTIONS:
1. The administration should provide funding for the teacher to attend a workshop on Thematic Units. (This would address the #1, #4, #5, and #6 ranked restraining forces and the #2 and #3 ranked driving forces.)
2. This teacher should be encouraged to implement Thematic Units and present her plans and outcomes before the entire faculty. (This would address the #2 and #5 restraining forces and all driving forces.)
3. Teachers who agree to share their Thematic Unit plans will receive money from the PTO for creating additional instructional materials. (This would address the #2 , #3 and #6 restraining forces and #1 and #3 driving forces.)
4. This teacher can become a lead teacher within the building, training colleagues in the use of Thematic Units. (This would address restraining forces #2,#4, #5, #6.)

HISTOGRAM

The **Histogram** is a depiction of data on a bar graph which represents how often a class of data occurred. One of the main purposes of using a Histogram is to predict improvements in a system. The system must be stable, however, or the Histogram cannot be used to make predictions. If the system is unstable the Histogram might take different shapes at different times. Therefore, the Histogram is often used with a **Control Chart**.

A Task Force studying a system may gather statistical data about the system and then draw a Histogram to help them assess the current situation. Then, in order to test a theory, the Task Force may change one or more processes within a system and, after gathering additional statistical data and redrawing another Histogram, check to see if the modifications improved the system.

The Histogram is used when one wishes to analyze the variation within a system. One must have a set of either related attributes (counts) data or variables (measurements) data. Although we will describe how a Histogram is prepared and how the shape of the Histogram may vary, we will not do the actual calculation of the statistics. Instead, we refer the reader to any elementary statistics book for the actual calculations.

In the example that follows we have selected a case study from a seventh grade science class where the teacher wanted to have her students analyze their study habits and the relationship to their success rate in science. The class participated in discussions and agreed on possible factors affecting their school success and study habits. Each student agreed to monitor the amount of time s/he spent talking on the telephone for one month. They also agreed to keep track of the grades they received in science class during the month. At the end of the first month, the task force combined all data. The total number of minutes the class members spent talking on the telephone was 95,250. That represented 3,175 minutes per student for the month, or an average of 53 minutes per day for 30 days. The total number of minutes spent studying for the same period of time was 31,399. This meant that each student spent an average of 17 minutes studying science per day.

The task force recorded the data and made a Frequency Distribution chart. This was posted and the class discussed ways to improve their grades. At the end of the first month, the class agreed to cut the amount of talking on the telephone in half and use that time to study science. As before, each student again kept track of his/her time spent on the telephone and all science grades. The class wanted to see if making a small alteration in their daily habits would dramatically affect their science grade.

Procedure

1. Select the Data to be Analyzed

We have assumed that the Task Force or the individual studying a system has collected either the attribute data or the variable data. In our case study the students kept tract of both telephone time and grades received.

2. Record the Data

A frequency table is constructed similar to those shown below.

Frequency Distribution
Distribution of grades for Mrs. Appleton's seventh grade science class for November, 1991.
(Before reducing the time spent on the telephone.)

Grade	Absolute Frequency	Relative Frequency %	Relative Cumulative %
A	01	3.33	3.33
B	03	10.00	13.33
C	06	20.00	33.33
D	12	40.00	73.33
F	08	26.66	100
Total	30	100	

Frequency Distribution
Distribution of grades of the students from Mrs. Appleton's science class for December, 1991 (After reducing the time spent on the telephone in half.)

Grade	Absolute Frequency	Relative Frequency %	Relative Cumulative %
A	6	20.00	20.00
B	9	30.00	50.00
C	13	43.33	93.33
D	2	6.66	100
F	0		
Total	30	100	

3. Draw the Histogram

Draw the x-axis (horizontal) and the y-axis (vertical). They should be of approximately of equal length and of sufficient size to best display your data. Then draw a bar for each "Grade" with the corresponding "Frequency" for which it occurred.

The histograms showing the distribution of grades of the students from Mrs. Appleton's science class from November, 1991 (before the self-imposed telephone restrictions) and from (after the self-imposed telephone restrictions) December, 1991 are shown below.

Distribution of grades from Mrs. Appleton's students during the month of November, 1991.

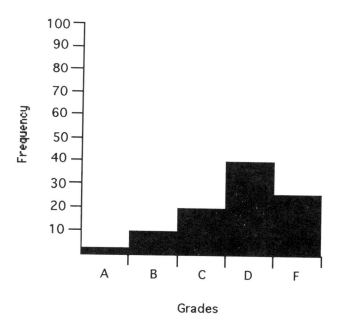

Distribution of grades from Mrs. Appleton's students
in December, 1991. (After altering the time spent
on the telephone.)

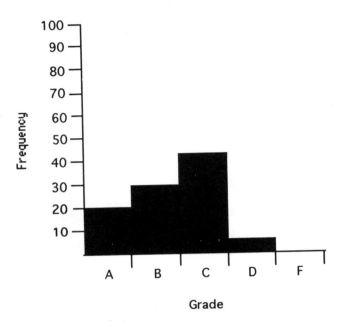

4. Analyze the Shape of the Histogram(s)

Histograms have six common shapes, namely 1) symmetrical, 2) skewed right, 3) skewed left, 4) uniform, 5) random, and 6) bimodal. These are shown below.

The Common Shapes of Histograms

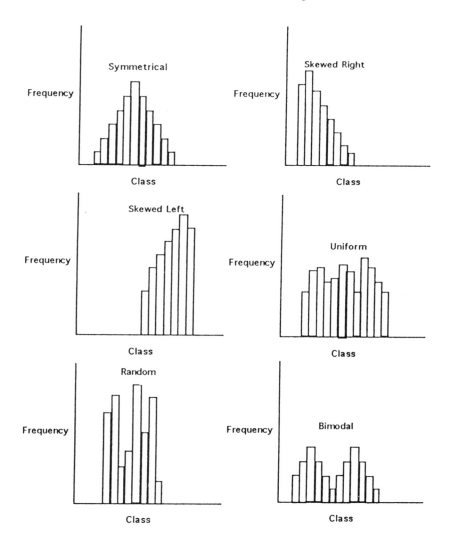

The symmetrical figure, called a bell-shaped curve, usually represents a "normal" distribution which indicates that the system under investigation is probably under control. Ideally the mean (average), mode, and median of the class data are equal and that 99.73% of total area under the curve is plus or minus 3 standard deviations.

Histograms can also trail off either to the right or left. Whereas the skewing to the right is known as a positive skew, the trailing to the left is known as a negative skew. These can occur when the data has values greater than zero, as in our case study.

The uniform and random distributions can indicate that the system under investigation is out of control. By the same token, a uniform distribution may be the result of not having sufficient number of classes in one's data, while the random distribution may result if one has multiple sources of variation in the system under study. In either case, these distributions usually provide little information.

The bimodal shaped histogram may indicate that the system under study is the result of several sources of data.

The first Histogram in our case study with Mrs. Appleton's science class is skewed left.

The skewed left is "negatively skewed," *i.e.*, it has a larger number of instances occurring with lower grades (C—F) and a few in the higher grades (A—B). As mentioned above, this skewed distribution occurs when the data within a system has a possible zero point and all the data collected have a value larger than zero.

The second Histogram is also skewed to the left, however, the class grades did improve. In this case one could make the case that the majority of students in Mrs. Appleton's class were able to achieve a grade better than "C" (93.3%) after making a slight change in their study habits.

After analyzing the data, these students decided to embark on a continuous improvement project to see how each could improve his/her performance in all classes. Next, they agreed to monitor the amount of time spent watching television while tracking their grades. The graphic data was a powerful tool indeed!

NOMINAL GROUP PROCESS

This technique is a structured process which helps the group identify and rank the major problems or issues that need addressing. This technique is also good for identifying the major **strengths** of a department/unit/institution. The technique gives each participant an equal voice, a key element of the group process.

The example below is from Mr. Jones' Social Science class. The session was called by the teacher because of his concerns of a lack of quality in his classroom. Students, a representative number of parents and Mr. Jones participated in the process and were to arrive at a consensus as to the perceived problems and/or weaknesses that inhibited quality.

For the **Nominal Group Process** (NGP) it is recommended that each group have a facilitator that is not part of the task force/unit. The facilitator may have to encourage some members of the team who are reluctant to contribute/participate; likewise, the facilitator may have to restrain members who normally try to control such processes. All members need to feel comfortable with the process and comfortable in participating. Each facilitator will require a stopwatch during the workshop.

Each group should consist of 5 to 10 persons. Since large units will have several groups, it is possible, although unlikely, that each group may perceive different problems/weaknesses. If this should happen, the facilitator may have to review the results and plan another session for the entire unit before the final ranking can be assigned.

Procedure

1. Introduction to the Process (5 Minutes)

The facilitator provides instructions regarding the process but does not influence the group's decision. The facilitator keeps the group working within the time limits.

The facilitator tells the participants that the NGP allows them to explore areas systematically and to arrive at a consensus. The process consists of developing a list and ranking perceived problems. The results of the ranking are discussed, and the perceived problems which are the most important to the group are identified.

2. Presentation of the Question (15 Minutes)

The facilitator should direct the question to be considered to the group. For example, the facilitator, as in this case, might be instructed to ask the group: "What do you consider to be the major problem of your unit that is affecting quality?"

The facilitator should repeat the question and then ask each participant to write short and specific 3 to 5 word answers for each perceived problem on **Form A** (see below). The facilitator should request that each member complete Form A silently and independently, reminding the participants that they have 5 minutes for this task. At the end of 5 minutes if it appears that several members have not finished, the facilitator should state that s/he will allow 2 additional minutes. If most members have already finished, the facilitator should not allow the extra time.

FORM A
Listing of Perceived Problems
What do you think are the major problems in your unit that inhibit quality?
Please use the form below and write out short but specific answers.

Item #	Perceived Problem
1	
2	
3	
4	
5	

3. Development of a Master List (20 Minutes)

While the group is developing their list of perceived problems, the facilitator should use an overhead and project **CHART I.**

At the end of the time allotted for listing the perceived problems of the unit, the facilitator should ask the participants to stop writing. Then in a round robin fashion, the facilitator will ask each to read aloud one of the perceived problems on his/her list. The facilitator will tell the participants that if they come to a problem on their list that has been given, they need not repeat it. If one item is phrased differently from another but appears to be the same, the facilitator will ask the group members to indicate by a show of hands if they think the items are the same. If a majority of the group feel the items are the same, the perceived problem will not be listed again; otherwise, both items will be listed. It may be necessary during this time for the facilitator to ask the participants not to speak out of turn. There should be **no discussion** of the list at this point. For a period of time the participants should not be influenced (to avoid coercion) by the opinions or remarks of others. This must be adhered to early in the process. Otherwise, those less assertive members will not raise problems which they alone might perceive: for instance, that another member likes to control department meetings. As each perceived problem is given, the facilitator will record the item on the **CHART I**. The facilitator must **not** suggest categories or combinations. The items should be numbered and recorded as presented by the participants without editing, unless the item is too long, in which case the facilitator may try to shorten the phrasing of the perceived problem without changing the meaning. If at the end of 20 minutes some group members have items that have not been presented, the facilitator will ask each member to give the one **most important** perceived problem remaining on his/her list.

A sample of some of the initial results of the perceived problems that resulted from the NGP in Mr. Jones' Social Science class are shown below.

Chart I

Perceived Problems that Inhibit Quality in Mr. Jones' Social Science Class.

Item #	Perceived Problem	Initial Value	Final Value	Final Rank
1	Class size too large			
2	Textbooks are out of date			
3	Classroom is in disrepair			
4	Students are tardy			
5	Too many students are absent			
6	Too many interruptions (announcements, etc.)			
7	Class periods are too short			
8	Teacher is unenthusiastic			
9	Teacher hasn't kept up new techniques & information			
10	Class activities are too routine (boring)			
11	Coercive, punitive discipline policy			
12	Students don't complete homework assignments			
13	Mr. Jones coaches football & uses class time to work out new plays			
14	Tests are too hard			

4. Master List Item Clarification (15 Minutes)

The facilitator should point to each perceived problem on the master list and read the item aloud. The facilitator should ask if each item is understood. If an item is unclear, the facilitator should ask the individual who generated the item to address and clarify it. The facilitator should **not** attempt to either condense the list nor to permit the group to discuss the relative importance of the perceived problems at this point. Remember, the purpose of this step is **clarification.**

5. Initial Ranking of the Items (15 Minutes)

The facilitator should distribute **Form B** (see below) to each member of the group and should request that each member select and rank the **five (5)** most important perceived problems of the unit. The most important perceived problem should be assigned a #5; the next most important item should be assigned a #4; and so forth with the #1 being assigned for the least important. The participants then record their rankings on **Form B** whereupon the facilitator should collect the forms and tally the results on the master list giving each item an initial score.

Form B
Initial Ranking of Perceived Problems
Please refer to the master list (Chart I) that describes the perceived problems and indicate in the table below what you think are the five major problems.

Item Number from the Master List	Initial Subjective Ranking Value
	#5 (Most Important)
	#4
	#3
	#2
	#1 (Least Important)

Using the listings from our aforementioned example in Chart I, the members of the task force in Mr. Jones' class assigned the following values to the listed perceived problems.

Chart I
Perceived Problems that Inhibit Quality in Mr. Jones' Social Science Class.

Item #	Perceived Problem	Initial Value	Final Value	Final Rank
1	Class size too large	7		
2	Textbooks are out of date	23		
3	Classroom is in disrepair	17		
4	Students are tardy	40		
5	Too many students are absent	20		
6	Too many interruptions (announcements, etc.)	1		
7	Class periods are too short	3		
8	Teacher is unenthusiastic	29		
9	Teacher hasn't kept up new techniques & information	31		
10	Class activities are too routine (boring)	45		
11	Coercive, punitive discipline policy	8		
12	Students don't complete homework assignments	30		
13	Mr. Jones coaches football & uses class time to work out new plays	27		
14	Tests are too hard	35		

6. Discussion of Initial Ranking (30 Minutes)
    The facilitator should ask the participants to discuss the results of the ranking. The participants may wish to **elaborate, defend,** and to **dispute** the rankings. They may not add items. Items may be discussed even if they did not receive a high score. The members should be reminded that this is their opportunity to express opinions and to persuade others. The facilitator should attempt to keep the discussion orderly and to prevent anyone from dominating.
    At this point similar items may be combined into a single category. In the above example a total of 14 separate items was eventually reduced to nine. These are shown below.

Class size too large	Too many interruptions
Textbooks are out of date	Class periods are too short
Classroom is in disrepair	Teacher is unenthusiastic
Students are tardy	
Coercive, punitive discipline policy	
Students don't complete homework assignments	

7. Break (20 Minutes)
     The facilitator should encourage the participants to take a
break and to move about, since it is rumored that if one sits too
long, the blood drains from the brain to the lower extremities.
Some members of the group may find this a welcome relief from
the previous discussion (or debate, if that should occur). Others
may want to take the discussion into the hallway. Likewise, the
facilitator should devise innovative means to have the members
return promptly after the break session is scheduled to end.

8. Final Listing and Ranking of Items (15 Minutes)
     After the items have been discussed the facilitator should
distribute a **copy of Form C** (see below) to all group
members. The facilitator should request each member to rank the
top five choices as before: assign **#5** to the one item they
consider the most important; **#4** to the second most important;
etc. At the end of the allocated time the facilitator should record
the final values to each item on the master list.

Form C
Final Ranking of Perceived Problems
Please refer to the revised master list (Chart I) that describes the
grouped perceived problems and indicate in the table below what
you think are the five major problems.

Item Number from the Master List	Initial Subjective Ranking Value
	#5 (Most Important)
	#4
	#3
	#2
	#1 (Least Important)

The results of the Master List should be recorded and typed on **Form D** (see below). When this was done in Mr. Jones' class mentioned above, the following data were obtained.

Form D
Summary and Rank of the Perceived Problems that Inhibit Quality in Mr. Jones' Social Science Class

Item #	Perceived Problem	Initial Value	Final Value	Final Rank
1	Class size too large	7	0	9
2	Textbooks are out of date	23	17	5
3	Classroom is in disrepair	17	2	7
4	Students are tardy	40	29	4
5	Too many students are absent	20	0	
6	Too many interruptions (announcements, etc.)	1	32	3
7	Class periods are too short	3	5	6
8	Teacher is unenthusiastic	29	97	2
9	Teacher hasn't kept up new techniques & information	31	0	
10	Class activities are too routine (boring)	45	0	
11	Coercive, punitive discipline policy	8	1	8
12	Students don't complete homework assignments	30	110	1
13	Mr. Jones coaches football & uses class time to work out new plays	27	0	
14	Tests are too hard	35	0	

Below are the various charts and forms you will need to conduct the NGP in your class.

Chart I
Perceived Problems that Inhibit Quality in our Class

Item #	Perceived Problem	Initial Value	Final Value	Final Rank
1				
2				
3				
4				
5				
6				
7				
8				
9				
10				
11				
12				
13				
n				

FORM A
Listing of Perceived Problems.
What do you think are the major problems in this class that inhibits quality?
Please use the form below and write out short but specific answers.

Item #	Perceived Problem
1	
2	
3	
4	
5	

Form B
Initial Ranking of Perceived Problems.
Please refer to the master list (Chart I) that describes the perceived problems and indicate in the table below what you think are the five major problems.

Item Number from the Master List	Initial Subjective Ranking Value
	#5 (Most Important)
	#4
	#3
	#2
	#1 (Least Important)

Form C
Final Ranking of Perceived Problems
Please refer to the revised master list (Chart I) that describes the grouped perceived problems and indicate in the table below what you think are the five major problems.

Item Number from the Master List	Initial Subjective Ranking Value
	#5 (Most Important)
	#4
	#3
	#2
	#1 (Least Important)

Form D
Summary and Rank of the Perceived Problems that Inhibit
Quality.

Item #	Perceived Problem	Initial Value	Final Value	Final Rank
1				
2				
3				
4				
5				
6				
7				
8				
9				
10				
11				
12				
13				
n				

OPERATIONAL DEFINITION

An **Operational Definition** is a very precise statement of what is expected from process objectives. It is probable that most of the troubles within the classroom are the result of operational definitions which are imprecise or undefined. An operational definition is a prerequisite for collecting data, and it must be clearly understood by everyone, *e.g.* the members of the task force, teachers, secretaries, students, etc.

Major problems arise in everyday events within schools because of unclear or undefined operational definitions. For example, students may want a clear definition of how their grades are going to be determined, including such simple and basic items as to what are they expected to know when they complete a course, how are they to be tested, and what are the classroom rules. Teachers are usually evaluated by the administration every year; never by students or parents. However, for most faculty, evaluation systems are not only statistically invalid but they also drive in fear (as do the tests most teachers give to students).

Operational definitions are used for **every** process that is trying to be improved. It is not necessarily right or wrong, but it must be **accepted by all members working on the system or process**. In addition, if the conditions change as one is examining the process the operational definition may change as well as any new measures added.

Procedure:
1. Statement of the Problem
Before any characteristic of a system or process is examined, the actual problem or issue has to be clearly defined. This is best done in form of a question such as, "How can I increase the success rate of students identifying major bones in the body and give examples of three types of joints.

2. Identify the Criterion to be Applied to the Object or the Group
The criterion to be measured is the success rate of third grade students identifying the major bones of the body and giving examples of three types of joints.

3. Identify the Test
The actual testing method must be precisely described including the evaluation procedure. In this example, the student must identify ten major bones of the body from numbered bones on a skeleton. In addition, they must name and give an example

of three types of joints. (The students have previously been taught all major bones and joint types. They have participated in a variety of exercises using differing instructional modes to learn. There have been group activities utilizing the skeleton to experiment with types of joints.) Students will have the option to leave their seats and examine the skeleton closely as well as test out joint theories.

4. Describe the Decision Process

The decision process is what permits one to confirm or deny success. In this example, students will assess each other's answers using a scoresheet each group has developed and checked against a master sheet.

PARETO DIAGRAM

The **Pareto Diagram** is a TQI tool that is used to identify the few significant factors that contribute to a problem and to separate them from the insignificant ones. It is based on the work of Vilfredo Pareto, an Italian economist (1848-1923) and was made popular by Joseph Juran in the 1940's. However, it was Alan Lakelin who came up with the 80/20 rule of the Pareto Diagram. The rule says that about 80 percent of the problem comes from about 20 percent of the causes.

The Pareto Diagram is a simple bar chart with the bars being arranged in descending order from left to right. Although many consider it a problem solving tool, it is really best for guiding a team to the problem areas that should be addressed first.

In the example below we have selected a case study from a high school auto shop where requests for repairs (known as "work orders") were not being completed in a timely fashion. Many of the repairs were not accomplished simply because the "work order" form was not completed correctly. The students and shop teacher identified six categories which attributed to the majority of errors, namely, 1) unclear requests, 2) principal's signature absent, 3) method of payment for parts not indicated, 4) date on which the work was to be performed was absent, 5) location of automobile not specified, and 6) work order request misfiled. The shop teacher appointed a task force and asked them to collect and analyze the data. As part of their study they used the Pareto Diagram which is shown below.

Procedure
1. <u>Select Categories to be Analyzed</u>

The members of the task force should seek to identify those data that they need to collect to address a particular problem, such as time, location, number of defects, number of errors and to place them into a category. The number of categories should be kept to 10 or less.

2. <u>Specify the Time period in Which the Data will be Collected</u>

Obviously the time period that is selected will vary according to the system under study. It may be hours in the measuring the time it takes accounting to cut a check or years in case of testing an improvement theory. However, the time selection should be constant for all diagrams that are being compared.

In the above example, the shop teacher chose to compare the 6 categories over the past academic year.

3. Record the Data

A table is constructed and it has a category column and a frequency column as shown below.

Category	# of Violations
Unclear requests	130
Principal's signature absent	74
Method of payment absent	46
Date to perform absent	40
Location of auto not identified	38
Work order misfiled	32
Total	360

The frequency table is constructed which shows the category, frequency, relative percent, cumulative frequency, and cumulative percent.

Category	Number Occurrences	Relative %	Cumulative Frequency	Cumulative %
Unclear request	130	36.1	130	36.1
No Principal's signature	74	19.7	204	55.8
Method of payment absent	46	12.8	250	68.6
Date to perform absent	40	11.1	290	79.7
Location of auto not identified	38	10.6	328	90.3
Work order misfiled	32	8.9	360	99.2
Total	360	99.2%		

4. Draw the Graph

Draw the x-axis (horizontal). It should be long enough to best display your graph and it may vary from several inches to 6 or 7 inches. The width of each bar should be equal. It the case study we are examining the x-axis of 3.6 inches was selected and the scaling factor of 0.60 inch was selected to represent each of the categories.

Draw two vertical lines (y-axis) of equal length as shown below. They should be as long as the x-axis, if not longer. Again, they should be long enough to best display your graph.

Label and scale the axes. In this case study the x-axis will represent the categories being compared, the y-axis on the left will represent the number of occurrences, and the right y-axis will represent cumulative percent.

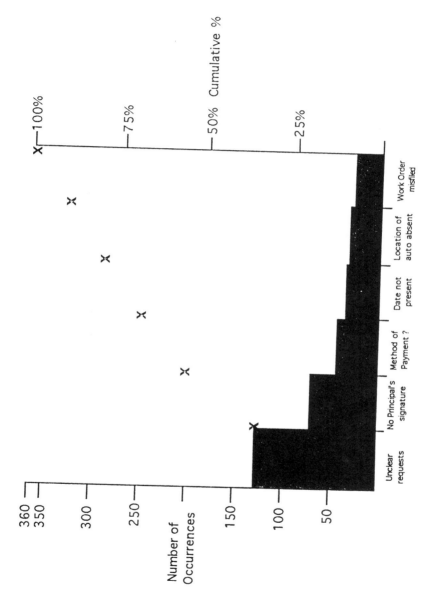

After the graph is drawn plot the cumulative frequencies and draw a line connecting the marks (**x**) as shown below.

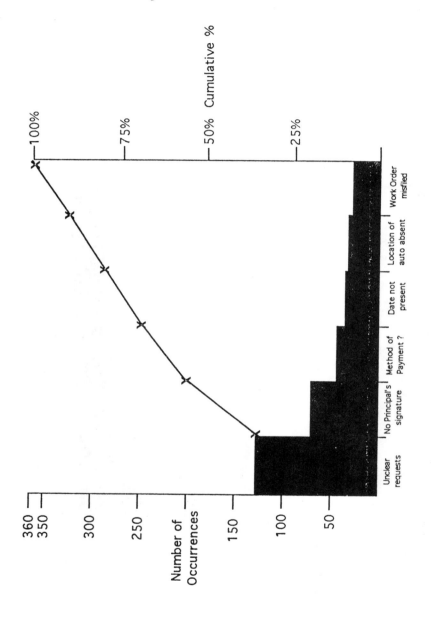

5. Analyze the Diagram

It is not unusual for 80 percent of the problem to be caused by a few categories and the Pareto Diagram will easily demonstrate this. In the above example over 55 percent of the occurrences were due to the first two categories.

One must be careful when using this powerful tool. It is true the Pareto diagram can point out chunks of data that can be used by a task force to analyze causes and then direct their efforts towards a few categories, however, there are data that can not be categorized easily. Some data, without further analyses, may be misleading if they are too general. The above data could be misinterpreted if the shop teacher simply concentrated on the first two categories.

RELATIONS DIAGRAM

The **Relations Diagram** is used as a planning tool. It is rarely used alone. Instead, when used with either the **Scenario Builder** and/or the **Affinity Diagram**, the **Relations Diagram** is a powerful tool to arrive at root causes and effects of a process or a problem.

When a task force uses the Relations Diagram to examine a complex problem over an extended period of time it will most likely be able to not only direct its efforts towards the major root causes of the problem(s) in an efficient manner, but it will also be able to constantly update and modify the necessary actions that might result from observed changes in the "system" under study.

Procedure
1. Statement of the Problem
    Although it is possible to use the Relations Diagram by identifying a problem/issue and then stating it in a brief and specific manner, it is much more efficient to have examined a complex problem/issue with other tools before using the Relations Diagram. For example, we recommend that the task force first utilize one of the other tools such as the **Nominal Group Process** and/or the **Affinity Diagram**, to arrive at a consensus on the process/issue under investigation, then analyze the findings further with the Relations Diagram.

    In this example, a high school drama class was attempting to establish a set design and construction shop. They determined that a team was the best way to work through the problem. Their school district could not underwrite such a project, however, the class was determined that the added capability such a shop would provide was worth examining. After doing an analysis with an Affinity Diagram, the team posted the following header cards to the question "What are the issues associated with us establishing a set design & construction shop?"
    1. Get the support of parents.
    2. Get the support of local business.
    3. Demonstrate a need to the principal.
    4. Get the support of the student body.
    5. Develop and design a plan for the design & construction shop.
    6. Prepare informational materials and programs
    7. Develop and carry out a fund raising campaign.
    8. Organize a volunteer effort to collect equipment and materials.

In order to examine the root cause and effects of issue, they next did a **Relations Diagram**. This is shown below.

2. Recording the Perceptions
    Place the header cards from the **Affinity Diagram** in a circular pattern around the problem/issue being examined as shown below. This can be done using an overhead projector, but a large sheet of flip chart paper is usually better.

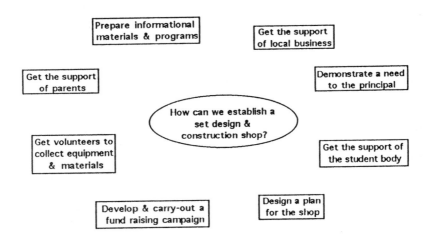

3. Demonstrate Interrelationships
    One should ask if there is a "cause-and-effect" between the header groups. If a relationship exists, draw a line to connect the headers. An arrow is placed from the header that is a cause of something having an effect on the other header.

    In the example below the task force decided that it was necessary to gain the support of the principal before going ahead with their plans. As a result, they drew arrows away from the cause and towards the header that it would effect or have influence over.

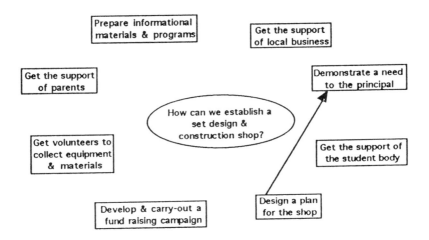

The inter-relations are continually examined until all headers are compared to each other. When this was done with the aforementioned example the following diagram was finally constructed.

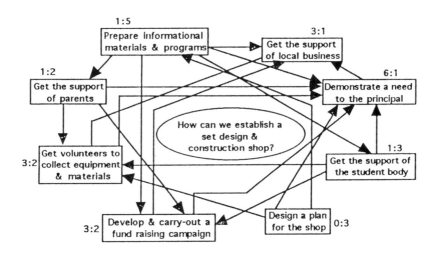

4. Analyze the Interrelationships

Count the number of arrows that are directed towards each header and the number that leave. Express this as the #Towards : #From. Write the numbers next to their respective headers as shown above.

The **root causes** are those headers that have the greatest number of arrows going **FROM**; the **root effects** are those headers having the greatest number of arrows going **TOWARDS**. In the above example the two root causes suggest that the task force should design and draw plans for the shop and develop informational materials and programs prior to going to the principal for his approval and support.

RUN CHART

A **Run Chart**, also called a tier chart, is a line graph of data where the observed values can be either measurements (variables) or counts (attributes). The data is plotted on the vertical axis while the time is plotted on the horizontal axis.

One of main benefits of a run chart is to examine the functioning of a system over time. Similar data plotted together in a histogram may not reveal an important trend in the system that might require corrective action.

A run chart is constructed from data that is collected as the system is in operation. A run chart is often used by a task force as the initial tool in gathering information about the system under study. Usually more than 25 points are required for a valid run chart.

A run chart is a simple TQI tool and can be used with a wide variety of data. They are good for a single snapshot or for following trends. Various units within the school could make excellent use of run charts by posting good and poor trends for all to see and analyze. (Note: these charts should never be used as a threat or employees will refuse to offer their suggestions as how the system can be improved.) Depending upon the data the time factor can be seconds, minutes, hours, days, weeks, or years. Depending upon the data it may be possible to add the statistical upper control limits (UCL) and lower control limits (LCL) and make the run chart a "Control Chart."

Procedure
1. Select the Data to be Analyzed

We have assumed that the Task Force or the individual studying a system has collected either the attribute (counts) data or the variables (measurements) data. In the case study below, Mrs. Salmon was interested in discovering the average amount of time it took her students to achieve mastery for each unit of study. She wanted to examine her assignments and teaching styles for each unit and was going to focus on those units where the students were having the most difficulty with mastery.

2. Record the Data
Record the data in the order which it was collected.

Average time (in days) to achieve mastery per unit

Class period	Unit 1	Unit 2	Unit 3	Unit 4	Unit 5	Unit 6
#1 (8-8:50 AM)	13	15	14	16	15	14
#2 (9-9:50 AM)	14	13	14	13	13	14
#3 (10-10:50 AM)	13	14	16	15	15	14
#4 (11-11:50 AM)	19	23	20	18	21	16
#5 (12-12:50 PM)	16	16	17	17	16	14
#6 (1-1:50 PM)	14	16	16	15	15	14

3. Draw the Graph
    The first thing one has to do is to scale the chart and this will vary depending upon the type of data collected, *i.e.* variables or attributes.
    In scaling for the variables data one starts by finding the largest and smallest values in the data. In our case the largest was 23 and the smallest was 13. The difference between these are determined (23-13=10). Then a rule of thumb is to divide the difference (10) by 66% of the number of lines on your graph paper. The chart paper used in our case study is shown below. It has 30 lines, therefore, 30 x 0.66= 19.8, or approximately 20. Therefore, 10 ÷ 20 is 0.5. Always rounding to the higher number each line will have an incremental value of 1.0.
    Next the lines should be numbered from the middle of the chart. Since our values range from 13 to 23 minutes the value which is one half is 5 minutes. Since the center number is 5 minutes + 13 minutes or 18 minutes, we can set the center line at either 15 minutes or 20 minutes and assign an incremental value of one minute to the other lines.
    Scaling for attributes data is identical to that of the variables scaling except the first line of the chart is assigned a value of zero and the increment values are added from the bottom up.
    The data points are plotted on the graph paper as shown in and the points are connected with straight lines.

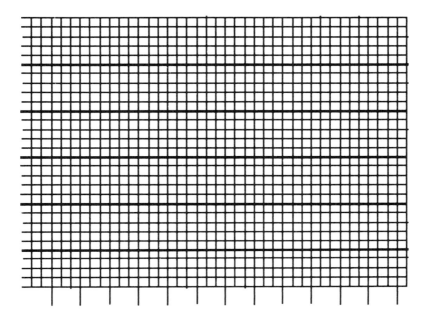

It should be mentioned that almost any chart paper can be used to plot the data of run charts and that the process of scaling would be the same.

The chart should be carefully labeled so that the results can be clearly understood by all members of the task force. An example of a completed run chart is shown below.

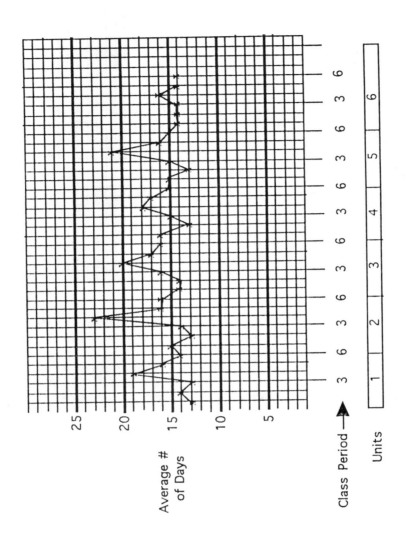

4. <u>Analyze the Chart</u>

One should look for runs of 7 or more points showing increases or decreases as well as for other patterns.

In our case a pattern was discovered: students in "Period 4" took significantly longer to achieve mastery than students in all the other classes. Period 4 is just before lunch. Students may be tired, or hungry and distracted from their studies. (It could also be that Mrs. Salmon is tired and hungry and is not providing the necessary leadership.) She also discovered that the second period class averaged only 13.5 days to complete mastery in all the units. Her task now is to match this data with her teaching styles for the fourth and second periods. Based on that information, she will examine the learning styles of her students prior to making any adjustments in the class. Mrs. Salmon also will engage the students in the continuous improvement project, utilizing one or more of the other tools.

SCATTER DIAGRAM

Scatter Diagrams are used to test the possible interrelationships of two factors. If a relationship appears to exist, the factors are said to be correlated. However, a cause-and-effect relationship can be verified only with the use of control charts.

A scatter diagram is a useful tool that can be used by action teams to analyze causes of poor processes or systems.

1. Select the Data to be Analyzed

In the following case study a teacher wanted to test whether the grade of the students in a fourth grade mathematics unit was related to the time they watched television (TV). The parents were asked, as part of their TQM contract, to record the amount of time in minutes that their child spent watching TV over a week and to submit this log to the teacher. At the end of the report period the teacher plotted the results.

2. Record the Data

Student ID Number	Hours per Week Viewing TV	Math Grade in %
001	<1.0	96
002	2.5	98
003	14.0	60
004	21.0	72
005	21.0	56
006	2.5	88
007	3.0	83
008	7.0	86
009	8.0	71
010	3.0	91
011	3.0	86
012	18.0	60
013	21.0	56
014	<1.0	93
015	10.0	75
016	9.0	76
017	10.0	77
018	2.5	92
019	6.0	70
020	7.5	73
021	2.5	99
022	14.5	60
023	9.0	77
024	8.5	69
025	4.0	80

3. Draw the Diagram

The first thing one should do is scale the diagram so that both axes are approximately the same length. The length of the axes should be long enough to accommodate the entire range of values and the entire length of each axis should be used. In our example the time per week the students watched TV ranged from less than 2.5 hours to 21 hours. The x-axis usually contains the data believed to be the influencing or independent factor while the y-axis contains the dependent or responding factor. In our example the teacher believed that the more the students watched TV the less they studied and, as a result, their grades suffered. Therefore, the independent factor is time watching TV and the dependent factor is the grade.

The diagram should be labeled, dated, and the points should be plotted. The completed diagram is shown below.

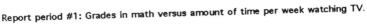

Report period #1: Grades in math versus amount of time per week watching TV.

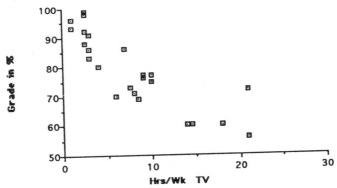

4. Analyze the Diagram

Although it looks as if there might be a negative correlation between the amount of time the students watched TV and the grade that they received in the mathematics, there may be other factors that influenced the grades, such as the number of absences, etc. Clearly, however, the amount of time the students watch TV might be a possible root cause for poor grades in math.

SCENARIO BUILDER

The **Scenario Builder** is a planning tool which quantifies roughly the outcomes that may result if one or more proposed changes to a system are implemented. It is useful for helping to analyze the most likely outcomes of an element of change on a complex system. It is a tool that asks "what if?" and concentrates the efforts of team members to propose most likely outcomes, both positive and negative. It is a powerful tool that combines many of the features obtained from an affinity diagram, the nominal group process, the force field analysis, and the systematic diagram. Like the **Affinity Diagram** it attempts to organize complex issues; like the **Nominal Group Process,** it forces the group into identifying and ranking the most likely effects that the proposed change may bring; like the **Force Field Analysis**, it concentrates on both the positive and negative driving and restraining forces and the action steps that should be taken to overcome the resistance of implementing the change; and, finally, like the **Systematic Diagram**, it helps to identify possible action items that are necessary in order to implement a broader goal.

The **Scenario Builder** should not be used until the task force members are familiar with the affinity diagram, the nominal group process, the force field analysis, and the systematic diagram. The **Scenario Builder** is **NOT** a replacement for the aforementioned tools, but it is a tool that one may wish to consider **IF** the situation under examination requires two or more of the tools for elucidation. Although the **Scenario Builder** requires a minimum of 3 hours of concentrated effort to complete, it still may save the task force many hours if, for example, three TQI tools are required to arrive at similar conclusions.

Procedure
1. Spell out the recommended changes

In using the scenario builder, the group has defined the system that requires modification. In fact, the team members should have solidified the change(s) that must be implemented in order to improve the system.

The recommended change ("C") is placed in the middle of the hexagon (see Scenario Builder Figure). The task force members should assume that the appropriate recommendations will be accepted in order to implement the change.

2. Record the Perceptions

The task force members should list at least three beneficial outcomes of the proposed change, and, if possible, three undesirable outcomes of the proposed change. The three beneficial outcomes should be listed in the squares labeled 1 through 3; the three undesirable outcomes should be listed in the squares 4 through 6. (Sometimes it is difficult and/or almost impossible to identify three truly unacceptable outcomes as a result of implementing improvements in processes or systems. However, the group should attempt to identify at least two undesirable outcomes.)

Following the above pattern, the group should label four scenarios that are likely to occur as a result of the outcomes identified in the squares labeled 1 through 6, and if possible, two should be positive and two should be negative scenarios. In any event, at least one should be either positive or negative.

The aforementioned pattern should be repeated with the triangles and the ellipsoids. At least one of the perceived outcomes should be either positive or negative at any of the levels.

Scenario Builder To Determine The Effect of Change

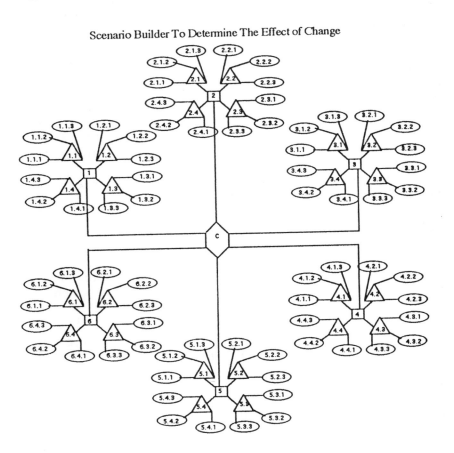

3. Score the Scenarios

Scoring of the scenarios can be done either as they are listed, or afterwards. But all six, first level scenarios should have at least a 70 percent perceived probability of occurring. To score the scenario builder the group assigns a number of +1 to +10 to any positive scenario that might occur if the change is implemented, and -1 to -10 to any negative scenario that might occur if the change is implemented. For example, the group may decide that a positive scenario A, identified and placed in square 1, would surely result if the change were effected and thus they assigned a value +10. The +10 means that the positive scenario would occur 100 percent of the time if the change were implemented and **IF** nothing were done to stop it. Likewise, a +3 should be assigned a value of 30 percent; +4, forty percent, etc. The group may decide that positive scenarios B and C should be assigned values of +7 and +5 respectively. Similarly, the task force might decide that negative scenario D would almost definitely occur (100% of the time) if the change were implemented, therefore, they would assign it a value of -10, whereas the negative scenarios E and F were only assigned values of -3 (30%) and -4 (40%) since they were less likely to occur if the change was implemented. If a **very positive** scenario would occur if the change is effected, and if its effect could not be altered, it should be assigned a value of +50. Likewise, if a disaster would occur if the change is implemented, and if its effect could not be altered, it should be assigned a value of -50.

The values for the first level scenarios, 1 through 6, should be recorded on a scenario builder tally sheet as shown below. Likewise, the values for the second level scenarios, 1.1 through 6.4, should be recorded. Finally, the values for the third level scenarios, 1.1.1 through 6.4.3, should be recorded. The scoring guidelines for the scenario builder are shown in the following table.

Positive Scenario	Negative Scenario	Would Likely Occur Percent of the Time	Effect Can Be Altered?
+1	-1	10%	Yes
+2	-2	20%	Yes
+3	-3	30%	Yes
+4	-4	40%	Yes
+5	-5	50%	Yes, Requires Effort
+6	-6	60%	Yes, Requires More Effort
+7	-7	70%	Yes, Requires Much Effort
+8	-8	80%	Yes, With Difficulty
+9	-9	90%	Yes, But Unlikely
+10	-10	100%	Not Likely
+50	-50	100%	Never

Scenario Builder tally sheet for estimating perceived effects of change on a process or a system and the prospect that a given event will occur.

1. ___	1. ___	1. ___	1. ___
1.1 ___	1.2 ___	1.3 ___	1.4 ___
1.1.1 ___	1.2.1 ___	1.3.1 ___	1.4.1 ___
1.1.2 ___	1.2.2 ___	1.3.2 ___	1.4.2 ___
1.1.3 ___	1.2.3 ___	1.3.3 ___	1.4.3 ___
Total ___	Total ___	Total ___	Total ___

2. ___	2. ___	2. ___	2. ___
2.1 ___	2.2 ___	2.3 ___	2.4 ___
2.1.1 ___	2.2.1 ___	2.3.1 ___	2.4.1 ___
2.1.2 ___	2.2.2 ___	2.3.2 ___	2.4.2 ___
2.1.3 ___	2.2.3 ___	2.3.3 ___	2.4.3 ___
Total ___	Total ___	Total ___	Total ___

3. ___	3. ___	3. ___	3. ___
3.1 ___	3.2 ___	3.3 ___	3.4 ___
3.1.1 ___	3.2.1 ___	3.3.1 ___	3.4.1 ___
3.1.2 ___	3.2.2 ___	3.3.2 ___	3.4.2 ___
3.1.3 ___	3.2.3 ___	3.3.3 ___	3.4.3 ___
Total ___	Total ___	Total ___	Total ___

4. ___	4. ___	4. ___	4. ___
4.1 ___	4.2 ___	4.3 ___	4.4 ___
4.1.1 ___	4.2.1 ___	4.3.1 ___	4.4.1 ___
4.1.2 ___	4.2.2 ___	4.3.2 ___	4.4.2 ___
4.1.3 ___	4.2.3 ___	4.3.3 ___	4.4.3 ___
Total ___	Total ___	Total ___	Total ___

5. ___	5. ___	5. ___	5. ___
5.1 ___	5.2 ___	5.3 ___	5.4 ___
5.1.1 ___	5.2.1 ___	5.3.1 ___	5.4.1 ___
5.1.2 ___	5.2.2 ___	5.3.2 ___	5.4.2 ___
5.1.3 ___	5.2.3 ___	5.3.3 ___	5.4.3 ___
Total ___	Total ___	Total ___	Total ___

6. ___	6. ___	6. ___	6. ___
6.1 ___	6.2 ___	6.3 ___	6.4 ___
6.1.1 ___	6.2.1 ___	6.3.1 ___	6.4.1 ___
6.1.2 ___	6.2.2 ___	6.3.2 ___	6.4.2 ___
6.1.3 ___	6.2.3 ___	6.3.3 ___	6.4.3 ___
Total ___	Total ___	Total ___	Total ___

4. <u>Interpret the Scores</u>

The team should examine the first level scenarios, labeled 1 through 6, and they should have values ±7, *i.e.* all should have a greater than 70 percent chance of occurring if the changes were implemented.

The task force should continue to build upon the **major** positive and negative scenarios through levels two and three. As before they should concentrate their efforts on only the scenarios with values of ±7 or greater.

5. <u>Describe what will likely happen to each even and then what ACTION STEP needs to be taken to accentuate the positive and minimize the negative outcomes as well as the DESIRED OUTCOME</u>

With the likely events of both positive and negative outcomes resulting in the implementation of the task force's recommendations to change a system being evaluated and quantified, action steps can now be identified to either recommend the change and to minimize the possible negative outcomes, or to, in fact, abandon the change as it might be disastrous to the classroom or school.

6. <u>List and analyze any scenario that has a number greater than ±100</u>

The scenarios that have a high score usually means that if the recommended changes were implemented and if the perceptions of the task force members were representative of the institutional culture, then the scenarios would take place.

7. <u>Suggest what one or two systems should be improved to maximize the positive and minimize the negative</u>

Case Study

Here is an example of how the **Scenario Builder** was effectively used with students in a twelfth grade English class.

The students in Ms. Amie Mosier's twelfth grade English class were not doing well. A task force consisting of five students and Ms. Mosier was formed. After conducting a Nominal Group Process session with the class, they arrived at the conclusion that the students would learn more and do better quality work if the students could work cooperatively in groups. Following the aforementioned directions:

1. <u>Spell out the recommended change(s)</u>

The recommended change ("C") is: **Students will work in groups on all classroom assignments in order to receive better grades in English**.

2. Record the Perceptions

The task force members should list approximately an equal number of beneficial outcomes and undesirable outcomes of the proposed change. These are shown below along with the scoring.

3. Score the Scenarios

Scoring of the scenarios can be done either as they are listed, or afterwards. But all six, first level scenarios should have at least a 70 percent perceived probability of occurring. To score the scenario builder the group assigns a number of +1 to +10 to any positive scenario that might occur if the change is implemented, and -1 to -10 to any negative scenario that might occur if the change is implemented. If a **very positive** scenario would occur if the change is effected, and if its effect could not be altered, it should be assigned a value of +50. Likewise, if a disaster would occur if the change is implemented, and if its effect could not be altered, it should be assigned a value of -50. The aforementioned table was used and the following numbers were assigned to the scenarios if the recommended change ("C") is implemented: **Students will work in groups on all classroom assignments in order to receive better grades in English**.

1. Students will get along well and will work effectively in the groups. (+7)

   1.1   Students will realize the importance of group success. (+7)

      1.1.1 Self esteem will rise because the group will be successful. (+9)

      1.1.2 Students will bond with a different group of students. (+6)

      1.1.3 Some will be frustrated because there will be less individual recognition.(-3)

   1.2   Students will achieve a quality group product. (+8)

      1.2.1 Students will take pride in workmanship realizing they've produced a quality product. (+10)

      1.2.2 Students will recognize excellence and know they can achieve it. (+10)

      1.2.3 Students will be frustrated at the amount of work involved in achieving quality work.(-2)

   1.3   Students will spend too much time chatting/gossiping and little time working on the assignment. (-2)

      1.3.1 Students will broaden their circle of friends. (+5)

      1.3.2 Students will practice better communication skills. (+5)

             1.3.3 Students will not achieve quality work because they will not focus on the assignment. (-8)

    1.4   Students will broaden the assignment , causing them to be inefficient in their use of time. (-3)

             1.4.1 Students will become so enthusiastic they will continue to find new ways to explore the assignment. (+4)

             1.4.2 Students will learn many different off-shoots about the assignment, thus broadening their knowledge base. (+4)

             1.4.3 Students will not finish the assignment on time. (-6)

2. After Ms. Mosier trains students in cooperative learning, groups will work effectively producing quality assignments. (+10)

    2.1   Students will enjoy cooperative learning and will agree to work in groups. (+8)

             2.1.1 Students will become active learners and have fun in the classroom. (+8)

             2.1.2 Students will expand their friendships. (+7)

             2.1.3 Students will not focus on the assignment. (-3)

    2.2   Students will feel good about being helpful to their classmates. (+50)

             2.2.1 Self-esteem will increase. (+10)

             2.2.2 Students will realize how working together increases success. (+10)

             2.2.3 Some students will do the work of others rather than helping them. (-7)

    2.3   Training students will take up a great deal of class time. (-8)

             2.3.1 Ms. Mosier will consider this is important. (+10)

             2.3.2 Students will learn how to work cooperatively. (+7)

             2.3.3 Training will take away valuable class time, causing Ms. Mosier to feel stressed. (-8)

    2.4   Students who are not in groups with their friends will not put all their focus and energy into accomplishing the assignment. (-5)

             2.4.1 Students will get to know other students. (+5)

             2.4.2 Factions within the classroom will begin to break down as students work together with others. (+4)

2.4.3 Some students will become angry and refuse to work together. (-7)

3. Students will appreciate individual differences in their classmates and will recognize how each contributes to the success of the group. (+9)
   3.1   Students will recognize that people learn differently. (+50)
       3.1.1 Students will learn that some are "smart" in other subjects but "slow" in English. (+50)
       3.1.2 Teaming will become more important than individual success. (+7)
       3.1.3 Racial tension will be reduced as students work together. (+10)
   3.2   Students will be frustrated with those who not contribute to the project. (-10)
       3.2.1 Clicks will form within the group. (-10)
       3.2.2 Hard feelings will result. (-10)
       3.2.3 Racial tension will increase. (-10)
   3.3   Leaders will evolve to direct the group. (-50)
       3.3.1 All members of the group will develop significant leadership qualities. (+7)
       3.3.2 Some of the leaders will become pushy. (-50)
       3.3.3 Some students will ignore the leaders. (+10)

4. Students will resist working together and will do individual projects within the group. (-8)
   4.1   Students will work harder for their own gain than they otherwise would. (+3)
       4.1.1 The quality of each person's work will be higher than normal. (+2)
       4.1.2 Students will learn about independent study. (+3)
       4.1.3 There will be an overlap among student's work. (-7)
   4.2   The group assignment will not be cohesive. (-7)
       4.2.1 The individual parts of the assignment will good quality. (+3)
       4.2.2 Students have will not learn to work cooperatively. (-10)
       4.2.3 The group assignment will not be completed since the group will not tie it all together. (-9)
   4.3   Students will become angry because each thinks s/he is doing all the work. (-8)
       4.3.1 Adrenaline will make all students work harder. (+2)

4.3.2   Some students will quit because they will feel unappreciated. (-4)

4.3.3   Groups will break apart because students will refuse to work together. (-9)

5. Some students will simply not participate in the group, and a few students will undertake responsibility for completing the group assignment. (-7)

    5.1   Some students will get the assignment done. (+3)

        5.1.1   The assignment will be completed. (+3)

        5.1.2   The goal of working together in a group will be achieved. (-10)

        5.1.3   Students will be angry with other group members for not helping. (-8)

    5.2   There will be dissension between the students. (-10)

        5.2.1   Natural tension will cause students to practice communication skills. (+2)

        5.2.2   Students will break into factions...those working and those not. (-7)

        5.2.3   Students will complain to Ms. Mosier that the assignment is unfair. (-8)

    5.3   Some students will not do any work. (-10)

        5.3.1   Some students will relax. (+1)

        5.3.2   Working students will be angry with those who are not. (-9)

        5.3.3   Group goals will not being met since students will not learn to work together. (-10)

6. Tensions will be high since students will refuse to work with anyone other than their friends. (-8)

The task force entered the scores of each scenario into the table that follows.

Scenario Builder tally sheet for estimating perceived effects of change on a process or a system and the prospect that a given event will occur.

1. +7
1.1 +7
   1.1.1 +9
   1.1.2 +6
   1.1.3 -3
   Total +26

2. +10
2.1 +8
   2.1.1 +8
   2.1.2 +7
   2.1.3 -3
   Total +30

3. +9
3.1 +50
   3.1.1 +50
   3.1.2 +7
   3.1.3 +10
   Total +126

4. -8
4.1 +3
   4.1.1 +2
   4.1.2 +3
   4.1.3 -7
   Total -7

5. -7
5.1 +3
   5.1.1 +3
   5.1.2 -10
   5.1.3 -8
   Total -19

6. -8
6.1 ND
   6.1.1 ____
   6.1.2 ____
   6.1.3 ____
   Total ____

1. +7
1.2 +8
   1.2.1 +10
   1.2.2 +10
   1.2.3 - 2
   Total +33

2. +10
2.2 +9
   2.2.1 +50
   2.2.2 +10
   2.2.3 - 7
   Total +72

3. +9
3.2 -10
   3.2.1 -10
   3.2.2 -10
   3.2.3 -10
   Total -39

4. -8
4.2 -7
   4.2.1 +3
   4.2.2 -10
   4.2.3 -9
   Total -31

5. -7
5.2 -10
   5.2.1 +2
   5.2.2 -7
   5.2.3 -8
   Total - 30

6.2 ND
   6.2.1 ____
   6.2.2 ____
   6.2.3 ____
   Total ____

1. +7
1.3 -2
   1.3.1 +5
   1.3.2 +5
   1.3.3 -8
   Total +7

2. +10
2.3 -8
   2.3.1 +10
   2.3.2 +7
   2.3.3 -8
   Total +11

3. +9
3.3 -50
   3.3.1 +7
   3.3.2 -50
   3.3.3 - 9
   Total -74

4. -8
4.3 -8
   4.3.1 +2
   4.3.2 -4
   4.3.3 -9
   Total -27

5. -7
5.3 -10
   5.3.1 +1
   5.3.2 -9
   5.3.3 -10
   Total -35

6.3 ND
   6.3.1 ____
   6.3.2 ____
   6.3.3 ____
   Total ____

1. +7
1.4 -3
   1.4.1 +4
   1.4.2 +4
   1.4.3 -6
   Total +6

2. +10
2.4 -5
   2.4.1 +5
   2.4.2 +4
   2.4.3 - 7
   Total + 7

3. +9
3.4 ND
   3.4.1 ____
   3.4.2 ____
   3.4.3 ____
   Total ____

4. -8
4.4 ND
   4.4.1 ____
   4.4.2 ____
   4.4.3 ____
   Total ____

5. -7
5.4 ND
   5.4.1 ____
   5.4.2 ____
   5.4.3 ____
   Total ____

6.4 ND
   6.4.1 ____
   6.4.2 ____
   6.4.3 ____
   Total____

4. Interpret the Scores

4.1   Examine the scores of the six, first level scenarios

The team should examine the first level scenarios, labeled 1 through 6, and they should have values ±7, *i.e.* all should have a greater than 70 percent chance of occurring if the changes were implemented. All scenarios did have a score greater than ±7.

4.2   Build upon the second level scenarios that have a 70 percent chance or greater perceived probability of occurring

The task force continued to build upon the **major** positive and negative scenarios through levels two and three. As before they concentrated their efforts on only the scenarios with values of ±7 or greater.

The task force, therefore, had to consider the following scenarios: 1.1, 1.2, 2.1, 2.2, 2.3, 3.1, 3.2, 3.3, 4.2, 4.3, 5.2, and 5.3.

5. Describe what will likely happen to each event and then what ACTION STEP needs to be taken to accentuate the positive and minimize the negative outcomes as well as the DESIRED OUTCOME

With the likely events of both positive and negative outcomes resulting in the implementation of the task force's recommendations to change a system being evaluated and quantified, action steps can now be identified to either recommend the change and to minimize the possible negative outcomes, or to, in fact, abandon the change as it might be disastrous to the organization.

SCENARIO 1: The students will get along well and work effectively in groups (+7) since they will realize the importance of group success (+7). Therefore self-esteem will rise because the group will be successful (+9) and this will cause the students to bond together (+6).

While working together to produce a quality "product (+8)," the individuals will take pride-in-workmanship (+10) and will recognize excellence and know they can achieve it (+10).

ACTION STEP: The task force will report its finding and recommendations back to the class.

DESIRED OUTCOMES: The students will realize that cooperative learning and teaming is the way things are done in real life situations.

SCENARIO 2: After Ms. Mosier trains the students in cooperative learning, groups will work effectively together (+10). After the training the students will enjoy working in groups (+8) as they will become active learners (+8). In addition, they will expand their friendships (+7). Group projects will make students feel good about helping their classmates (+50) and self-esteem will increase (+10). Students will realize the importance of group success, although some students may end up doing the work of others rather than showing them how the work should be done (-7).

Ms. Mosier knows that it will take time to train the students in TQI tools (-8) and that this time will come from regular class time (-8), but the training is very important (+10) if the students are to learn how to work as a team (+7).

ACTION STEP: Ms. Mosier will take time from the regular classes to teach the appropriate TQI tools which encourage teaming.

DESIRED OUTCOMES: The students will begin to work as a team and realize success in English.

SCENARIO 3: Students will appreciate individual differences in their classmates and will recognize how each contributes to the success of the group (+9). As a result students will recognize different learning styles (+50) and the differences in preferences for subjects (+50). Since teaming will become more important than individual success (+7), racial tension will be reduced as the students work together (+10).

The possibility exists that the students will become frustrated with those who do not contribute to the project (-10) and various subunits will result (-10) which will increase hard feelings (-10) and increase racial tension (-10).

As in any group project, leaders will emerge and direct the group project (-50). Actually, this may be a +50 if the leaders help the group to realize their own potential and don't become pushy (-50). Some students will totally ignore pushy leaders (+10).

ACTION STEP: Each group will have to constantly remind its members about the benefits of team work.

DESIRED OUTCOMES: The students will realize the importance of leadership in helping the group obtain success.

SCENARIO 4: Students will resist working together and will do individual projects within the group (-8). The group will not be cohesive (-7) since most students will not learn to work cooperatively (-1). As a result the group assignments will not be completed (-9). Students will become angry as each student will think that they are doing the majority of the work (-8) and the group will break apart because they will refuse to work together (-9).

ACTION STEP: Ms. Mosier must instill into the students the importance of teaming and how to use the TQI tools in order to achieve success.

DESIRED OUTCOMES: The students will learn the necessary skills to work together as a group.

SCENARIO 5: Some students will simply not participate in the group, and a few students will undertake responsibility for completing the group assignment (-7). (The task force members concluded that this scenario was so similar to #4 that it did not need to be discussed further since it would be resolved by the action step taken under scenario 4.)

SCENARIO 6: Tensions will be high since the students will refuse to work with anyone other that their friends (-8). No action step is recommended since this may fade after the work teams are formed and success is achieved.

6. <u>List and analyze any scenario that has a number greater than ±100</u>

The scenarios that have a high score usually means that if the recommended changes were implemented and if the perceptions of the task force members were representative of the institutional culture, then the scenarios would take place.

One scenario has a number greater than ±100 , namely 3.1, which reads:

3. Students will appreciate individual differences in their classmates and will recognize how each contributes to the success of the group. (+9)
3.1 Students will recognize that people learn differently. (+50)
    3.1.1 Students will learn that some are "smart" in other subjects but "slow" in English. (+50)
    3.1.2 Teaming will become more important than individual success. (+7)
    3.1.3 Racial tension will be reduced as students work together. (+10)

(It should be mentioned that before the end of the year Scenario 3 did occur!)

7. <u>Suggest what one or two systems should be improved to maximize the positive and minimize the negative</u>

After analyzing the results of the scenarios and the results that were obtained by the end of the school year, the action team decided that a major dysfunctional system was at the root of poor learning in their high school, namely, the students were not taught how to work together in order to obtain quality results. In a letter to the school board and the principal, the students suggested that a course in TQI procedures be taught at the ninth grade level, if not sooner.

SYSTEMATIC DIAGRAM

The **Systematic Diagram** is used as a planning tool to determine the specific action steps that are necessary to accomplish a broader goal, especially if a number of people, departments, or units are involved. The **Systematic Diagram** is best used with an **Affinity Diagram** or a **Relations Diagram**.

Procedure
1. Statement of the Problem/Goal
   We will build upon the example presented in the **Relations Diagram** section when a task force consisting of drama students and their teacher was attempting to establish a set design and construction shop. The goal is drawn on the left hand side of the paper. This can be done using an overhead projector or a large sheet of flip chart paper.

END

```
┌─────────────────┐
│ Establish a Set │
│ Design and      │
│ Construction    │
│ Shop            │
└─────────────────┘
```

2. Generate Levels of Events and Actions Necessary to Accomplish the Ends
   The first level of events and actions are usually broad, but as one moves from left to right the tasks become very specific as one level builds upon the other. In the example that follows the task force members know that if they are to accomplish their goal, they will ultimately require approval and support from the principal, parents, business community, and students. In order for those to occur, however, the task force recognized that it will need to develop a rationale, a design, and informational materials. The steps are incorporated in the completed Systematic Diagram below.

301

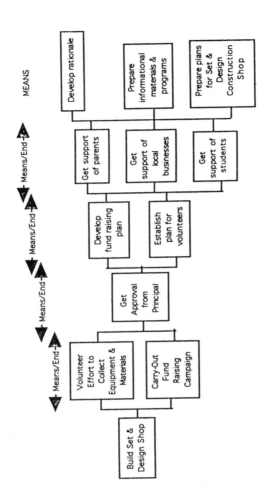

3. Analyze the Diagram and Assign Tasks

After the Systematic Diagram is completed the task force members should analyze their findings and discuss them with the rest of the class. Then specific tasks or action steps with specific time lines should be assigned. It is a good idea to post the Systematic Diagram with the names of the person(s) having the responsibility to accomplish a specific task (action).

Formula for Determining the Cost of Waste in School Districts

The following formula will allow you to determine the cost of waste (not doing the job right the first time) in your local district.

1. Number of students who did not return to school last year.
   _____

2. Dollar amount of state aid to education per pupil in your district. _____

3. **Total state aid dollars lost in your district last year.** (Multiply 1 & 2). _____ (Assume the same level of non-returning students over a 4 year period.)

4. **Total state aid dollars lost in your district for 4 years** (multiply 3 x 4 years). _____

Calculate this loss in terms of faculty, staff, programs, and instructional materials. List what your district will lose as a result of not receiving the money in 4.

_____

_____

_____

_____

_____

Assume that half the non-returning students go on welfare in 2 years or less.

5. Number on welfare (divide 1 in half). _____

6. Number of teen mothers (divide #5 in half). These girls will receive Aid to Families with Dependent Children (AFDC), WIC (Women, Infants and Children—A health and nutrition supplement program), Medical Assistance, and Food Stamps. (For the purposes of this exercise, we will assume each teen mother has only one child.) _____

7. Amount of AFDC paid per household per year (Multiply #6 by your state AFDC amount for a single parent with one child x 12 months) _____

8. Amount of Food Stamps paid per household per year (Multiply #6 by your state Food Stamp allowance for a single parent with one child x 12 months.) _____

9. Cost of AFDC and Food Stamps for a 4 year period (add #7 and #8 together, then multiply the sum times 4).
   _____

10. Number of single individuals on welfare (divide #5 in half). These individuals will receive cash assistance 3 months per year. They are not the caretakers of dependent children, but will also receive Medical Assistance and Food Stamps. _____

11. Total cash assistance per year (Multiply #10 by your state cash assistance for single individuals per month times three). _____

12. Cash assistance paid over a 4 year period. (Multiply #11 times 4). _____

13. Total food stamp allowance per year (Multiply #10 by your state food stamp allowance for a single individual x 12).
_____

14. Total food stamp cost per 4 years (Multiply #13 x 4).

_____

Assume that 33% of all non-returning students are unemployed. Calculate the loss in tax revenue to your district and community. Assume a high school graduate could earn approximately $10,000 per year without further education or training.

15. 33% of line one is the number of former students that are probably unemployed. _____

16. Using your state income tax rate, figure the amount of lost tax revenue per person. (Multiple the per person tax rate times the line 15). _____

17. The federal tax rate for a single individual earning $10,000 per year, with only the standard deduction and personal exemption ($5,300) is $972 [1990]. (Multiply $972 x line 15)

18. Loss of federal and state tax dollars over for one year. (Add lines 16 & 17). _____

19. Cost in tax dollars for 4 years (multiply line 18 by 4).

_____

20. **TOTAL COST PER YEAR in lost state aid to education, taxes, cash assistance and food stamp programs** (add lines 3,7,8,11,13 and 18). _____

21. **TOTAL COST FOR 4 YEARS in lost state aid to education, taxes, cash assistance and food stamp programs** (add lines 4, 9, 12, 14, and 19). _____

Customer/Supplier Contract

Dear Parent,

You are my supplier. I am your customer. You supply me with your child every day. As my supplier, I expect you to ensure that:

A. Your child
1. will be in school on time, every day unless illness prevents attendance.
2. will have a good night's sleep.
3. will come to school having had breakfast.
4. will complete all homework and that it is in the book bag prior to departure for school each day.
5. will arrive at school with all books and materials
6. will **not** bring any weapons or sharp objects to school.
7. will **not** bring any drugs or alcoholic beverages to school.

B. You will:
1. inform me when your child is unhappy about school (or this class).
2. attend any parent conferences at the mutually agreed upon time.
3. inform me when you have concerns about the child or the class.
4. reinforce the class emphasis on problem-solving by carrying out this plan at home with your child.
5. help your child with goal setting and plans to reach those goals.

_____

Signature - Parent/Guardian   Date

305

Customer/Supplier Contract

Dear Parent,

You are my customer and your satisfaction is very important to me. Therefore, I agree to the following:

1. Keep a folder of your child's continuous improvement projects that can be accessed by you and your child at any time, thereby ceasing dependence on inspection.
2. Teach your child how to track his/her own progress and assess his/her own work for quality.
3. Evaluate your child on the basis of mastery of quality work, resulting from continuous improvement projects thereby allowing him/her to have pride in his/her work.
4. Drive fear out of the classroom, thereby enhancing your child's self-esteem.
5. Provide a wide variety of instructional approaches to allow your child to succeed no matter his/her learning style.
6. Provide classroom assignments and projects that are exciting, meaningful and purposeful, thereby enhancing your child's enthusiasm for learning.
7. Teach and provide opportunities for your child to work cooperatively in groups on team projects.
8. Teach your child to assume responsibility for his/her own education by providing him/her with the necessary tools for learning.
9. Teach and provide opportunities for your child to learn the importance of helping all classmates to succeed.
10. Teach your child problem-solving techniques and allow him/her to practice this whenever personal or group problems occur.
11. Teach your child skills in critiquing his/her own work and that of all classmates for the purpose of continuous improvement.

_____   _____
Signature (Teacher)   Date

PROFESSIONAL WORK PLAN AGREEMENT

As a student in _____ class, I agree to:

Come to class everyday, on time, with all necessary books and materials, and prepared to learn.

Be respectful of myself, my classmates, the teacher and anyone within our educational family.

Come to class without any weapons or objects that could harm others.

Come to class with my homework neatly completed.

Come to class ready to participate in any group activities.

Willingly help any of my classmates anytime they or the teacher ask me to.

Offer helpful suggestions to classmates so they can continuously improve to achieve quality work.

Assist my classmates in the review of their work and accept suggestions from others about ways to improve my work.

Practice the problem-solving model to achieve self-discipline.

Continuously improve any assignments and/or projects until I have achieved quality work.

Learn about Total Quality Improvement techniques and tools.

_____
Signature (student)   Date

PROFESSIONAL WORK PLAN AGREEMENT

As your teacher, I agree to:

Provide you with a class mission statement and long-range class goals.

Discuss the goals with you and answer the questions—WHY, WHY, WHY?

Work with you to establish short-term class goals as well as personal goals.

Provide you with training in Total Quality techniques and tools, including giving you a Quality Manual.

Provide you with examples of quality work.

Drive fear out of the classroom by eliminating my biases and by not employing coercive, punitive discipline tactics.

Provide meaningful, interesting assignments and projects that relate to the real world.

Teach lessons using a variety of teaching techniques so you can succeed regardless of your learning style.

Work with you on continuous improvement projects until you achieve quality.

Maintain a folder of your work, including your continuous improvement projects. This will become the basis for any evaluations.

Listen and respond quickly to any suggestions you have for improving the class.

Encourage you to work in groups through group assignments and projects.

Signature (teacher)   Date

QUALITY INDEX RATING PROFILE

In order to determine the "quality index" (QI) of your classroom processes and systems, please refer to the table below an assign points (1-5) for each category subsection based on described criteria. Enter your scores in the table at the end of this section and calculate your QI.

Self-Assessment Quality Index of Classroom Processes & Systems.

1.0   **Leadership** (15%)

This category examines your commitment to leading the students to achieving quality work.

1.1   Describe what quality means to you. If you have a formal statement, please include.

1.2   How has the quality policy and/or mission statement been deployed among the students.

1.3   Describe your leadership, personal involvement, and visibility in communicating the quality program to your colleagues, parents, the community, administration, and other groups.

1.4   Describe your preferred teaching styles.

1.5   Describe the nature of any on-going education/training you have had to keep up with the latest trends in your content area.

1.6   How do you define quality in your own work, and explain the ways you exemplify that to your colleagues.

1.1   Describe what quality means to you. If you have a formal statement, please include.

Points	Criteria
1	No formal statement.
2	Quality work is only mentioned at the beginning of the year, with no formal statement or examples of quality work
3	Formal statement is given to students and shared with parents and administrators.
4	A formal statement is presented to students at the beginning of the year; quality work is displayed for all to use as a model; students know what quality work means to their own success and the success of the class and school.
5	The formal statement relates to WORLD CLASS quality results with the teacher and students committed to continuous improvement in the processes and systems of the classroom and the outcomes.

1.2   How has the quality policy and/or mission been translated to the students?

Points	Criteria
1	Mainly "talk" about quality
2	There is a quality manual on display in the classroom with examples of quality work enclosed
3	Quality manual and/or policy statements about quality are distributed to all the students
4	There is training provided to all students on quality procedures and goals
5	The quality policy is deployed with a clear direction, commitment of the teacher and students and everyone works together to integrate the classroom activities.

1.3   Describe your leadership, personal involvement, and visibility in communicating the quality program to your colleagues, parents, the community, administration, and other groups.

Points	Criteria
1	Traditional management role of directing and controlling.
2	Visible in concern for quality issues within the school.
3	Visible in expressing the quality mission outside the school to parents, school board, industry, city officials, and the state department of education.
4	Active in supporting adhocracy and collaborative learning within the classroom and implements suggestions resulting from student input. Is a supportive leader for ALL students as progress is monitored and constantly seeks ways to improve the learning process.
5	Recognized as a leader outside the school for instituting quality.

1.4   Describe your preferred teaching styles.

Points	Criteria
1	Mostly lecture with some question and answer periods.
2	Use of lecture, demonstration, and question and answer periods.
3	More traditional methods interspersed with some group work.
4	A variety, adapting to learning styles of students and including some collaborative learning and discovery learning.
5	Mostly student led, collaborative learning with goal setting a major focus. Mastery learning of basic facts is accomplished in a variety of ways. Students with different learning styles are interspersed to provide all with opportunities to contribute in a variety of ways.

1.5   Describe the nature of any on-going education/training you have had to keep up with the latest trends in your content area.

Points	Criteria
1	Meet the local or state in-service requirements for annual increments each year.
2	Subscribe to at least one professional journal, and attend at least one workshop/conference each year.
3	Maintain communication with local and state curriculum specialists, read and implement the latest information, attend as many conferences as possible with the school year.
4	Make recommendations to the librarian for future purchases, send for information on the latest trends in the content area, encourage specialists to come into the classroom to provide demonstrations and/or offer suggestions for improvements, read journals and newspapers to implement the newest trends and make meaningful assignments in concert with world events.
5	Actively engaged in national, state and local organizations, and maintain a network with other professionals. Maintain an on-going, well-planned continuing education program that is well thought out and revolves around a global perspective.

1.6   How do you define quality in your own work, and explain the ways you exemplify that to your colleagues.

Points	Criteria
1	No thought has been given to quality.
2	Quality is defined by the traditional evaluation by management.
3	Quality is defined by the achievements of the students, and this information is presented in written form to my colleagues.
4	The quality of work is reflected in the student's enthusiasm for learning and achieving quality work. As a TQ leader, I am available to assist my colleagues.
5	The quality of work is reflected in the "World Class" quality of students' work and their enthusiasm for helping classmates achieve success. The numbers of students choosing to pursue a career in my content area, or who are enrolling in advanced courses in the content area is also a measure of the quality of my work. Finally, we are all having fun while learning.

2.0   Classroom Environment. (10%)

This category examines the overall climate of the classroom and its accessibility to achieving quality for all students.

2.1   Describe the arrangement of furniture and equipment in the classroom.

2.2   Describe the climate of the classroom in terms of respect, care and concern for students.

2.3   How does the teacher present a "Success" climate for students.

2.4   Describe how discipline is maintained in the classroom.

2.1   Describe the arrangement of furniture and equipment in the classroom.

Points	Criteria
1	Furniture is arranged in rows. Equipment and supplies are locked in cabinets not accessible to students.
2	Furniture is clustered in small groups. Equipment is not readily available to students.
3	Furniture is periodically rearranged to compliment lessons and student activities. Some equipment is available to students most of the time.
4	Classroom furniture becomes a functional workstation for student groups and they arrange it as needed.
5	Equipment and furniture are extensions of the work taking place within the classroom. Students may move the furniture to suit their needs. Equipment is kept out and ready for students use. Everyone understands the need to respect others and property is properly handled and cared for.

2.2   Describe the climate of the classroom in terms of respect, care and concern for students.

Points	Criteria
1	Interaction between teacher and students and between students is infrequent.
2	All students are greeted in a friendly manner each day.
3	The teacher takes care to let students know he/she is available to "talk" outside of the classroom.
4	The teacher presents him/herself as a role model for caring and respects all students. There are no visible biases for students or groups of students.
5	The teacher maintains a supportive, caring role when students are ill or troubled and makes time for them.

2.3   How do you present a "Success" climate for students?

Points	Criteria
1	There are some success posters in the room.
2	The teacher posts examples of student work, and provides some individual rewards for "excellence".
3	The teacher is the cheerleader for the group. Students have no fear in the classroom. Students' self-esteem is affirmed even when mistakes are made. Mistakes are accepted as necessary risks towards growth. There is no blaming.
4	The teacher openly displays an unconditional belief in the ability of ALL students to perform quality work and maintains high expectations of self and the students. To this end, the teacher constantly and patiently strives to assist all students to achieve quality work.
5	Students engage in meaningful activities, which allow them to want to achieve quality work. They are encouraged to work collaboratively and help others achieve success. The group goal is to have every student achieve success and in the process gain pride of workmanship and have fun.

2.4   Describe how discipline is developed and maintained in the classroom.

Points	Criteria
1	Traditional punitive methods are developed and implemented by the teacher.
2	Students understand the classroom rules and those who choose to break them are reprimanded.
3	Students assist in establishing classroom rules and the consequences of breaking them.
4	Students are held responsible for their own behavior and disruption may involve "time-out" and includes a contractual arrangement with the teacher to resume regular classroom activities.
5	Discipline problems are few since all students are empowered and accepted equally. Students have no fear in coming to the classroom. All students learn ways to communicate through speaking and in writing that allows them to resolve problems without major disruption to the class. Students are expected to resolve problems with others involved, rather than having teacher or administration solve the problem.

3.0   Information and Analysis (5%)

This category examines the scope, validity, use, and management of data and information that underlie the total quality system in the classroom. Adequacy of data and information is examined to support a prevention-based quality approach using "management by fact."

3.1   In what areas (materials, student satisfaction, student involvement, parent satisfaction, students entering post-secondary institutions, students adequately prepared for the next level of instruction in any given curricular area, number and type of discipline problems, student retention, time for achieving mastery in any curricular area, etc.) do you have data to illustrate quality trends by function, and/or process in your classroom? Please list. If you have any, please enclose examples of quality trends.

Points	Criteria
1	No data or just the standard evaluation data.
2	Standard retention data, with some information on curricular trends.
3	Use of statistical methods to monitor critical processes and systems.
4	Cost of quality analysis data are collected and available for all (including students) to examine.
5	Within the classroom all processes and systems are analyzed from statistical data and use the Plan-Do-Check-Act (P-D-C-A) cycle to improve the processes and systems.

4.0   Strategic Quality Planning (5%)

This category examines your planning process for empowering students to achieve quality work and the short and long-term priorities to achieve or sustain any leadership position.

4.1   Summarize your specific principal quality goals, objectives, and plans for the short-term (3-6 months) and longer term (1-2 years).

Points	Criteria
1	Standard goals, based on the district's or the state's goals
2	Numerical objectives related to quality, cost effectiveness, and customer satisfaction.
3	Management by policy deployment where all students have work plan assignments related to the quality goals of the classroom.
4	Quality goals exceed those of the district and/or state, and everyone is committed to achieving those goals.
5	All objectives of the classroom key on achieving "World Class" capabilities in quality related performance which includes process and system orientations.

5.0   Human Resource Utilization (15%)

This category examines the outcomes of your efforts to develop and utilize the full potential of all students for quality and to maintain an environment conducive to full participation, continuous improvement, and classroom growth.

5.1   What are the teacher's key strategies for increasing the effectiveness, productivity, and participation of all students.

5.2   Please describe how the teacher educates students in quality improvement.

5.3   What percentage of current students have ever received education in quality improvement concepts and processes?

5.4   Describe how the teacher positively reinforces students for contributions to quality improvement (e.g. recognition of teams, awards, etc.)

5.5   What has the teacher done to ensure the quality of work life in the classroom, to maintain a supportive education environment and to empower all students to actively participate in the learning process?   If you have examples, please include.

5.1   What are your strategies for increasing the effectiveness, productivity, and participation of <u>all</u> students.

Points	Criteria
1	No formal strategy.
2	Strategy is dependent on the curriculum
3	Formal and flexible strategy which encourages the students to participate in assessing the classroom climate and offer suggestions for improving it. Students are empowered to work for the success of all.
4	The classroom environment is completely without fear, and cooperative learning opportunities are a pivotal part of each day; therefore all students have a part in the success of the group.
5	The teacher assumes the role of TQ teacher, challenging students to reach untapped potentials. Students evaluate their own work as well as others' for quality, offering suggestions and encouragement.

5.2   Please describe how you educate students in quality improvement.

Points	Criteria
1	Students receive no education in principles of total quality improvement (TQI).
2	Students are educated only on subject matter skills and receive no TQM or TQI training.
3	All students are educated on the principles of TQM and TQI.
4	Students are educated on the principles and processes of quality including SPC and PDCA, and utilize these in their daily work.
5	Learning is based on the continuous improvement of all students as the keystone to the success of all.

5.3   What percentage of current students have ever received education in quality improvement concepts and processes?

Points	Criteria
1	0%
2	Less than 25%
3	25 to 60%
4	61 to 90%
5	91 to 100%

5.4   Describe how you positively reinforce students for contributions to quality improvement (e.g. recognition of teams, awards, etc.)

Points	Criteria
1	Traditional grades are the reward for achievement.
2	Typical performance reviews focusing on individual efforts.
3	Commendations and other rewards are dispensed at the discretion of the teacher.
4	Commendations and other rewards are dispensed at the discretion of both the teacher and students.
5	Team recognition and incentives for efforts are based on the improvement of the processes and systems where the teacher's role is to support and facilitate the efforts of the team. Information about team rewards is sent home. There is a system in place for distributing information to parents, community members, and school colleagues.

5.5   What have you done to ensure the quality of work life in the classroom, to maintain a supportive education environment and to empower all students to actively participate in the learning process? If you have examples, please include.

Points	Criteria
1	The classroom environment reflects an attitude of: be quiet, do your work and don't question or make suggestions.
2	Administration's suggestions are considered and discussed.
3	Only certain selected students' suggestions and ideas are discussed.
4	Participative management approach where all students are encouraged to make suggestions, discuss options and collaborate with others to implement group decisions.
5	Upside down pyramid where the teacher's role is to be a leader and to support quality work and all students are performing that work. Adhocracy at its best.

6.0 Quality Assurance of Products and Services (15%)

This category examines the classroom's systematic approach based primarily upon quality improvement processes and systems, including the control of procured curriculum materials, equipment, and services.

6.1   What methods do you use to evaluate student's academic performance?

6.2   How do you define waste in your classroom, and what preventive measures do you take to reduce waste?

6.3   How do you elicit improvements in quality to those supplying goods and services to you, including those students coming to you?

6.4   How do you evaluate and integrate the quality of skills your students use that they've learned from other classes within your school?

6.1   What methods do you use to evaluate your student's academic performance?

Points	Criteria
1	Traditional paper/pencil evaluation with teacher grading
2	Students grade each other's quizzes
3	Teachers grade all unit tests, and students are able to continue improving their grade until mastery is achieved.
4	Students turn in a portfolio of work at the end of each unit, along with a self-evaluation. The teacher then evaluates the level of achievement for mastery learning at the 80% level.
5	Students work together to evaluate each other's work and provide appropriate feedback for revision/discussion. A portfolio of work is included reflecting cross-curricular, critical thinking and writing or computational assignments. The teacher's assessment reflects mastery learning at "World Class" levels.

6.2   How do you define waste in your classroom and what preventive measures do you take to reduce waste?

Points	Criteria
1	No formal evaluation of "waste," such as the retention rate of students.
2	"Waste" is considered as students who do not pass and is determined solely by inspection such as paper/pencil tests or as "scrap" because the job has to be redone.
3	"Waste" includes measurable external failure costs such as the cost of drop-outs to society, illiteracy, teen pregnancy rates, drug and alcohol problems, juvenile delinquency, and truancy.
4	Process orientation regarding waste is considered such as time, steps, complexity, special projects, etc. to get ALL students to minimal standards.
5	"Waste" is recognized as a result of poor processes and systems and includes all aspects of the educational system; and as a result, an ongoing effort utilizing, K-12 curricular teams, cooperative learning, cross-curricular teams, and mastery learning is employed.

6.3   How do you bring about improvements in quality to those supplying goods and services to you, including those students coming to you?

Points	Criteria
1	There is no effort made to improve the quality.
2	There is an informal agreement to discuss student deficiencies with former teachers and parents.
3	Suppliers (former teachers and parents) are provided with instruction in TQM and encouraged to incorporate the principles. Textbooks and instructional materials are continuously examined to meet improved curriculum and teaching techniques.
4	Through the teacher's efforts, former teachers within the district have process oriented quality improvement capabilities.
5	The teacher has an active partnership with all suppliers (including parents) to set and improve quality. There is cross training throughout the curriculum

6.4   How do you evaluate and integrate the quality of skills your students use that they've learned from other classes within your school?

Points	Criteria
1	No formal tracking system
2	No effort is made to meet with other teachers, but concern is vocalized about the skills of the students
3	Evaluation of skills from cross-curricular classes is done once a year
4	Active interaction between all teachers across the curriculum
5	Partnerships are formed, and assignments are constructed so that skills from across the curriculum will amass to achieve quality. Suppliers are expected to improve continuously.

7.0 **Quality Results** (15%)

This category examines quality improvement based upon objective measures derived from customer requirements/expectations analysis and from operations analysis. Also examined are current quality levels in relation to those of competing organizations.

7.1   Enclose in graph form some key improvement data in your students

7.2   Briefly describe one or two continuous improvement projects(s) which have led to the results in 7.1

7.3   Please describe how you compare your classroom with other classrooms within or outside of your product or service area (benchmarking)

7.1   Enclose in graph form some key improvement data in your students

Points	Criteria
1	Graphs are not generated.
2	Traditional quality indicator information is used (i.e. the grade).
3	Traditional information is evaluated regularly in the classroom using graphs that are understood by all students
4	Field intelligence data are gathered by the teacher and evaluated in graphical form, (i.e. the number or percent of those passing the AP test, number enrolling in college, number going on to a more difficult level of instruction, etc.)
5	Information related to strategic quality objectives is regularly used and is posted in graphical form throughout the classroom for all to see; reports are provided to the school board, administration, and are sent home to all parents.

7.2   Briefly describe one or two continuous improvement
        project(s) which have led to the results in 7.1

Points	Criteria
1	No project groups or no measurable results available
2	Project groups are put together quickly with effort put into the nature of the project and how it might lead to quality improvement.
3	Mastery learning is utilized and results are charted, but cooperative learning is only utilized occasionally.
4	Project groups are established with assignments that are cross-curricular and meaningful.
5	All students are engaged in project groups that study issues and result in cross-curricular meaningful work, and value added work is accomplished by the teacher remaining a supportive leader. The main work, using quality tools and methods, is done by the students.

7.3   Please describe how you compare your classroom with other classrooms within or outside of your product or service area (benchmarking)

Points	Criteria
1	No comparable data is available.
2	Standard accounting information such as: standardized test scores, students passing, etc.
3	Passive collection and analysis of data from outside sources such as parents and former students.
4	Benchmarking of competitors, (i.e. percent of your students going on to next highest level of schooling, those taking the most difficult classes, compared to other like classes).
5	Instituted an active program to obtain comparative "benchmarking" data on all functions and services from the BEST in those areas whether they are competitors or not (i.e. continuous search for the premier approaches to teaching/learning your subject matter).

8.0 Customer Satisfaction (25%)

This category examines the organization's knowledge of the customer, overall customer service system, responsiveness, and ability to meet requirements and expectations.

8.1   How do you determine your customers, and their satisfaction level outside your classroom?

8.2   How do you determine your internal customers and their satisfaction level inside your classroom?

8.3   In what functional areas, processes, or systems do you have defined, measurable product and/or service quality criteria? Please list.

8.4   What methods do you use to determine customer satisfaction?

8.5   Summarize trends in customer satisfaction and list measurements you have in specific areas.

8.6   What happens in your classroom that significantly promotes continuous improvement to increase customer satisfaction?

8.1   How do you determine your customers and their satisfaction level outside your classroom?

Points	Criteria
1	There is no formal collection system to measure customer satisfaction.
2	A complaint follow-up process is in place but the information provided is infrequently used.
3	A formal complaint handling system is in place and provides feedback to the teacher. Complaints are treated as "special cases"
4	A **P-D-C-A** process is used with the information gathered from customer (i.e. alumni, students, parents, employers, postsecondary institutions) satisfaction surveys. Processes are in place to monitor key indicators of customer satisfaction.
5	The teacher maintains a comprehensive data collection system that leads to **Quality Function Deployment** within the classroom relating to processes and assignments

8.2   How do you determine your internal customers and their satisfaction level inside your classroom?

Points	Criteria
1	No formal program exists.
2	Communication of satisfaction is mainly "hearsay".
3	Satisfaction is determined routinely through surveys.
4	Satisfaction is determined routinely though surveys and a P-D-C-A process is used to improve the relationship between students and other teachers within the building or district.
5	All functions are engaged in quality for internal customer (student, other teachers); satisfaction and communications are horizontal.

8.3   In what functional areas, process, or systems have you defined, measurable product and/or service quality criteria? Please list.

Points	Criteria
1	None
2	Teacher measures certain products
3	Teachers measures at least 50% of the products or services
4	Teacher and students measure at least 50% of the products or services
5	There is a total quality system oriented towards data gathering

8.4   What methods do you use to determine customer satisfaction?

Points	Criteria
1	No analysis is done.
2	There is some tracking of passively gathered data (keeping a mental count of reports of satisfaction).
3	There is regular tracking of passively gathered data (maintain records with information and source on a yearly basis).
4	Active accumulation and analysis of data in areas of customer satisfaction.
5	Management (teacher) is actively involved with all internal and external customer satisfaction measures and actually gathers information from employers, parents, graduates, and post-secondary institutions.

8.5   Summarize trends in customer satisfaction and list measurements you have in specific areas.

Points	Criteria
1	There is no information.
2	Information is just hearsay such as "enrollment in this class is up, therefore I must be doing something right".
3	Specific measurable data are available through external sources such as employers or postsecondary schools showing increasing customer satisfaction with the results of the student's work in class.
4	Valid questionnaires are regularly sent to other teachers, parents, postsecondary institutions, and employers to identify trends.
5	The teacher generates and monitors the data which evaluates key quality criteria showing constant year-to-year improvements.

8.6   What do you do that significantly promotes continuous improvement to increase customer satisfaction?

Points	Criteria
1	Nothing
2	Quality successes are recognized through awards, certificates, etc.
3	In addition to recognition awards, the teacher sends kudos personally to students and parents.
4	The teacher has applied for the classroom quality award and has demonstrated measurable improvement.
5	The teacher has become actively involved in the Quality Movement not only locally, but also nationally. The teacher has published papers and/or made speeches about the quality processes and systems.

The following rating sheet would be used if the previously suggested characteristics and weighted values are used for evaluating a classroom for a "quality" award.

QUALITY AWARD RATING SHEET

Applicant: _____

Reviewers:_____

Date:_____

Document notes, questions, etc. on reverse side. Note: ALL RATINGS ARE FROM 1-5

1.0   Leadership (15%)

    1.1   _____
    1.2   _____
    1.3   _____
    1.4   _____
    1.5   _____
    1.6   _____
    Total ÷ 6   _____
    Total ÷ 6 x .15   _____

2.0   Classroom Environment (10%)

    2.1   _____
    2.2   _____
    2.3   _____
    2.4   _____
    Total ÷ 4   _____
    Total ÷ 4 x .10   _____

3.0   Information & Analysis (5%)

    3.1   _____
    Total x .05   _____

4.0   Strategic Quality Planning (5%)

    4.1   _____
    Total x .05   _____

5.0   Human Resource Utilization (15%)
    5.1   _____
    5.2   _____
    5.3   _____
    5.4   _____
    5.5   _____
    Total ÷ 5   _____
    Total ÷ 5 x .15   _____

6.0   Quality Assurance of Products & Services (15%)
    6.1   _____
    6.2   _____
    6.3   _____
    6.4   _____
    Total ÷ 4   _____
    Total ÷ 4 x .15   _____

7.0   Quality Results (15%)
    7.1   _____
    7.2   _____
    7.3   _____
    Total ÷ 3   _____
    Total ÷ 3 x .15   _____

8.0   Customer Satisfaction (25 %)
    8.1   _____
    8.2   _____
    8.3   _____
    8.4   _____
    8.5   _____
    8.6   _____
    Total ÷ 6   _____
    Total ÷ 6 x .25   _____

Total Award Rating = Sum of weighted totals from 1.0 to 8.0 =

_____

We suggest the following interpretation of the scores:
Score 1.0—2.9   :   Traditional Teacher
Score 3.0—3.9   :   Progressive Teacher
Score 4.0—5.0   :   Total Quality (TQ) Teacher

In our experience most teachers have an initial score of between 1.8 to 2.4. Most likely this is the direct result of the educational experiences provided in the schools of education at our traditional colleges and universities. After 45 to 60 hours of training in TQM and one year of applying the P-D-C-A cycle in their classrooms, most teachers advance to a score of approximately 3.5. This "Progressive" teachers notice great changes in the classroom. We believe that it will take these people an additional two years of TQM experience and the support of an enlightened administration to become a **Total Quality Teacher.**

The Quality Teacher

This text will clarify TQM processes and procedures and demonstrate how they can be used in the classroom. It is an introductory guide to teachers interested in implementing total quality management (TQM) in their classroom. In Chapter One, we summarize briefly the TQM approaches of two quality experts, namely Dr. W. Edwards Deming and Dr. Philip Crosby. Chapter Two shows how TQM works with students, especially the "at-risk" population. Chapters Three-10 examine a specific point of the Quality Index Assessment and discusses specific ways to integrate each within the classroom. (Most of the indices are modifications of the Malcolm Baldrige Criteria.) Each chapter ends with the Quality Index Assessment criteria for that point. In Chapter Eleven, we suggest the conditions that are necessary for successfully implementing TQM in the classroom. Finally, the Appendix contains the Total Quality Improvement tools, examples of Customer-Supplier contracts, and a personal Quality Index Profile demonstrating how you would rate on the overall assessment.

Dr. Kenneth G. Wilson, a 1982 Nobel Prize recipient in Physics, said that he is impressed with the classroom case studies and the total quality management tools and that he recommends this book for K-12 math and science teachers.

Susan Costentino of Middlesex, New Jersey is a member of the Quality New Jersey Focus on Education Team. She said the "...book is informative and meaningful. I now know where to begin [TQM] in my fifth grade classroom."

Mr. Ben Daviss said: "Thanks! You're making revolution."

A high school principal in Florida said that this book is "must reading for all teachers." She also stated that she wished that *The Quality Teacher* were available when she first started her teaching career."

Cornesky & Associates Press
PO Box 2139
Bunnell, FL 32110
(904) 437-5401
(904) 439-4317 FAX

ISBN 1-881807-01-0